D1221553

TEXAS
Cooking

Center Point
Large Print

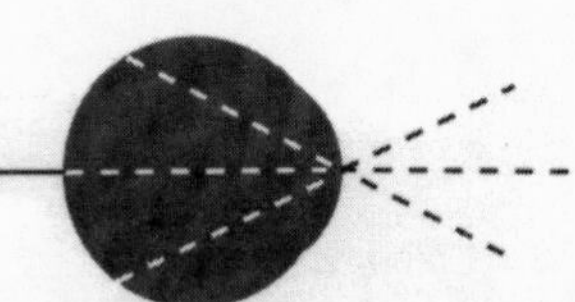

This Large Print Book carries the
Seal of Approval of N.A.V.H.

TEXAS
Cooking

Lisa Wingate

CENTER POINT PUBLISHING
THORNDIKE, MAINE

This Center Point Large Print edition
is published in the year 2005 by arrangement with
NAL Signet, a division of Penguin Group (USA) Inc.

The text of this Large Print edition is unabridged. In other aspects, this book may vary from the original edition. Printed in Thailand. Set in 16-point Times New Roman type.

ISBN 1-58547-524-6

Library of Congress Cataloging-in-Publication Data

Wingate, Lisa.
Texas cooking / Lisa Wingate.--Center Point large print ed.
p. cm.
ISBN 1-58547-524-6 (lib. bdg. : alk. paper)
1. Women journalists--Fiction. 2. Businessmen--Fiction. 3. Cookery--Fiction.
4. Texas--Fiction. 5. Large type books. I. Title.

PS3573.I53165T495 2005
813'.6--dc22

2004013423

To my boys—

for taking me once again
to the aimless paths
of childhood,

for making sure that
inchworms and ant hills
never go unnoticed,

for reminding me
that the best things in life
are often the little things

Chapter 1

FOOD and stories go together. They have been paired since the first tribes of man gathered around campfires in caves, or tents, or crude brush shelters. They are like an ancient couple married longer than anyone can remember, bringing warmth and comfort, wisdom and laughter to those who sit with them. Many of the oldest stories are about food and where it came from—like the Native American legends about how the People got the first seed corn, or how the buffalo came to be, or the biblical one about the Garden of Eden and how Adam and Eve brought about their fall from grace by eating the forbidden fruit.

In my family, some of the best stories are about food, like the one about the time my grandmother tried to create sauerkraut in a five-gallon crock and filled the basement with a gas so noxious no one could go down there for months. Or the time my great-aunt decided to try the new Mexican cooking fad on Easter Sunday, and created something so horrible even the dogs were afraid of it.

Cooking talent, in my family, is like eye color. You never know who's going to get what. I got blue eyes, no cooking talent. I'm not bitter about it. I have no cooking interest, either.

My mother spotted this deficiency in me early, and gave up trying to mold me into a culinary genius. She decided that, along with my grandmother's curly red hair, I inherited Gran's nondomestic personality. Just like my grandmother, I didn't fit the traditional mold that society sets out for girls. I was scab-kneed and red-headed, tall and not the least bit refined, and determined to do everything my brother could do. I rejected all things girlish, including cooking. I spent my formative years reading about adventure, or running the fringes of the neighborhood looking for adventure, but never in the kitchen, unless my grandmother and my great-aunts were gathered there, and the room was filled with wild Irish stories.

My mother, a prim schoolteacher, was often scandalized by what was said at those gatherings of the Collins clan, but she let me sit and listen anyway. Perhaps she knew it was important for me to fit in somewhere, or perhaps she was just happy to see me finally in the kitchen, peeling potatoes or snapping green beans, finally learning how to cook, or so she thought. The fact was that I learned a lot about my family, and listened to some wonderful Irish stories, but I didn't absorb a teaspoonful of cooking knowledge.

Which is why it's so strange that cooking took me on an adventure as wild as any of my great-aunts' tales, and changed everything I thought I knew about myself. It all began with cooking. A story about cooking. Texas cooking.

I was so aghast when I got the offer, I sat silently staring out the window with the phone buzzing in my ear.

"Collie?" Laura Draper's voice brought me back to reality. "Collie, are you still there?"

"Laura, are you sure you dialed the right number?" I

asked. "I don't *know* anything about cooking. I don't know anything about Texas. I cover D.C. stories, remember? *Washington,* D.C. Real stuff."

Fortunately, Laura ignored my burst of attitude. "You can't do *any* kind of stories sitting in bed with the covers pulled over your head, Collie." Only a really good friend can put you in your place like that and get away with it. "Now get off your butt and check your fax machine. I sent the proposal over two days ago, in case you hadn't noticed."

"I hadn't," I muttered.

"I'm not surprised," she fired back. "It's an eight-story run, and the pay isn't bad. Eight thousand plus expenses."

A huge sigh trembled through me, and the sound of it made my eyes burn. It was filled with the sense of hopelessness that had become the biggest part of me. "It just isn't my kind of story. . . ."

"Stop it, Collie!" The volume made me hold the phone away from my ear. After so many weeks of quiet, her voice seemed like thunder rolling through my brain. "You're going to have to face the fact that you're out of luck in D.C., at least until this lawsuit thing is old news. I *know* you've got bills to pay. Go to the stupid fax machine, pick up the stupid assignment, and get on the stupid plane. I need the first article by the fifteenth."

"Of June?" Swinging my feet around, I stood up like a coma patient finally wobbling out of bed.

My joke bombed. "Very funny. The fifteenth of April. One week. Don't miss deadline. Enjoy the warm weather." Click.

So there I stood in a darkened room full of unwashed clothes and empty food containers, staring at the papers in the fax machine, wondering how I had come to this point. It's a long way down from award-winning Washington correspondent to unemployed freelance writer. The bottom of the pit is filled with dirty laundry and dried-up Chinese food. Testify in a lawsuit against your employer, and this is where you end up.

I never guessed the way out would be through Texas.

I pondered the idea as I sat on the plane reading the outline for the article series—quirky stuff about summer food festivals and bed-and-breakfast inns with famous recipes. Touchy-feely stuff. Not my kind of thing. It would have been more suited to any number of feature writers who were actually *from* Texas, and I'm sure Laura knew that. The fact that she'd given it to me only pointed out what a good friend she was, and what a charity case I had become.

"So, you never did tell me why you were headed to Texas in the first place." The guy beside me was an engineering consultant from D.C. Earlier on, we had been commiserating about being sent to Texas on business.

"I have a series of articles to do there." I hoped I was sounding cordial but romantically uninterested. Three months of wallowing in self-pity had left me a little rusty on social niceties.

He smiled, looking interested in more than just my work. "In Dallas? It sure would be nice to have someone from D.C. to talk to while I'm stuck there."

"In San Saline," I interjected before things could go any farther. I could force myself to go to Texas and write articles about cooking, but romance was out of the question. Not now. Probably never again. "I guess that's a suburb of Dallas."

He laughed so loudly the lady across the aisle stopped her needlepoint to look at us. "Not quite. San Saline's in central Texas, an hour or two west of Waco. You're headed to the middle of nowhere." He gave a rueful snort that made my stomach drop. "You've got a lot to learn about Texas." Leaning back in his seat, he crossed his arms over his chest and closed his eyes, still grinning like a Cheshire cat. "There's nothing out there but jackrabbits and goat farms. Like the commercial says—'It's like a whole other country.' "

"Oh," I muttered, and that was the end of the conversation for the rest of the plane ride. He fell asleep with his glasses askew and his mouth hanging open, and I sat reading my papers, having a waking nightmare about dropping off the edge of the world.

I was trying to find San Saline on the map as the plane landed.

Beside me, my seatmate woke up and straightened his glasses.

"Down here." He pointed over my shoulder to a small dot with a tiny name beside it.

"Oh," I said, folding up the map as the plane stopped at the gate. "Thanks."

"No problem." Standing up, he pulled his carry-on from the luggage bin. "So, are you in Dallas overnight?"

My mind quickly made the decision *not* to be in Dallas overnight, as I grabbed my luggage and followed him from the plane. "No. I'm going to pick up my rental car and get going."

"Can I buy you supper before you take off?"

"No . . . really . . . but thanks."

For a moment, we stood pinned together in uncomfortable silence at the end of the gateway, waiting for a group of reuniting relatives to finish hugging and move out of the path. It reminded me that I hadn't even called my mother to tell her I was going to Texas. I'd have to think of some way to explain what I was doing here. Anything but the truth. I couldn't possibly tell my parents that the prodigal daughter, the one they were so proud of, was now largely unemployed and writing recipes for a women's magazine. I hadn't even worked up the guts to tell them that I had been fired from my job, and why. *Lies beget more lies,* my grandmother would have said.

The crowd finally cleared, and my traveling partner followed me across the hall to the rental-car counter. I had the uncomfortable feeling he was going to ask for a ride somewhere, but as the agent handed me my keys, he seemed to give up the idea.

"Well, have a good trip," he said, turning toward the baggage-claim area.

"Thanks." Clutching my rental-car keys, I watched him disappear into a sea of blue jeans, boots, ball caps, and cowboy hats; then I took a deep breath and dove in myself. One girl from D.C., heading for Nowhere, Texas.

The drive turned out to be prettier than I expected. As I traveled west out of Dallas–Fort Worth, the countryside opened into an ocean of rolling grass-covered hills dotted with pink and white poppylike flowers. In places, the ground was carpeted with thick blue wildflowers, blanketing the roots of gnarled trees that looked like crooked old men yawning after a hundred-year nap.

"This isn't so bad," I muttered, passing old farmhouses and metal tractor sheds. All in all, it was serene, peaceful. Not too crowded, not too empty. Just what I needed to break out of my rut. It didn't *look* like the middle of nowhere. Except for the details of vegetation, it looked a lot like Maryland, where my family had vacationed for years on a guest farm. That picture made me think of my parents again, and I spent the next forty miles pondering what to say to them and how much to tell. There was something surreal and definitely not right about the fact that I had concealed from them everything that had happened in the past three months. Actually, a couple of skilled performances over the phone were all that had been required. Thirty-six years old, and I was still hiding from my parents . . .

Near Waco, I stopped for a snack and a drink at the exit where I was to leave the interstate for a two-lane highway that led due west into what, on the map, was a section with nothing but towns in microscopic print.

The cashier, who underneath his John Deere cap didn't look a day over fifteen, cocked a brow at my roasted soy beans and bottled water. "Health nut?" he drawled.

I laughed, thinking of the mountain of pizza boxes and greasy egg-roll containers I'd put in the Dumpster before leaving home. "Trying to get back in the habit. Is this State Highway Eighty-four?"

He drew back, looking at me as if I were a leper. "Man, you from New York or someplace?"

"D.C." *Not that it's any of your business*. "Why?"

"You talk like a Yankee." He grinned an impishly charming grin that made me forgive his ignorance. "Yeah, that's Highway Eighty-four, right out front."

"Is it the road to San Saline?"

Craning his neck again, he squinted at me. "Well . . . it *eventually* goes to San Saline. It's, like, two hours that way."

"Oh." I tried not to make obvious my dismay. "Is there a better way to go?"

"Well, you can go on Farm Road . . ." He paused, looked me over carefully, then shook his head. "No, ma'am. You better stick to the highway." As if to say a Yankee couldn't possibly be trusted with the more complicated shortcut.

"All right. Thanks for the information."

"We've got a huntin' lease in the San Saline area," he went on as I tucked my change into my wallet. "We go down there a lot during deer season, and in the spring to get rattlers."

"Rattlers?" I repeated absently, fumbling with the latch on my purse.

My hesitation turned out to be a mistake. Shutting the cash drawer, he leaned on the counter and made himself comfortable. "Yeah, rattlesnakes. You know.

Diamondbacks? They're all over the place down there. I mean, we've got 'em here, too, but down there you can catch 'em and get lots of money for the big ones at the Snake Days."

"Snake Days?" I was half-mortified, half-fascinated, like Buck Rogers landing on a new planet.

"Like a . . . fair?" He said it slowly, as if maybe I didn't speak English. "All the towns down there have one. If you bring in the biggest snake, or the most pounds all told, you can get five hundred dollars."

In pure amazement, I said, "Oh. What do they do with the snakes after?"

"Fry 'em up and serve 'em with gravy. Usually hundreds of pounds of 'em."

"And people eat that?" My stomach rolled over at the concept.

"Uh-huh."

"They do this every year?"

"Uh-huh."

"Don't they ever run out of snakes?"

He laughed so hard tears came to his eyes, and it took a long time for him to answer. "Not hardly. Rattlers are like weeds around here. They're everyplace."

That wasn't comforting news, considering my present destination. "Yuck. You're kidding."

"No, ma'am. Last year my uncle and me caught one eight foot long and over six pounds. It was the biggest one at the Lometa Diamondback Jubilee. That's the skin on the wall." He pointed to a long piece of wood overhead with an enormous snakeskin shellacked to it.

He went on as I stared at the skin. "We were drivin'

through this pasture just south of Lampasas, and we stopped to open the gate by this cattle guard. They aren't supposed to shut those gates on the county roads, but . . ."

The story went on for another ten minutes before another customer came in and saved me from hearing any more. Taking one last glance at the record-setting snakeskin, I hurried out the door, into the car, and onto the highway, having learned my first three lessons about Texas: Stay off the farm roads if you're a Yankee. Snakes are everywhere. And everyone has a story. If you pause for more than an instant, they'll tell it to you—whether you want to hear it or not.

I kept a watch for eight-foot rattlesnakes as I left Waco and traveled into hilly country, which gradually grew more and more unpopulated, ceased to look anything like Maryland, and started to look more like the edge of the world—at least the edge of the populated world. Miles passed with the only sign of humans being one or two cars and a smattering of gateways with ranch names on them. Occasionally, houses and barns were visible at the ends of the driveways, but mostly there were just gates and dirt driveways, winding off into nowhere like the wagon trails of old.

The sun slid slowly toward the horizon ahead, dimming the landscape, making it seem even emptier. Or maybe it *was* growing emptier. It was hard to say. All I knew for sure was that it was the least populated place I'd ever been.

The car lurched suddenly, the tires making an ominous *clump-clump* as they ran over something I couldn't see. My heart hammered upward as I glanced in the rearview, watching a fragment of wood fly airborne in the car's wake, then tumble end over end and disappear beyond the glow of the taillights. I started wondering whether there were any nails in it, and what I was going to do if a tire went flat, and if I could get the spare on alone, and how far I might have to walk to get help, and whether rattlesnakes came out at night, and how I would explain it to my mother if something happened to me in the middle of Nowhere, Texas, when I wasn't even supposed to be here.

I was relieved when I crested a hill and saw the lights of a town nestled in a valley in the distance. Civilization. At last. I would get a hotel room and travel on in the morning.

As I came closer and exited the highway, my hopes evaporated like a mirage in the desert. The town wasn't much more than a highway crossing with a feed mill and a tractor dealership on one side, and a crumbling main street on the other. The sidewalks had clearly been rolled up for the night. Not a light was on, anywhere. No motel. No convenience store. No restaurant. Nothing but darkened buildings, locked-up churches, and what looked like a smattering of houses squatting among the trees on a hillside. The lights I had seen were nothing more than a few yard lamps, three flickering streetlights, and a dim neon sign in front of the tractor dealership.

Stopping in the middle of the main street, I stared blankly at the flickering green neon outline of a tractor. *Friendly's Tractors*, the words said in faded black paint. *Home of True the Tractor Man.*

"Save me, True the Tractor Man," I muttered, and a comic-book image came into my mind—greasy ball cap, worn-out coveralls, a cross between Barney Fife and Gomer Pyle. I could practically see his silhouette in the dirty window glass of the tractor showroom. . . .

Shaking my head at myself, I put the car in drive again and stretched in my seat. I was more exhausted and food-deprived than I thought. I was starting to hallucinate. I needed a bed, a meal . . . and some gas. The gauge was below a quarter tank. The highway sign said, *San Saline, 58.*

My mind did a little mental algebra. Ten-gallon tank, maybe . . . three gallons left, maybe . . . Thirty miles per gallon, maybe . . . thirty goes into fifty-eight . . .

No problem. Straightening my shoulders, I stepped on the gas, and the car went . . . nowhere. The needle sank past empty with *Titanic* speed. The engine coughed, wheezed, then died, and the car coasted slowly downhill, coming to an unholy rest beneath the flashing neon sign of True the Tractor Man. Saying a silent prayer, I tried to start the car again, but nothing happened.

All at once, I was marooned in Nowhere, Texas.

Cursing my luck, I dug my cell phone out of my purse and flipped it open. A tow truck, I'd just call a tow truck and this would all be . . .

The phone flashed two little words. *No signal. No signal. No signal.*

"Oh, I can't believe this!" Slamming my hands on the steering wheel, I let my head fall against the headrest, and closed my eyes. *Think, Collie, think. Think of something.*

No good ideas came to mind. Walk the half mile or so to the lights on the hillside and hope there were houses. Sit where I was and wait for a car to come along. Lock the doors, curl up in the backseat, and wait for morning. The soy nuts were gone. I might starve to death before then. . . .

A knock on the window made me jerk upright. Clutching a hand over my exploding heart, I looked sideways into a pair of jeans and slowly upward into a face hidden from the neon glow by the shadow of a ball cap. Alarm bells zinged through my head as I rolled the window down a crack. It was well after dark. I was a female alone on a deserted street. A man was knocking on my window. . . .

"Are you True the Tractor Man?" came out of my mouth. In spite of my fear, I flushed from head to toe at the stupid remark.

A warm, friendly laugh rose from beneath the ball cap, and I felt better instantly. "Are you lost?"

"I'm out of gas and my cell phone won't work," I blurted. *Stupid, stupid, stupid.* If he was a psychotic killer, he would now know I was helpless. "I mean, I don't . . . No. I'm all right. Can you call a tow truck for me?"

Hands in his pockets, he leaned closer to the window crack, and I could just make out the neon-lit outline of a masculine chin and a shadowed profile that told me he was younger than I had originally thought, probably in his thirties. "The nearest tow truck's an hour away."

"Oh, God." I groaned, feeling that familiar sense of despair come over me. Nothing, but nothing, went right for me anymore. "Is there a motel around here?"

"No, ma'am." He had a slow Southern drawl that made the words sound almost like a foreign language. "Nearest motel's in San Saline." I couldn't really see his face, but I could have sworn he was smiling, as if the whole conversation were a little amusing. "You're not from around here, are ya?"

"No," I bit out, aggravated, desperate, uncertain of what to do next.

"You from New York or someplace?" The second time in a day I'd been asked that question. Only this time it wasn't funny.

"D.C. Why?"

"I figured someplace like that." He nodded, his chin disappearing into the shadow, then appearing again. "Where ya headed?"

Jamming my fingers into my hair in frustration, I pulled the tired, frizzed-up mess out of my eyes. "San Saline. I have a room waiting for me there at the Hawthorne House Bed-and-Breakfast. Can you give me *any* ideas as to how I might get there *tonight*?"

"You need some gas." He chuckled at his own joke. The playful sound of it whittled the edge off my temper.

"You're right. Is there a gas station near here?"

"Not that's open."

"And the tow truck's an hour away?"

"Yup."

It came to me then that he was enjoying giving useless one-sentence answers to my questions, so I thought very carefully before I spoke again. "Have you any idea as to where I might *get* some gas at this hour, and, if so, will you tell me what it is?"

He grinned, a glimmer of straight white teeth barely visible in the shadow of his ball cap. "Sure. You just sit there, and I'll get some gas out of the tank out back."

"You will?" I breathed with the wonder of a child being told Santa just filled the Christmas stockings. "That would be just . . ." I realized he had already left me and was headed toward the building.

Looking out the front window, I watched him cross the dim parking lot with a long-legged, unhurried gait, then disappear behind a row of tractors. For a fleeting moment, I was given to the terrifying thought that he wasn't coming back.

Get real, Collie. Just stay in the car. He'll be back in a minute, and you'll be on the road. When you get back to Dallas, you can sue the rental-car company for giving you a defective gas gauge. Yes, sue the rental car company. That would feel good. . . .

Five minutes ticked by, and I started to worry again. Then he appeared out of the darkness like Batman coming to the rescue. Batman in well-worn jeans and a ball cap. Lugging a gas can. My hero.

"Pop that gas-cap cover," he called as he passed my window.

I did, listening to the vacuumlike sound as he opened the cap, then the sweet *swish-swish* of gas going in. Within moments, he put the cap on and closed the cover.

"That oughta do it," he called, stepping into the shadow of the sign pole, so that I could barely see him. "See if she'll start."

I turned the key, and the car sputtered stubbornly for a moment, then roared to life. "Sounds good," I called. "What do I owe you for the gas?"

"Not a thing, ma'am." Stepping forward, he tipped the brim of his ball cap. "It's been a pure pleasure." He turned away and headed toward the building before I had a chance to tell him thank-you.

Rolling the window down, I stuck my head out and called, "Thank you!"

He waved a hand over his shoulder to tell me it wasn't necessary. "Have a good trip to San Saline. Straight down this highway. You can't miss it. Watch out for deer."

Watch out for deer. Eight-foot rattlesnakes and now deer. If I ever made it to San Saline, I was going to call my *friend* Laura Draper and demand hazard pay.

Even so, as I pulled onto the highway and cruised into the star-filled Texas night, I was strangely glad I had come. It felt good to be out of bed, gone from my apartment, and doing something again. I had a sense of regaining myself, which was strange, considering that nothing around me was familiar. In the bright moonlight, I could see the shapes of the hills becoming steeper and sharper, the thick stands of brush changing to wispy grass, dotted here and there by thick clumps of twisted, heavy-limbed trees. Through the open window, a cool, dry breeze brought a heavy floral scent, reminding me of the blue flowers I had admired earlier. I would have to ask somebody what they were called. . . .

The quiet, as usual, caused my mind to drift. It wandered, as always, to the past three months, to the very start of everything that had gone wrong. I could see my boss of ten years, a man I trusted and thought I could count on, leaning confidently back in his chair on the other side of the conference table.

"There's no meat to this thing. They'll never bring it all the way to trial. Small out-of-court settlement and a retraction on the back page, that's all it will amount to. It'll all be over in a month," he said. He had called all of us in to be briefed by the lawyers on what we should and shouldn't say in regard to the libel lawsuit brought against the newspaper by Senator Williams.

At the time I wasn't worried. The fact that my name was even involved was purely accidental—a slip in the editing room that gave me the byline for an article I had not written, but only edited and touched up for J. Ross Bennett, my boss. I knew the facts behind the article had to be airtight. If Bennett had information that candidate Williams had taken illegal campaign contributions, then it was true. I was a little surprised to hear him even mention printing a retraction of the article. Bennett's facts were always reliable. He knew every back alley and closet in D.C., and he knew where to get information. Libel suits were nothing new for him, and he always won.

It'll all be over in a month. Bennett was right. It was all over for *me* in a month. Job, reputation, contacts, work relationships, personal relationship. Crunch.

Over me like a steamroller over Wile E. Coyote. Amazing how much your life can be changed by one simple miscue in the editing room.

Bennett was wrong about the case settling out of court. Before I knew it, I was testifying against the paper, and when I testified, I did the one thing the paper didn't want me to do. I told the truth. I told everyone in the court that my part in the article went only as far as editing and touch-up. When I did it, the look in Bennett's eyes told me he was going to hang me out to dry. He had wanted me to accept responsibility for the article and simply claim reporter's privilege, refusing to reveal my sources. He said that the paper's case would look cleaner that way. He promised that the paper would defend me to the fullest, and that in the end, the case would amount to nothing if I played it their way.

If I had known then what would come of telling the truth, I might have decided to lie.

Liars never prosper, my grandmother would have said. I was proof that people who tell the truth don't either. The people who prosper are the ones who keep their heads down and stay out of firing range.

Like Brett—Mr. "Collie, I think we should cool it until this deposition thing is over." Mr. "I love you, Coll, but you've got to understand. . . ." Mr. Couldn't be bothered to return my messages. Mr. Too busy to come by. Mr. "You understand, don't you, Coll?" Mr. "I've met somebody else. I didn't mean for it to happen, but you've been so tied up with this lawsuit."

Thinking of it still made my blood boil. My hands

kneaded the steering wheel, imagining his neck. His and my ex-boss's. The two-faced shmucks. When it came right down to it, they couldn't stand a woman who could compete on their ball field.

Cut it out, Coll. This is pointless. It's over. It's over. It's done. My mantra of the past month or so. It never did any good before, but this time I felt my anger flow out the window like cigarette smoke and vaporize into the night.

Amazed, I smiled and gave myself a mental pat on the back. I was getting better—healing, if you could call it that. Coming back from the dead.

Shaking my head, I took a deep breath of the fragrant night air and tried to think of something else. The work ahead of me was a safe subject—depressing, but safe. First to San Saline to the Hawthorne House Bed-and-Breakfast, operated by the same family for 150 years, famous for its authentic Texas food, especially delicacies made from some kind of native fruit called the prickly pear. Then to the Bluebonnet Festival in Burnet for an annual chili cook-off. I hoped that wasn't one of those festivals that included live snakes. Then to a town farther south called Fredericksburg, a tourist destination famous for German food and antique stores. Next, to the riverwalk in San Antonio for famous Tex-Mex recipes near the Alamo—that was to occupy the space of two articles. After that, to the Salt Creek Ranch to help prepare a chuck-wagon supper for visiting "dudes"—people, undoubtedly, much like myself. Following Salt Creek, I was to go to a town called Copperas Cove for a Civil War reenactment, including food of the period, particularly chess pie and caramel pie. My final assignment was another bed-and-breakfast on the way back to Dallas in a town called West, which was famous for Czechoslovakian food, especially Kolaches.

Rubbing the kindling ache between my eyebrows, I considered it all. The whole thing still seemed a little *Twilight Zone*-ish, as if I could not possibly *really* be heading off on such a pointless project, as if I were dreaming and would wake up in my bed any moment with the dirty laundry and the food containers. Glancing at the fax, barely visible in the dim light on the seat beside me, I reaffirmed the reality of my position. At the bottom of the page, Laura had scrawled, *Work from the Hawthorne House in San Saline, or get rooms in other towns as you go. Your choice. Topics are flexible; fax me with any other article ideas. Everything within easy driving distance. Have a good time. Relax. Laura.* And then this annoying smiley-face with a mocking, one-sided smirk, laughing at me from the bottom of the paper.

The car topped a hill, and the lights of San Saline appeared in the valley below like a shimmering oasis. Filled with something akin to euphoria, I gazed across the distance at the flickering lights nestled in the tree-lined valley ahead. Finally, I had arrived. It looked more promising than the last town—like there might actually be a place where I could get food.

A flicker of motion crossed the bottom of my vision, and I glanced at the road just in time to see a deer bound from the ditch in front of me and bolt into my lane, then freeze in the headlights. Gritting my teeth, I hit the brake and swerved into the oncoming lane, hoping the deer would stay where it was. My heart froze in my throat, then jumped back to my chest and started beating again as I passed the deer and moved into my own lane. Slowly I descended the remainder of the hill and entered the city limits of San Saline, where something familiar caught my eye from the roadside.

Welcome to San Saline, the sign said. *Visit Friendly's Tractors II, Home of True the Tractor Man*. Shaking my head, I thought of my encounter beneath the sign in the last town. It all seemed funny now.

Chuckling at myself, I drove slowly down the main street of San Saline, which I was happy to see had more to offer than my previous stop. Centered around a quaint town square with an old, German-style courthouse, it contained several antique stores, a hardware store, a pecan shop, a resale boutique, a dollar store, a ladies' dry-goods store that looked like it was straight out of the 1950s, Harvey's Boots-'n'-More, and a pizza parlor. Just off the square were a couple of churches, a café that looked like it was a revamped adobe cow barn, a car dealership, a Dairy Queen, and, of course, Friendly's Tractors, complete with the same flickering green sign.

Staring at the sign, I almost missed the driveway of the Hawthorne House Bed-and-Breakfast, located just past the Sale Barn Café and Friendly's Tractors.

I turned into the driveway and proceeded slowly through the ivy-covered stone gateway toward the main house. Even in the darkness, it was an imposing structure, nearly two and a half stories of ancient white stone with tall, narrow windows and a sloping tin roof. A generous porch and second-story balcony circled the front and south side, supported by huge columns of stacked white stone cylinders that looked like they had been chipped into shape by hand. Between the center pillars hung a sign that told me I was in the right place. *Hawthorne House Bed and Breakfast, Est. 1867.*

An ample, gray-haired woman appeared on the porch as I sat reading the sign. She stood holding a shawl around her shoulders, peering at me like I might be someone suspicious.

Parking the car, I climbed out and limped stiffly up the walk, realizing that I hadn't stretched my legs since Waco.

"Hello?" I said. "Is this the Hawthorne House Bed-and-Breakfast? I . . . I have a reservation."

Breaking into an enormous grin, the woman descended the steps in a stiff-legged hobble and stretched out a hand, welcoming me with surprising enthusiasm. "Oh, it's you," she said. "I've been getting worried about you. You should have been here a half hour ago. You didn't hit a deer, did you?"

"No." I wondered if she had me confused with someone else.

"Well, that's good. That's good." Laying a hand on my shoulder, she guided me along a pathway that led around the side of the house to a row of four cottages out back. "I'm glad you made it. I was just about to call and get the constable out of bed to go after you."

I stopped walking, certain she had me confused with

someone else. "I'm sorry, but you must have me confused with someone. I'm just here to rent a room."

"Oh, no, ma'am." Herding me on, she patted me like a puppy. "You're just who we were expecting. True the Tractor Man called just after eight-thirty and said to be on the lookout for a blue car with a frizzy redheaded lady that talks like a Yankee. Said if I didn't see you in an hour and a half, I'd better call and tell the constable to go on up the highway, because you'd probably hit a deer or got lost."

"Oh," I said meekly, somewhere between insulted, grateful, and amazed. *A frizzy redheaded lady that talks like a Yankee*. Not exactly a flattering description. I had a feeling it wasn't meant to be. Following her onto the porch of the first stone cabin, I waited for her to unlock the front door, and said, "This is really cute. Were these cabins part of the original estate?"

Nodding, she opened the door and guided me inside. In the light, she looked younger than I had originally thought, perhaps in her sixties, round-faced, ample-bodied. "This was the first structure built by my husband's great-great-great-grandfather when he homesteaded the place. The other three were built later as workers' quarters, but this one is our biggest and our best. Jasper just finished redoing it. It has a phone *and* a TV. We have that satellite cable here, so we get *ninety-nine* channels, but you have to watch the one we're watching in the big house. If you want me to change the channel, just ring me on the phone, and I'll do it right away. We like to make our guests happy. Since you missed supper, I fixed you a basket there on the table—bread, some chicken salad, deviled eggs, watermelon pickles, and a slice of homemade pecan pie. There's tea and lemonade in the little refrigerator. And a bowl of fruit." She paused for a breath. "Is there anything else I can get you?"

"I . . . uh . . . I can't think of anything." I wasn't used to such royal treatment. In fact, it made me uncomfortable and mildly suspicious. Where I come from, if someone treats you like that, they want something. Everyone in D.C. has an agenda.

"Anything special you want to watch on television tonight?"

I shook my head.

"Well, then, I'll let you alone. I work across the street at the café in the mornings, so our guests—well, you're the only one we have right now—usually take breakfast over there. That is, if you're up and about before ten-thirty. Otherwise, you'll have to take lunch."

"No, I'm not a late sleeper. I'm good on a few hours a night." Although at the moment I felt like I could sleep for a week. "Did the editors from *Southern Woman* explain why I'm here?"

Reaching out, she patted me on the upper arms, and for a moment I had the uncomfortable feeling I was going to be hugged. I have never been the hugging type, especially not with strangers. "Oh, yes, and we are so excited! Having our little community in the *Southern Woman* is just the most exciting thing that has happened around here in years. The whole town is buzzing about it."

"Well . . ." I tried to think of a nice way to tell her the

article was just supposed to be a small piece about her bed-and-breakfast and a few traditional recipes, not an advertisement for the town of San Saline. "What they really want is a little material about your establishment, some traditional recipes, and information about where they came from."

"Mm-hmm, mm-hmm." I had the distinct feeling she hadn't heard a word I said, as she stepped onto the porch. "You just come by the café tomorrow morning, and you'll have more stories than you can write, I can promise you that. Now, I'll leave you alone. I've got to get back to the house. I'd best get Jasper to bed before he starts snoring in his chair, or he'll be there until morning."

Standing in the doorway, I shook my head, watching her hobble down the stone path. She wasn't going to be an easy interview. I didn't have the first clue how to do pointless human-interest stuff. I wasn't very interested in humans—not the folksy down-home kind, at any rate. I liked to study people with powerful secrets and dirty little lies. . . .

But when you haven't got steak, sometimes you have to eat hot dogs and try to pretend. Anyway, I didn't have the energy to worry about it. All I wanted was a meal and a good night's sleep in the cute iron bed on the other side of the cabin. Tomorrow morning I'd put on my reporter's cap and see if I could come up with something interesting to say about the food in Nowhere, Texas. If not, I'd just have to call and explain the problem to Laura, say thanks-but-no-thanks for the assignment offer, and get on the plane home.

Chapter 2

THE sound of snakes crawling woke me sometime in the gray hours of dawn. Pulling the covers up to my neck, I stared at the rough-hewn cedar beams on the adobe ceiling. I listened as a slithering sound crossed the tin roof just over my head.

Rattlers are like weeds around here. They're everyplace. A heebie-jeebie ran through my body, raising a rash of goose bumps, and I pulled the covers tighter, listening as the sound moved to the other side of the roof, near the fireplace. I wondered if a rattlesnake could climb up the outside of a chimney, down the inside, across the floor, and up the posts of an iron bed. Then I wondered if one might have done it already.

I was out from under the covers and into a squat on the bed with a speed and agility I hadn't known since my days as an adolescent gymnast. Feeling clumsily on the wall behind me, I found the reading lamp and pulled the chain, filling the room with dim pink light. Throwing back the covers, I inspected the bed. Empty. Crawling to the other end, I peered over the footboard and checked the floor. Nothing. I held very still and listened for sounds on the roof again. Silence.

"Good God, Collie, get a grip." I suddenly felt very stupid. Good thing I was alone in the room. Rattlesnakes on the roof! Geez, what an imagination. Amazing what a half-asleep mind can come up with.

Pulling the covers over the bed, I propped the pillows and lay down again, watching yellow light gather slowly around the edges of the window blinds. In a half hour or so, it would be late enough to call my mom. I still wasn't sure what I was going to tell her. *Hi, Mom, I'm in Texas doing an important story on . . .* On what? What possible assignment could I be doing here for *American Business Daily*? Why did I still feel compelled to lie about my job situation, anyway? Thirty-six years old and I was still hiding my detention slips from my parents. There was something really pathetic about that.

Hi, Mom. I'm in Texas doing a story, but I can't tell you yet what it's about. Not a lie, exactly. It might work, assuming I could get Mom to swallow it. Trying to hide the truth from her was like trying to hide an egg from a ferret. Once she got curious, she just kept sniffing until she found what she was looking for and cracked it open.

My best hope was to wait until after eight o'clock and call Dad at work at his electrical-supply business. He would relay the message to Mom, and that would take care of it. Then I could—

A horrible scream broke the morning silence, and I bolted from the bed, my heart hammering.

"Help! Help!" It came again, a child's voice from somewhere outside—a desperate sound between a cry and a scream. "Mama! Mama! Help!"

I thought instantly of the snake on the roof, and panic rushed through my sleep-laden limbs like wildfire. There really was a snake, and someone was in trouble. I stood frozen, my mind spinning. *Call 911? The main house? No time. Get something to kill it.*

Frantically, I stuck my feet into the red pumps I'd had on the night before, caught one heel on the hem of my knee-length nightshirt, and stumbled across the room, knocking over the fireplace tools. Grabbing the fireplace stoker and a paring knife from the kitchen cabinet, I rushed to the door, threw it open, and bolted into the yard, listening for the cry to come again.

"Mama!" It repeated, this time from somewhere in front of the main house. "Help! Help! Help!"

Heart racing, I held the stoker in front of me and stumbled through the wet grass to the front of the house as the cry rose to a blood-curdling pitch, almost unrecognizable, animallike. Suddenly it stopped.

I froze, listening with the knife and stoker held ready, waiting for the cry to come again.

"I'm almost afraid to ask what you're doing there." A voice from the porch startled me, and I whirled around clumsily, my heels sinking into the wet sod. Two men were sitting in the porch chairs drinking coffee. The older one, wearing a cowboy hat and faded overalls, stood up, looking confused. "Is there something I can help you with?"

"I think someone's being attacked by a rattlesnake!" I said, panting. "I heard a snake on my roof this morning, and then I heard someone screaming for help." They made no move to assist me, and my frustration grew epic. "Didn't you hear it? Someone was screaming! Just a moment ago! It sounded like a child. Over there somewhere!" I waved the fireplace stoker toward the wisteria bushes by the fence.

Finally the younger man dragged himself from his

chair and came down the stairs. "You going to kill the snake with those?" He motioned to the stoker and the paring knife, his eyes squinting skeptically beneath the brim of his ball cap. "Did you know a diamondback can propel himself as far as five feet when he strikes?"

I held the weapons out, more than ready to be rescued. "It was all I could find. Please! Someone's in trouble."

The cry came again from the bushes, sounding even more frantic, more contorted and strange.

"See! There it is!" I waved the knife frantically, my mind racing in overdrive.

To my complete dismay, my would-be rescuer snatched his cap from his head, slapped it against the thigh of his jeans, broke into a huge grin, then doubled over and guffawed with laughter.

Openmouthed, I looked from the now-silent bushes to him, then to the old man who was standing at the edge of the porch, trying not to laugh.

"What is going on!" I stomped my foot, and the heel of my shoe sank in and caught, making me stumble around like a drunk.

The old man on the porch hobbled down the steps with his hands out, ready to catch me if I fell down. "Ma'am, I'm sorry." His lips twitched beneath a thick gray mustache. To his credit, he didn't laugh. "That ain't a person making that noise. . . . It's a peacock. My wife should've told you about the peafowl. Usually she warns people ahead of time that they sound kind of like a kid screaming for Mama. They always do that in the morning."

Dumbfounded, I stared at him, slowly lowering my weapons, wishing I could melt into the soil like a snowman and disappear. *This has to be a bad dream.* Looking down at my bare legs and the red pumps half-buried in the dirt, I got a mental image of just how ridiculous I must look, standing there in my silk Tweety Bird nightshirt, hair sticking up everywhere, no makeup, armed with a paring knife and a fireplace poker. It was, without idiomatic doubt, one of the most humiliating moments of my life.

The younger man stood up finally, still gasping for breath, and the older man reached over and jabbed him in the shoulder. "For heaven's sake, Jimmy, cut that out. She ain't the first person to be fooled by those peafowl."

Struggling to stitch together the scraps of my dignity, I stumbled sideways onto the stone path where the old man stood. "I'm sorry to have upset your morning," I said, trying to ignore their stifled chuckles. "I . . . It's been a weird night."

The old man looked at me with genuine sympathy, then shot an irritated glance at the younger man. "I'm real sorry, ma'am. What you heard on your roof this morning was probably just the peacocks, too. They make a weird noise draggin' those tail feathers across the tin." He gave me a friendly, apologetic grin. "I guess now you'll have a funny story about Texas to tell the folks back home."

"I suppose so." *Not a chance. Never.* "Excuse me. I need to go get dressed now. Glad I could liven up your morning." I turned around and headed toward my cabin with as regal a bearing as was possible.

An hour later, after a bath in the little claw-footed tub, a cup of coffee at the quaint drop-leaf breakfast table, and a little time spent surveying the charming antique decor of the cabin, I was feeling better about the whole thing. It even seemed a little funny. I chuckled at myself in the mirror as I finished my makeup and slipped on a casual blue pantsuit. Combing my hair into a twist at the back of my head, I clipped it into place and stared at myself in the mirror. I looked like a person I could barely remember—the consummate, confident professional I once was, and would be again, once my peacock-chasing, snake-killing, recipe-writing days in Texas were over. When I got back to D.C., I was going to start knocking on doors. And I wasn't taking no for an answer. I'd start wherever I had to with another newspaper and work my way up from there. I didn't know who to be if I wasn't Colleen Collins, newspaper reporter, the person I had been since my high school days in my mother's journalism class. The job was who I was, and without it, I'd be mush in my bed forever. If I worked hard, I could finish up this recipe thing in a few weeks and be back in D.C. getting on with the rest of my life, with eight thousand dollars in my pocket.

Meanwhile, I needed to call my folks. I checked the clock. Seven-thirty—eight-thirty in Baltimore. They would both be gone to work by now. Dad would be busy at the store, not a lot of time to talk. I could tell him where I was and not have to answer a lot of questions.

I dialed the number on the old black rotary phone and waited nervously for the call to connect. Static hummed in my ear like an army of bees about to swarm.

"Hi, Dad," I said when I recognized his voice on the line.

I heard the sound of papers rustling, and for a moment I wondered if he knew it was me.

"Well, hello, honey," he said finally. I could always count on Dad to be glad to hear from me.

It made me feel lousy about lying to him. But it wouldn't matter once I got back to D.C. and secured a new job. "You busy?" I knew he would say yes.

"As usual. Lots of contractor orders today. Have to get the electrical components together for delivery to a big new building in Baltimore. What's going on with you?"

If only you knew. "Nothing. I just wanted you to know I'll be in Texas on an assignment for a few weeks." The phone connection fuzzed, and I wondered if he heard me.

"Where?" he said. I could hear the cash register ringing in the background. "Your mom was hoping you could come up for the twins' birthday party weekend after next. We haven't seen you in months, Coll."

"Oh, I wish I could." A lie. I just wasn't up to a big family holiday—watching my parents dote on their only grandchildren, my younger brother's twin daughters. Listening to my mom hint at the fact that I was a washout in the marriage-and-family department. No possibility of grandkids here. It never bothered me until I turned thirty-five, and it became apparent that time had pretty well run out. "I'll be tied up in Texas for a few weeks on this assignment. I'll come see you guys when I get back. I promise. Meanwhile, you can get me on the cell, if you need me."

"All right, hon. I'll tell Mom."

A sigh of relief went through me. "Great. Tell Rob and Kathy hi for me. I'll send something for the twins' birthday. Maybe cowboy hats."

Dad chuckled that potbellied chuckle I had always loved. "Very good. We'll talk to you later, hon."

"All right. 'Bye, Dad." I hung up the phone with a growing sense of relief. That would probably take care of things. Mom was busy this time of year with teaching journalism and getting the school yearbook distributed. She probably wouldn't bother calling to check on me.

I sat with my hand on the phone for a minute, feeling guilty about the pack of lies I had just unleashed on my father. I was wrong in keeping the truth from them, and I knew it. I was wrong in keeping the deception going for three months, letting them think Brett and I were still together and I was still working for *American Business Daily.*

I didn't spend much time with my family anymore, and I wasn't even sure why. It just seemed as though, now that Rob was married and had the twins, the family focus was on babies, and I was outside the loop. It was easier to stay in D.C., stay busy working, and spend holidays on assignment, or traveling to some getaway with Brett. It was easier not to have to listen to my mother hinting about marriage, and that perhaps there was an underlying reason why Brett and I, in six years together, had never headed down the road to matrimony, and about how she had known the day she met my father that he was the one for her.

I wondered how it was possible to know something like that. I had thought Brett was for me. I had thought we were a perfect match—both dedicated to our careers, neither one jealous of the other's time commitments, neither one clingy or demanding, both working for the same newspaper, him in marketing and PR and me as a reporter. It seemed like a perfect setup, yet now I was finding out that the weave was so loose, the slightest wind tore apart the fabric of our relationship.

My eyes started to water, and I pushed away the thoughts before they could overtake me again. Grabbing my tape recorder and pad, I glimpsed myself in the mirror and shook my head. That just didn't look like a person who couldn't face up to her own parents. That looked like the Colleen Collins who did exactly what she wanted and didn't ask for anyone's permission.

"Go forth and conquer," I muttered, turning toward the door. "It's time to climb back into the ring."

I had myself psyched by the time I reached the café across the highway from Hawthorne House. Getting out of the car, I studied the ramshackle building. It didn't look much better in the daylight than it had the night before. Built of crumbling adobe covered with pink paint and framed on one corner by a wall of glass bricks, it looked like an unholy mating between an Indian pueblo and a 1950s diner. Embedded into the adobe on either side of the front door were gigantic wooden wagon wheels, which at some point had been painted pink with the building. Over the door hung a sign that read, *Sale Barn Café,* and below that in a haphazard combination of capital and lowercase letters, *Y'all come on in.* The odor around the place, wafting up from acres and acres of cattle corrals next door, was anything but welcoming.

Taking my notebook and tape recorder from the car, I closed the door, wishing I had eaten at the room before coming. The place looked like it should be housing the cows rather than feeding people. Apparently I was the only one who felt that way. The parking lot was filled with pickup trucks, a few cars, one tractor, a flatbed semi with hay on it, and two horse trailers with horses standing in them.

That otherworldly feeling came over me again as I walked to the front door. I was so far out of my element, the distance wasn't even measurable. *Y'all come on in* didn't feel like it applied to me.

The door jerked open just as I was about to reach for it. Two men in cowboy regalia stepped out, looking like they were about to go to a movie set somewhere. I couldn't help myself. I stopped for a moment to stare.

The one who was second in line held the door open for me, tipping his hat. "Morning, ma'am."

"Good morning," I said, and hurried through the door into the dimly lit interior.

I stopped beside the entrance to figure out the lay of the place, and at that moment everyone stopped what they were doing to look at me. At least it seemed that way. Scanning the room for a place to sit, I came to the uncomfortable conclusion that I was the only one in the room wearing a suit, or any form of business attire, even though it was nine o'clock Thursday morning. Tomorrow, I resolved, jeans and a T-shirt.

The only empty table was a booth near the swinging saloon doors to the kitchen. I hurried quickly across the room and slid into the seat. At the table beside me, a woman about my mother's age was having a heated discussion with an elderly couple, so I stared straight ahead at the kitchen doors, trying not to look like I was eavesdropping.

Mrs. Hawthorne came from behind the counter, pausing at the table next door to refill coffee cups. Her presence temporarily stopped the woman at the table from berating her elderly parents for forgetting to pay their monthly bills, and thereby having their utilities accidentally turned off. She had been in the process of threatening to take over their checkbook and their car. For their own good, of course.

I felt sorry for the old couple, and I was glad when Mrs. Hawthorne intervened. I wondered if her timing was not entirely accidental.

"How are you this morning, Miss Grace?" she said to the elderly woman.

The woman just nodded, looking despondent, and stirred her coffee.

"Oh, hell, we're in trouble with Francis again," her

husband said, straightening the hump in his shoulders and craning his neck so that he could look at Mrs. Hawthorne. "Mama forgot to pay the electric bill, and Francis had to go all the way over to Brownwood to get it turned back on. They been bickerin' at each other all morning."

Mrs. Hawthorne smiled, patting the old woman on the shoulder. "Oh, well, that isn't so bad. Everyone forgets things from time to time. You ought to check into that automatic draft. I have it on my electric and phone, and the company just takes the money right out of my checking account and sends me a statement. It makes things real easy." Without waiting for an answer, she turned around and set a coffee cup in front of me, giving me a quick wink that said she knew I'd been listening. "Good morning, Miss Collins. Did you have a comfortable rest?"

"Yes," I said, not wanting to elaborate on my morning fiasco. "But please, everybody calls me Collie."

She leaned against the back of the opposite seat, her brows drawing together into a worried knot. "I heard you had an experience with the peafowl."

I rolled my eyes, feeling blood come into my cheeks. News traveled fast. No wonder everyone was looking at me when I came in. "Yes, I did. But I'm happy to report that both the peafowl and I survived."

"Oh, that's good to hear." She patted me on the hand, seeming overly relieved that I wasn't mad about the birds. "Those peafowl are kind of a nuisance, but they keep the snakes away."

"They do?" I suddenly had a new respect for the peacocks.

Mrs. Hawthorne lowered herself to the seat across from me, heaving a huge sigh as she slid her ample body between the seat and the table. "Oh, sure they do. Peafowl, guineas, anything like that will kill the snakes. I do hate snakes, so it's worth it to me to have the peafowl around." She giggled again. "Jasper sure does get tired of them, though. He's about ready to butcher some and fry them up."

I swallowed hard, unsure of what to say. "Not really?" It made me wonder about the chicken salad from the night before.

Mrs. Hawthorne threw her gray head back and laughed so loudly I was sure everyone in the place would stare at us, but no one seemed to notice. "Oh, no. I'm just teasing. Don't worry; we won't feed you any peacocks."

Her laughter was infectious. "I was worried." I chuckled. I had a sudden strange sensation of sitting with my grandmother in her living room. It made me feel guilty that I hadn't seen her in almost a year. "So," I said, sobering up and opening my notepad. "What I really wanted to do this morning was spend a little time interviewing you, perhaps take a tour of the bed-and-breakfast, maybe look around the town a little. I'll be doing my own photography, so I'd like to get a picture or two of your house, and maybe one of a prickly pear tree to go with the jelly recipe."

Cocking her head to one side, she squinted at me as if I were speaking Greek. "What kind of tree?"

"A . . . prickly pear . . . tree?" I said a little more tentatively. "Are they in season this time of year?"

She slapped a hand over her mouth and laughter spilled around the edges as her face turned red with restraint. Fanning herself with her other hand, she shook it off finally, and said, "Pardon. That just struck me funny. Prickly pear isn't a tree; it's a cactus that grows around here."

My interest crept up. "Really?" I said. I'd never heard of people eating cactus. It sounded interesting and thoroughly Western—something that might make a satisfactory article for *Southern Woman.* "I didn't know cactus were edible."

Miss Grace at the table beside us perked up with sudden interest, interjecting before Mrs. Hawthorne could answer, "There was one year that all of us would have starved to death but for prickly pear cactus and jackrabbits." Beside her, her husband nodded, adding credibility to the story.

Francis, the daughter, rolled her eyes and huffed an irritated breath. "Oh, Mother, for heaven's sake. Don't start telling stories. I swear, nobody wants to hear that old stuff. It isn't true, anyway."

Miss Grace looked sideways at her daughter with a judicial countenance. "It most surely is true. Y'all young folks can't imagine it because y'all never had any real hard times, but when I was little, it was hard times around here."

Silently I flipped on my tape recorder, then sat mesmerized, noticing that almost everyone on our side of the restaurant had stopped to listen.

Miss Grace sat straighter in her chair and went on. "There was a terrible drought. People was coming south out of the dust bowl, setting up tents and squatting all over the place, begging for food and stealing things. There wasn't no work to be had, and even if you had money, there wasn't much food to buy. That one summer when I was six years old, my daddy got a bunch of old skinny cows from a man who didn't have no way to feed them and didn't want to sell them to the government slaughter program. Back then, the government was givin' folks five dollars a cow just to kill them and get them off the land. Now, Daddy knew from my Papaw James that the old-timers used to burn the thorns off the prickly pear bushes and feed them to the cows." She laughed, throwing her frail white arms into the air. "And Lord knows, we had plenty of prickly pear. Lots of other folks had cleared all the cactus off their pastures, but my daddy wasn't always a real enterprisin' man. Turned out that droughty summer, we were glad of it. Our cows held out while lots of others starved in the pasture. Daddy broke two of the cows to milk, and Mama carried the milk to town every day and sold it to the folks who had money. Sometimes she gave it away if folks needed it for a baby." She paused to take a sip of her coffee, and I looked around at the listeners—young cowboys, old farmers, two waitresses, a table of teenage girls, a group of women doing Bible study, and me, all listening, some turning around to watch, some just pausing in their meals and turning an ear our way.

"Daddy never killed one single cow for us to eat that

year, either," Miss Grace continued earnestly. "He shot jackrabbits and we boiled those, so as to keep all them cows for milkin' and breedin'. Daddy had another side business during Prohibition, too. He had a setup in an old cave near Lucy Creek, and in there, he brewed mash from them prickly pear fruit, and also made some pretty good pink wine. We wasn't supposed to talk about it, of course, but Daddy made a pretty good penny sellin' his produce. After it was over, he was a pretty well-off man."

Clapping her hands together in front of herself, she threw her head back and laughed. "He used to always tell folks he made his money in prickly pears and jackrabbits." Her laughter ended in a wistful sigh, and she picked up her spoon, stirring her coffee thoughtfully, as if she had forgotten we were there. "My mama always made the most wonderful prickly pear jelly. We children would run around in the summer, gathering up them fruit." She paused thoughtfully, looking first at her daughter, then at me, though I wasn't sure why. "I don't know what ever happened to that recipe. If I had that recipe, I believe I'd gather up a batch of cactus fruit this summer and make myself some jelly."

Two tables over, a young man in cowboy clothing stood up and picked up his check. "Well, I wish you'd come do it at the Salt Creek Pasture, Miss Grace. Then I wouldn't have to spend half the year poisoning them darned prickly pear bushes. Hey, maybe if I tell my boss your story, he'd let us leave 'em for the cattle to eat. Reckon?"

Everyone laughed as he made his way to the cash register.

A woman in the booth behind us turned around as he walked out the door. "Oh, I can tell you how to make cactus jelly, Miss Grace." Perhaps sixty years old, she had a newly teased beehive hairdo that looked like it was fresh from the beauty parlor. "My mother never made jelly of any kind, but when I married, my husband wanted the things his mother always made. I looked and asked, and looked and asked, trying to find someone who could tell me how to make cactus fruit jelly. Finally, I was given the recipe by a lady at the 1959 Lampasas County show." She paused, rolling her eyes upward and to one side, then looking back at us. "I guess I've been making that jelly for forty-odd years now. My husband liked it, and now since he is gone, I send some with the kids and grandkids when they come to visit, but that isn't too often since they've moved to San Angelo."

The conversation paused for a minute as she reached into her purse and took out a notepad and pencil, then primly set the pad on the corner of the table and held the pencil in a teacherlike fashion.

Trying not to be noticed, I flipped over the top sheet of my notebook and took out my pen to write down the recipe. The flow of the conversation was so perfect and natural that I supposed they had forgotten I was there. Suddenly I wasn't an outsider at all, but just one of the local folk waiting for my turn to add something to the conversation. The feeling was comfortable and warm, welcoming even—like being in my mother's living room on Christmas night after everything was finished and everyone was just sitting around talking.

As she went on, I found myself strangely at home, and strangely interested in the making of prickly pear jelly. Looking around, I noticed that the crowd had thinned, but almost everyone left had stopped what they were doing to listen to the conversation.

"Anyway," she went on, writing the recipe as she spoke, "all I do is pick about forty or so cactus fruit, wash them and remove the spines, put them sliced in a pot with about a cup of water, boil them until they are ready to juice, then strain them through an old flour sack. Use a half bottle of Certo, three and a half cups of sugar, and juice of two lemons to make the jelly, then seal it in jars or make freezer jell if you prefer."

Miss Grace nodded, reaching over to tap the corner of the paper with a look of recognition. "Yes, that's right. That is just the way my mother made hers. Now I remember. I remember clear as yesterday, but she threw the fruit into the pot spines and all, and just reached into the pot and sliced it with a big knife. I can remember standing on my stool by the stove watching her slice up that pink fruit, and smellin' that sweet, sweet smell." She smiled, looking at her daughter, who seemed to have lost her ire. "I can't believe I could of forgot that."

Francis smiled, reaching across the table and giving her mother's hand a squeeze. "Well, Mama, it just isn't something you've probably thought about in a while. You know, I don't think you ever told me that story about Grandpa and the cows."

Across the table from me, Mrs. Hawthorne cleared her throat and scooted loudly in the vinyl bench, obviously determined to add to the conversation. "You know, the secret to the best prickly pear jelly is to pick the fruit about half-ripe. It starts to have a bitter taste if you let it go too long. I pick mine with a big meat fork and . . ."

I lost track of the conversation. My thoughts were focused instead on Miss Grace and her husband, now sitting with eyes bright and chins tilted upward—and their daughter, Francis, looking at them with admiration and interest, suddenly reminded that her parents still had something worthwhile to say, something yet to teach her. Looking at the recipe together, they whispered about washing canning jars and picking cactus fruit. Whether they ever would, I couldn't say, but it really didn't matter. The unpaid electric bill and fight were forgotten, and the car keys remained in the old man's pocket.

Next to them, the woman with the beehive slowly folded her pad and tucked it away in her purse, then turned to finish her breakfast, smiling to herself. I wondered if she was listening to the remnants of the prickly pear conversation, or just lost in thought. Perhaps she was thinking of a young wife at the 1959 Lampasas County show collecting a coveted jelly recipe, or of a young mother standing over the boiling pot while her daughter perched nearby on a stool, watching the knife slice through the sweet pink cactus fruit. Perhaps she was thinking of her grandchildren and wondering when they would come visit and how many jars of jelly she would send.

It's strange, I thought, how memories are like boats floating out from their anchors. They drift through the edges of our consciousness, unnoticed, unexamined, mere shadows, until we run across the thing to which they are anchored. Wrapping our hands around the ropes, we pull them to the dock again, and they are as clear and as real as if we had experienced them yesterday.

Memories can be anchored to anything—a person, a place, a taste, a scent, an object, a melody. Even to something so insignificant as the tiny pink fruit of a cactus so worthless that most people clear it from the land without a second thought.

I stayed in the café as the breakfast hour waned and the customers paid their bills, stepping out the door into the bright midmorning sunshine and into daily lives I could only guess at.

"I'll wash things up and be ready to go in a jiffy," Mrs. Hawthorne called from the kitchen as the last customers left.

Looking over my notes, I turned to a clean sheet of paper, and my head filled with words. "No hurry," I called, and started writing, in longhand, which I hadn't done in years.

The pen glided over the paper in deep, rapid strokes as I pictured the café full again—the prickly pear-killing cowboy over there, the woman with the beehive hairdo at the next table, Miss Grace and her husband with their daughter, Francis. I listened to them talking again about prickly pears and jackrabbits, and milk routes to town, where milk was given free to people with hungry babies. I wrote about how their faces looked as they told their stories, and what their eyes said, and what they seemed to be feeling. I wrote about the way we are to each other, young people and old people—seldom really equal in our lives, seldom able to enjoy one another, one always a burden to the other, never able to really hear each other. Never really taking the time to listen. First the parents too busy for the children, then the children too busy for the parents.

And all the while, life goes on, the story ended, *boats full of memories floating out to sea, waiting for the moment when we gather on the dock and pull in the mooring lines.*

Setting the pen on the table, I stared at the words. It was my handwriting, yet not like anything I had ever written. Not like anything I had ever *thought*. Not like me at all.

Had my grandmother ever sat alone in some restaurant telling people about me and complaining that I never found time to visit? What stories might she have to tell that I had never heard, and how much more time did I have left to listen?

I wondered what she would tell me now, if I called her and told her everything that had happened in the past three months. Gran and I didn't butt heads as my mother and I often did. Gran and I understood each other. She had been a determined career woman before she married—a music teacher, a composer, and a writer, a woman ahead of her time, thirty-two and practically a spinster when she fell in love with a music professor, who in the end became her husband and my grandfather.

Gran had always understood my passion for my work. She loved reading my articles and jotting critiques and praises in the margins. When I was in journalism school, we spent long hours together, reading old newspaper stories she had written, working in her greenhouse, or occasionally making pathetic attempts at cooking meals. Like me, she couldn't cook, and she made no apologies for it. Perhaps that was why I never tried to improve on my cooking skills. I had always wanted to be just like my stubborn, redheaded Irish Gran.

Now that I thought about it, I couldn't remember ever having told her that.

Chapter 3

BY the time I left the café with Mrs. Hawthorne, I was already starting to have doubts about the sappy, sentimental article on my notepad. In the bright light of day, it seemed overly dramatic, overly emotional, and not at all something I wanted to have printed with my byline.

Mrs. Hawthorne looked at the scribbles with interest as we climbed into her car to take a couple of pictures of the town. "Have you finished your article already?" she asked.

"No." The word came out so quickly it almost sounded rude, and I felt like a teenager caught writing in a diary. "These are just notes." I folded the sheets back until I came to a blank one. "I did get the prickly pear jelly recipe written down, but I still need some more material—maybe one or two more recipes, a little historical information on your estate." I made notes as I spoke, determined, this time, to come up with something that sounded like a magazine article, not an adolescent philosophy lesson. "Oh, yes, and I want to make sure to get a few photos of a prickly pear plant, maybe one of the courthouse, a few of you and your husband on the porch of your house, and maybe one or two of you in your kitchen. I can't say which ones the magazine will use, but editors like to have several choices."

Mrs. Hawthorne nodded, giving me an earnest look as we pulled onto the highway behind a trailer full of unhappy-looking white goats. "Oh, I know you're right about that. My daughter-in-law works part-time for the *San Saline Record* newspaper. She'd love to meet you, since she's a reporter too, you know. Do you think you could come to dinner Saturday night? I think you met my son this morning when the peafowl woke you up."

She didn't wait for me to answer and didn't seem to notice when I blushed profusely. "Anyway, the editor at the *San Saline Record* just drives my daughter-in-law crazy about her pictures. He's always sending her back out to take new ones after the stories are already done. Say, maybe you could give her some pointers at dinner Saturday." She took one hand from the steering wheel and pointed toward my window. "Now, see, there is the *San Saline Record* office on your right.

That's been the *Record* office for over a hundred years—see, it says so right on that stone slab over the door there. That was the first two-story building on Main Street, built in 1868. That's where you go if you need to make copies or send a fax, or anything like that. My daughter-in-law, Becky, will fix you right up. They're closed for lunch from twelve to one. You already know the owner there, Truitt McKitrick—True the Tractor Man? You broke down last night at one of his tractor dealerships."

She paused for a breath or her train of thought ran off the track, I couldn't tell which, but the car was suddenly silent. She gave me a strange, measured look that was filled with a meaning I couldn't decipher. "You know, if you go over there this afternoon, he'll be in the office. He's always in the paper office on Thursday afternoons. He can help you with the fax machine." She gave me another strangely thoughtful, sideways look. "If the front door is locked, ring the buzzer. Sometimes he's upstairs above the newspaper office. He's got an apartment up there. But he doesn't mind coming down. He'd be happy to help you with the fax machine."

"Thank you, but I shouldn't need anything like that. I usually do everything by e-mail." And reliving my desperation of the previous night with True the Tractor Man hardly sounded like fun.

Brows knitting, she shook her head. "Well . . . our phone lines are a little cantankerous sometimes. . . ." A long pause, and then, "The peafowl like to roost on them, and it causes some problems."

The mental image made me chuckle, even though Mrs. Hawthorne was still looking at me with uncharacteristic gravity.

"That's all right. I can use my cellular," I said.

"Oh, well, probably not." She turned her attention to the road as the goat trailer stopped to make a left turn, and the goats stuck their shaggy heads through the bars, bleating at us. "We don't get very good reception. The nearest tower is on the other side of the hills. We're kind of in a dead zone. I think that's what they call it."

A dozen good jokes about San Saline *being* a dead zone came to mind, but I settled for, "I guess I'll just see how it goes, then." Looking ahead at the goats, I had a strange sense of how they were feeling. Trapped, not happy, no choice but to go where they were being herded.

It seemed more than a little ironic that we and the goats ended up in the same pasture. Mrs. Hawthorne explained that the man who owned the goats was notorious for not improving his pastures, and she knew we'd find plenty of prickly pear there in its wild state.

She waved at him as we passed over a row of what looked like metal speed bumps in the gateway. "Afternoon, Ed. This is Colleen Collins. She's a reporter all the way from *Southern Woman* magazine. We're just here to take some pictures of the prickly pear and bluebonnets. We won't bother the goats."

Ed gave a slow nod and a lackadaisical smile. "All right with me. Hope these goats don't bother ya too much. They ain't been fed today. They might be a little pesky."

"Oh, we'll be all right," Mrs. Hawthorne called back, then stepped on the accelerator to get us through the mud hole just past the gate. Away we went, bouncing down what looked like a rocky, overgrown wagon trail, the car mowing over three-foot-tall weeds and small cedar bushes while Mrs. H. and I tumbled around the seat like Weebles.

When we stopped and my equilibrium returned, I stepped from the car like Alice venturing into Wonderland. As far as it was possible to see, we were surrounded by an ocean of waving blue wildflowers. Here and there, patches of bright red and white blooms swam among the azure like schools of tropical fish, and short, flat-leafed cactus plants rose above the surf like sailboats lost at sea.

"It's beautiful," I breathed, feeling as if I had stepped into a postcard. "These are prickly pear bushes?" I pointed to one of the blooming cactus.

Mrs. H. swung her legs around and climbed from her seat with groan. "Yes, ma'am. And the blue flowers are bluebonnets. The hill country is famous for bluebonnets. Tourists come from everywhere this time of year to take pictures. And the red ones are Indian paintbrush, of course. The pink and white ones over there by the water are primrose, and those yellow ones with the red centers are called Indian blankets, but they're not in full bloom yet. They come a little later. One thing we do have here is lots of wildflowers."

"They're really incredible." Grabbing my camera, I started snapping pictures, more than would be needed for the article, so I would have some to hang on the wall in my office when I got home. I couldn't remember ever having been in a place with greater natural beauty.

"Oh, good gravy!" I heard Mrs. H. holler as my camera whirled from picture to picture, capturing the wonders around me so I could take them home to keep. "You'd better hurry up. Here come the goats!"

By the time I had snapped two more pictures, I could hear the thunder of a stampede. Lowering my camera, I glanced over my shoulder and saw them coming like a herd of rampaging mop heads, stringy white hair flying in all directions, mouths hanging open and pink tongues extended, making a bleating sound, something between a greeting and a threat.

Mrs. H. lumbered to the car. "You'd better get on in here! Those goats'll nip and peck you to death. They probably haven't been fed in a week."

"OK," I called over the din. But I couldn't resist focusing the camera and snapping shots of the oncoming army—so I could send them to Laura and tell her I wanted riot pay.

The goats overtook me before I made it to the car. Goats, I learned, are faster than they look, and they will eat almost anything. By the time I managed to drag myself into my seat and shut the door, I had been butted, buffeted, nibbled on, and nudged; there were slobber marks up and down my slacks, and a pair of hoofprints on my lapel from a goat that stood on its hind feet and tried to kiss me.

I surveyed the damage to my clothes as Mrs. H. wheeled the car around, and we sped toward the gate with the herd in determined pursuit. Jumping out at the gate, I pulled it open, let Mrs. H. drive through, then shut it just before the leaders skidded to a halt on the other side of the mud hole.

Safely across the fence, Mrs. H. and I looked into the disappointed faces of our pursuers and broke into gales of laughter. The goats stretched out their necks and bleated in response. I laughed until my ribs ached and I fell breathless into the passenger seat of the car. I couldn't remember the last time I had laughed like that, or if I had ever. In spite of my ruined suit, the experience was completely wonderful.

"That was great!" I gasped as we drove back to town. "I don't know when I've seen anything so funny. I think I need a goat to take home with me."

"Oh, honey, there's nothing harder to live with than a goat." Mrs. H. gave me a concerned look, then realized I was only joking. Chuckling, she shook her head at me. "Well, I didn't intend to stir up so much excitement, but that's why we love it out here. You just never know what the day will bring."

"That certainly is true." Looking in the visor mirror, I smoothed my hair, then replaced the clip. "Ten years living in D.C. without incident, and my first day in Texas I get mugged by a bunch of hungry goats."

Mrs. H. smiled sympathetically, looking at my slacks. "I'm afraid they've spoiled your nice suit. Shall I take you back to the house, or do you want to go on and finish your pictures now?"

"Let's just go ahead with the pictures." I did my best to brush the muddy goat marks from my slacks. Mostly they just smeared into dark streaks. In another place, in another time, I would have been mortified. Here, it didn't seem to matter. The truth was I was having fun. For the first time in months, I didn't feel the slightest twinge of depression. I suppose it's true what they say about laughter being good medicine.

Mrs. H. gave me a nod as we pulled into a parking space in front of the courthouse. "You hop out here and take your pictures. I'll be across the street at the newspaper office. When you're done, you can just walk on over. Looks like they're back from lunch." She strained to see around the corner of the courthouse. "Mm-hmm. I see Becky there in the window. You just come on over when you're ready."

"All right." Grabbing my camera bag, I climbed out of the car and stepped onto the courthouse lawn. As I walked away, I had the strangest feeling that Mrs. H. was still watching me. Glancing over my shoulder, I caught her in a strange, calculating expression, rubbing her chin, looking at me.

She waved when she realized I saw her, then put the car in reverse and backed away. As I turned back to my camera, I knew I was being sized up, but I couldn't imagine why.

The feeling left me uneasy and in no hurry to proceed to the newspaper office to meet up with Mrs. H.

I took my time photographing the old native-stone courthouse, then walked slowly around the square snapping pictures of the old buildings, many constructed from the same milk-colored stone blocks as the courthouse, and a few built of old red brick. Several bore carved marble name stones dating their construction to the late 1800s. In front of the stores was a yawning covered walkway with planters full of flowers, and wood or iron benches, some of which were occupied by old men in overalls, ball caps, or cowboy hats. They smiled and greeted me as I passed, then reclined in their seats, looking as if they had been there a while and didn't intend to leave anytime soon. A warm spring breeze danced along the street beside me, whipping a dust devil along, then disappearing into an alley. Watching it pass, I stood on the curb waiting for a pickup truck to go by so I could cross the street to the newspaper office. I had the sensation of being somewhere very old and very quiet, somewhere that, like the old men on the benches, hadn't been anywhere in a while and wasn't going anywhere anytime soon.

I took a deep breath, then walked across the street to the newspaper office.

Mrs. H. was lying in wait like a cat, and she pushed the door open with enthusiasm before I reached the curb. "Come in, come in. We were just talking about you. True is due back any minute with the Friday edition. It has some wonderful pictures of Monday's Pee Wee baseball practice. We're all just dying to see how they turned out."

I tried to seem interested as she introduced me to her daughter-in-law, Becky, a cute, round-faced girl who didn't look old enough to be out of high school.

She blushed when Mrs. H. called her an "ace reporter." "Oh, Mama Hawthorne, for heaven's sake."

Looking at me, she rolled her eyes. "I'm sure Ms. Collins isn't very interested in what goes on in a little bitty newspaper like ours."

Mrs. H. gave her the same parental warning look my mother used on me when she wanted me to be quiet. "Of course she's interested. Besides, she wants to say thank-you to True. You know, he practically saved her from disaster last night. She was stranded in Esther with no gas left in her tank. She could have been there all night, but he just happened to be working late on some inventory at the tractor dealership there. He saw her stuck on Main Street in her car, and—"

She stopped as the door swung open and in stepped a stack of boxes with jeans and cowboy boots sticking out the bottom. The stack stopped in the doorway to acknowledge the elderly African-American man who was holding the door open. "Thanks for getting the door, Malachi."

"No problem, Truitt, but you ought to carry them boxes a few at a time." The old man shook his head, peeking around the door and tipping his fedora hat at us. "That ain't gonna do your back no good, haulin' a heavy load like that."

The boxes replied as they moved past us, "You're right about that," and gave a warm, friendly chuckle I recognized from the night before. Becky cleared a path as he stumbled through the office, finally dropping the boxes on the floor in the back hallway. "Friday's edition," he announced. "Get 'em while they're hot." Without looking at us, he grabbed the top box and started toward the back door. "I'm going to deliver these to Harvey's before they close up."

"True." Mrs. H. hurried forward to stop him before he escaped. "There's someone here who wanted to meet you."

Openmouthed, I watched as Mrs. H. captured True the Tractor Man and dragged him to the front of the store. "True, this is Colleen Collins. She's a reporter all the way from *Southern Woman* magazine."

A reporter . . . from Southern Woman *magazine* . . . The introduction made me wince, but I forced a smile and looked at True the Tractor Man for the first time in the daylight. He was good-looking in a Western sort of way, with a darkly tanned face, deep blue eyes, and thick sandy-brown hair curling beneath the brim of his straw cowboy hat. He didn't fit my image of True the Tractor Man, at all. Today he was actually sort of . . . cowboy billboard–like.

He pointed a finger and gave me a surprised look as he reached out to offer a handshake. "The one who writes the recipes, right?" He glanced at Mrs. H. for confirmation, looking very pleased with himself for having figured it out.

The one who writes the recipes . . . I wished I could click my heels together three times and vanish from the spot. *There's no place like home*, I thought, and I wished I were home, curled in my bed with the covers pulled over my recipe-writing head.

"That's right." Mrs. H. patted me on the back, beaming like a teacher introducing her prize student at the spelling bee. "This is her."

I wasn't sure, but I thought she gave me a little forward shove. My mind clicked into gear, and I stuck my hand out to grasp his. "Colleen Collins," I said, blushing like a wallflower at a school dance. "Otherwise known as the frizzy redheaded lady who talks like a Yankee."

This time it was True the Tractor Man who blushed. Obviously he didn't know Mrs. H. had repeated his unflattering description of me.

"That . . . was you?" he said, releasing my hand and looking flustered. "Well . . . so . . . but . . . I guess you made it here all right?" He squinted at me, still not sure I was the same person he'd met the night before.

"I did," I said, not quite knowing what else to say. "And I want to thank you for helping me last night. I feel really stupid for getting myself stranded like that. I'd like to pay for the gas."

"No need. That kind of thing happens a lot during bluebonnet season. Tourists just don't know how to function when there isn't a Texaco around every corner." There was a note of contempt in his voice, and I knew I was being lumped in with the tourists—not smart enough to survive in his part of the world.

"Well, live and learn," I said flatly. *And I'd like to see your cowboy butt survive in D.C.*

Mrs. H. seemed to surmise that things weren't going along too famously, and she stepped in, giving Truitt McKitrick a peeved look. "I suppose we'd better be getting along and let you and Becky get the papers delivered. Don't forget, it's family game night at church, Becky. True, you ought to come over. It's potluck. A single man like you can always use a good meal." She glanced at me with a conspiratorial smile, as if I had some reason to care whether he came to family game night.

Truitt gave her a grin that was undoubtedly considered charming in his neck of the woods. I made sure to turn my interest out the window, so he wouldn't think I had any stake in the church potluck. The truth was I wanted to be out of the room and out of the conversation. I had work to do, and this was all a grand waste of time. And I had the disturbing feeling Mrs. H. was trying to set something up between Truitt McKitrick and me.

Truitt may have sensed the same thing. Shaking his head, he gave her a knowing look. "Now, Mrs. Hawthorne." There was a note of playful reproach in his voice. "You know I'm not going to get in the middle of that hen session at the church." Turning away, he walked to the back of the room, picked up a box of newspapers, and headed toward the back door. "You might take Miss Collins, though." Then he was gone, and the door slammed behind him.

I stood looking after him with my face red and my blood boiling. *Hen session!* Anyone who knew me knew I wouldn't be caught dead at such an event.

But, of course, he didn't know who I was. None of them did. All they saw was the frizzy redheaded lady who talked like a Yankee, ran out of gas in the middle of nowhere, knew nothing of goats, prickly pears, or peafowl, and wrote recipes for a women's magazine. Everything I had been before, all my achievements, all my credentials, didn't matter anymore. I was being looked down the nose upon by the tractor-fixing editor of an eight-page newspaper in Nowhere, Texas. In my profession, you can't get much lower than that.

But the phoenix rose from the ashes. And so would I.

Becky must have read some of what I was thinking, because she gave me an apologetic look as she walked past me to get a box of newspapers. "You just have to ignore him sometimes," she said. "He's always got his rear in a twist on print day . . . well, actually every day."

"Becky!" Mrs. H. gasped. "What a thing to say!"

Becky rolled her eyes and huffed with teenage self-righteousness. "Oh, Mama, it's the truth. He's a pain in the butt most of the time, and he thinks he owns the world, and I don't know why you like him so much."

Stepping forward, Mrs. H. braced her hands on her hips and rose up like a vengeful genie coming out of a bottle. "Now, you listen here. That isn't any way for a lady to talk, and not very Christian, either. I've known Truitt all his life, and he's a good person. After everything that's happened, you can't expect him to be like he was before."

Perking my ears, I stood very still, so as not to interrupt the conversation. On one hand, I had the distinct impression that this was none of my business. On the other, the reporter in me sensed a story coming on. The reporter, in these situations, always wins out.

With a disgusted huff, Becky opened a box and pulled out a bundle of newspapers. "You know what, Mama Hawthorne, you're a nicer person than I am. It's been five years, and I say it's time he got over it and stopped going around here acting like a jerk."

Mrs. H. didn't counter Becky's argument again, but instead stepped back, lowered her arms, and gave her daughter-in-law the same look of benevolent reproach she had given Francis in the café. "Well, Becky, you are not Truitt McKitrick, so it really isn't for you to say. The Lord lets us deal with things in our own time. It just isn't his time yet. Life happens the way it is supposed to, not the way we want."

Seeming properly shamed, Becky muttered, "I guess," and scooted out the door looking a few inches shorter.

I felt a little twinge myself, and I didn't ask for any more details about Truitt McKitrick. Mrs. H. didn't bring any up, either, but she was unusually quiet as we went back to the café for my car, and then over to Hawthorne House to take pictures and finish with the recipes. Her change of mood actually made the interview easier, because she told me what I needed to know, and not everything that passed through her mind. Still, it made me feel bad. I couldn't help thinking that I was part of the reason for the fight between her and her daughter-in-law.

I tried making a few jokes to cheer her up as she worked in the kitchen making hopping John, a dish with sausage, peppers, onions, black-eyed peas, and rice. Following that, she created traditional Texas red-eye beans. She told me the recipes as she went along because, she said, she'd never written them down, never really measured the portions, and couldn't remember how much went in if she wasn't cooking.

Her mood slowly started to turn around as she put water in the beans and put them on the stove to boil, then started making biscuits from scratch. This was a fascinating process for me, since I had never seen biscuits born anywhere but in a can. I told Mrs. H. as much, and she broke into giggles that interrupted the story she had been telling me about hopping John and red-eye beans being traditional meals for cattle roundups at the old Hawthorne ranch.

I snapped a few pictures of her laughing, with her head thrown back, and her face red against the flour-whitened apron.

"I brought home some of those canned biscuits once," she said finally. "I used to like to ride out with the men in the morning, back when we were ranching. I figured that, if I wasn't stuck in the house cleaning up all the mess from breakfast, I could ride all day long." Laughing again, she clamped one hand over her mouth and fanned her face with the other, then finally sucked in a breath. "I just knew that Jasper would never know the difference in the biscuits, and I thought I was so clever! I fixed a little bacon and gravy one morning and put those biscuits in the oven—buried the cans in the trash, even. Those darned biscuits came out of the oven as flat as pancakes and as hard as granite stone, but Jasper ate them and said they were good, so I thought I really had a wonderful thing figured out, and I kept feeding him those biscuits morning after morning; then I'd go out to ride with the men.

"One day, we had a crew on for cattle work, and they came in for breakfast. Those single men knew right away what those biscuits were, because, turns out, they had been cooking them in their cow camps. They called them whop biscuits, because you whop ’em on the skillet to get them open. Jasper looked at me like a choked horse. I never will forget it! Later on, he told me those were the worst things he’d ever ate, and he was afraid to say anything because here he thought I’d been making them myself. He’d been sneaking them out of the house in his pockets and burying them in the barn. He made me promise I wouldn’t ever bring whop biscuits in the house again.” Eyes rimmed with the moisture of laughter, she shook her biscuit cutter at me. “And I didn’t, either. That was the last secret we ever kept from each other. Truth isn’t a virtue in life; it’s a necessity.”

I nodded, thinking of all the trouble truth had gotten me into, then thinking of Brett and me, and how we had managed to get along for six years by not ever telling each other the truth, by not ever talking about any of the things that really mattered. Maybe that was why we were always so desperate to fill our time with activities—because we were afraid if things got quiet, we wouldn’t have anything to talk about. Maybe we would realize we were just passing time together instead of making a life, that the only thing keeping us together was the fear of being alone.

I thought of what Mrs. Hawthorne had said earlier. *Life happens the way it is supposed to, not the way we want*. I wondered if that was what was happening to me. I wondered if this journey I was taking, this time of being alone, feeling my way through unknown territory, was all part of some plan. A comforting thought, but probably not realistic.

When I looked up, Mrs. H. was watching me as if she were reading my thoughts. Turning over the bowl, she plopped the biscuit dough onto the counter in front of me, sending up a cloud of flour. "Here." She handed me a rolling pin and a small, round circle of metal with a wooden handle on it. "I'll show you how I roll out the dough and cut biscuits." She ripped the dough in half and started mushing her portion into a ball.

I looked at mine with trepidation. "I don't know *anything* about cooking," I admitted. "I don't want to mess up your biscuits."

She shook her head, making a *tsk-tsk* sound under her breath. "That must make it hard to write about."

You have no idea. "A little."

She smiled understandingly. "Well, this isn't cooking; it's therapy." She motioned to my plop of dough, and I felt obliged to clumsily pick it up and start working it into a ball as she went on. "Making biscuits is good therapy. You start out with a bunch of things that taste bad on their own—flour and shortening, dash of salt, and so forth. You mix them together and get something that looks like it'll always be a mess, then you work on it for a while, until it starts to look better." As she spoke, we kneaded, and my ball of dough started to resemble hers. "Then you roll it out flat." She demonstrated with her rolling pin, and I followed suit. "And you cut it out, piece by piece, until it's all lined up in the pan, orderly and just as it should be." She winked at me as I used the cutter to produce biscuits that were only slightly less professional-looking than hers.

I couldn't help looking at my work and feeling a sense of accomplishment. It really was kind of fun. "Not too bad, if I do say so myself."

Mrs. H. winked when I glanced at her. "Kind of gives you faith in the ability of a mess to work into something good."

I just smiled and finished with my biscuits, feeling a touch of that faith myself.

When we finished the biscuits, Mrs. H. invited me to the church potluck, but I politely declined, partly because I wanted to get back to my cottage to work on the article, and partly because, after what True the Tractor Man had said, I wouldn't have been caught dead at the local "hen session." Instead, I put my notebook and recorder in the cabin, then went to the grocery store to buy a few food items, so I could eat in my room.

The store was an experience in itself, another step back in time, with an old-fashioned butcher's section, a dairy case that looked like it had been there since 1950, and a smattering of everything from plumbing supplies to sewing thread. Strolling through the aisles, I forgot about hurrying back to my work, and walked slowly along, looking at items I didn't know still existed—Grandpa's Pine Tar Soap, Steen's Cane Syrup, Levi Garrett snuff, and dozens of other things I thought had long ago disappeared into history.

When I was finished, I paid for my items at the checkout stand, where the cashier actually read the price stickers and punched them in on the ten-key, a lost art where I came from. The uneven rhythm was pleasant, sort of nice compared to the sterile *beep-beep* of an electronic scanner. It was good to know there were still places where everything in life had not been reduced to a bar code.

The cashier looked over her shoulder as she counted my change from the register. "Got a customer for ya, Malachi," she called to an elderly African-American man dozing on the bench beside the soda machine.

The old man stood up and hobbled slowly forward to take the handle of my cart. I recognized him from the newspaper office earlier that day.

Taking my change from the cashier, I reached for the handle of the cart. "I can get those," I said. The thought of making him walk all the way to my car made me feel intensely guilty. I wondered what kind of a sadistic store manager would give such a job to an arthritic old man.

"No, ma'am." His drawl was slow and Southern, crackling like the paint on an old house. "I'll be pleased to carry these out for ya."

Determined to save him the trip, I tried again. "No, really. It's no problem. I only have a few things."

He studied me for a moment, his age-yellowed eyes barely visible beneath the brim of a fedora hat that looked as old as he did. Slowly his mouth curved into a grin. "Well, right nah I only got one customer, and if I cain't carry out these few things, I won't have a job. I been doin' this since I was sixty-two year old, and I'm pretty good at it. You wouldn't run an old man outa his job, wouldja?"

"I guess not." I gave up my fight for the cart and followed him as he hunched over the handle, moving slowly toward the door, one labored step at a time. Watching him, I thought of the people who slept in doorways and bridges in D.C., old, crippled, unwanted. I wondered where he lived, or if he had a place to live at all, and why there was no one to care for him, and why he was hauling groceries out to people's cars when he could barely walk the distance from the store to the parking lot. It seemed cruel and wrong, and I couldn't believe the people in this little town couldn't find a little charity in their hearts and take care of him.

I hurried ahead to open the trunk as he moved slowly across the parking lot; then I climbed in to start the car. But the car had other ideas. Just as it had the night before, it roared to life; then the gas gauge sank to empty, and the car died. After that it refused to start.

"Sounds like you got a problem," Malachi said as he came with my groceries.

"Oooohhhh!" Getting out, I slammed the keys against the roof of the car. "It won't start. Damn this car!"

Malachi put his finger to his lips, the corners of his eyes crinkling into cavernous lines. "Ssshhhh," he said, then pointed to the sky. "The Lawd is listenin' up there."

Aggravated, frustrated, now properly chastised, I thumped my fingers against my forehead, considering what to do next. It was probably a mile across town to

Hawthorne House, and I was tired, but I didn't have the number with me to call Mrs. H., and she was probably already gone to the potluck anyway. Undoubtedly the nearest cab was an hour away in the nearest real town.

"Ooohhh, I'll just walk," I growled finally, reaching for my grocery sacks. "Will it be all right to leave this car here?" As if I had a choice. "I'm staying over at Hawthorne House."

The old man shook his head, and for a minute I thought he was going to tell me no, and I was going to get irate.

Then he smiled again, pushing up the brim of his hat and looking at me through the droopy eyes of an old hound. "You just wait here a minute. Let me tell the little girl in there where I'm goin', then I'll drive ya right over to tha Haw-thone House myself."

I started to protest, thinking that I could walk the mile faster than he could get back and forth to the store, and into his car, wherever it was. "Oh, you don't have to—"

"I'd be pleased." He grinned, showing a row of even white teeth. "Nah you wait right here."

So I did, occupying myself while I waited by raising the hood of the car and looking at the engine like I had some idea of what might be wrong, which I didn't.

My cab rattled up in the form of an old Pontiac with torn bits of cream-colored vinyl roof floating in the breeze like banners. I waited, privately drumming my fingers on my arm, while the old man climbed out and slowly lifted the trunk, then set my grocery sacks in, one by one. When I tried to help, he gave me a sideways look that told me to mind my own business. After loading the last bag, he closed the trunk and opened the passenger door, waving me in like a valet.

"I apologize for this old car," he said, climbing into the driver's seat with a stifled groan of effort.

"I'm just grateful not to be walking." I noticed a Bible on the dash in front of me. The leather cover was cracked and worn smooth, the chapters and books carefully tabbed with yellowed Scotch tape and faded bits of paper.

Malachi looked sideways at me as we puttered from the parking lot at a speed only slightly faster than his walk. "I'm the preacher at the Riverbend Free Baptist Church, over toward Brownwood," he explained. "I been preachin' there for fifty years, since I was a young man a' twenty-five, and now I'm seventy-fo'. Used to be called the Riverbend Negro Baptist Church, but folks don't think that sounds good no mo'. We gotta be political right now." He chuckled, grinning at me. "I don't much get inta all that fuss. I figure the Lawd'll work them details all out in his time. When ya git old, ya just don't fuss about ever' little thing. Praise the Lawd!"

I couldn't help laughing with him. "So what's a preacher doing working at the grocery store?" I was thinking there should be someone in his congregation able to help provide for him.

He gave me a sly look as we rolled down Main Street and into the driveway of Hawthorne House. I could tell he knew what I was thinking and that I had assumed all the wrong things about him. "Well, I just do that part-time," he said. "It gives me the chance to git out and meet folk, and the money's good to have. I got three great-grandchildrens to help through college, and families in my congregation set back by sickness or hard times, and I put some in the church because we're a-savin' up for a baptistery with hot and cold runnin' water. Praise the Lawd!" Raising a hand skyward, he put the car in park. He smiled at me, and I smiled at him, and I felt a touch of "praise the Lord," myself. I suddenly wished I had the money to buy the old man a baptistery. But then, I suppose it wouldn't have meant as much.

I thanked him as he set the groceries on the porch; then I tried to give him some money for his trouble.

"Oh, it ain't worth that," he said, waving the twenty-dollar bill away.

"It's worth more than that." I looked him in the eye, and we both knew what I meant. He hadn't just given me a ride, he'd given me a quick lesson in the true nature of kindness.

Reaching out, he wrapped his hands over mine, folding the twenty-dollar bill in my fingers. "You come to my church some Sunday and put it in the offerin' plate." And he gave that sly smile again.

Then he hobbled back to his car, lowered himself slowly into the seat, and drove away with the rooftop vinyl fluttering like the wings of angels.

Chapter 4

AFTER I had finished tucking my groceries into the small refrigerator and the hand-hewn cabinets of the kitchenette, I pulled out the phone book and called the rental car company about the car. The peafowl must have been dancing on the phone line, because the connection was so fuzzy, I could barely hear the agent.

"Did you say you want me to drive it to Dallas for a replacement?" I hollered, having had quite enough of the runaround, and cars that wouldn't start, and fuzzy phone lines with peafowl on them. "Listen. You don't understand. This car is possessed. It only starts when it wants to. I've been stranded twice. I'm paying forty-eight dollars a day, and I want a car that runs!"

The connection fuzzed, so that she sounded like Charlie Brown's teacher. "Whaank-whank-whaaa-waaa-wheer-est rental agent to exchange the whaa-ar."

Blood boiled into my brain, and I stabbed my paring knife into the cutting board on the counter again and again. "Well, where in the world is that?"

"Whaaa-whank-wah-woh-cated at 1702 East Highway One-ninety in Copperas Cove, whaank-whah-waaa-wah."

"Listen!" I boomed, my voice ringing around the small room, probably punishing me more than her. "I am taking this thing to a garage in the morning, here in San Saline, and I'm sending you the bill for the towing and whatever. I have work to do tomorrow, and I am *not* spending my day driving to Copperas Cove. I'm looking at the map, and that's at least ninety miles from here!"

I couldn't understand what she said next—just static, and the faint sound of a voice. I think she was saying she couldn't hear me very well.

"I'll call in the *morning,*" I hollered into the phone, then *"Good-bye."* And I hung up, frustrated beyond belief.

Grabbing the paring knife again, I took out my aggravation on a defenseless apple. "Good God, how do people live like this!" I seized a hunk of cheese from the refrigerator and whacked it into squares. "*No* phone, *no* e-mail, *no* taxis, *no* deli, *no* movie theater, *no* rental cars. This is *hell!*"

Outside, the peafowl started a round-robin screaming session, like a bevy of lost souls crying out for absolution.

"Hell . . . with *peafowl,*" I muttered, setting my food on the little table and sitting down to eat. Looking out the window as the sky to the west burned amber, I could see the peafowl silhouetted in the wide-limbed trees and lined up on the T-shaped telephone pole in the yard like a bunch of overgrown vultures.

As the sun sank lower, they stopped calling and tucked their heads drowsily against their chests. The air drifting through the window screen turned gray and cool, laced with the scent of blooming wisteria and freshly mowed grass. Somewhere in the distance, the whir of a lawn mower hummed low like a father's lullaby. Then even that stopped, and the air was silent.

Letting my eyes drift closed, I took a long breath of

the spring fragrance, rolling my head drowsily as the breeze caressed my cheek, lifting stray strands of hair from the back of my neck, teasing like a lover. Beyond the sound of my own sigh, there was nothing but quiet, as if nothing existed but me and the breeze. No cars rumbling, no horns honking, no voices passing, no insects bleating. Nothing but the clarity of silence.

Opening my eyes, I reached across the table for my pad, turned past the notes and recipes to a blank sheet of paper, and began filling it with words. I wrote about old Malachi, how he leaned on the handle of the grocery cart, moving in his slow bow-legged shuffle, how the breath groaned from his throat as he lifted each sack of groceries, how his eyes were yellowed like the pages of an old Bible, how the lines around them were deep from laughter. I wrote about the old car with the angel wings and the faded fedora and the worn Bible. I wrote about the size of the heart in a man who could barely walk, yet would carry burdens for others to the last of his strength.

In the end, I wrote about myself, and how in my life I may have passed a hundred like Malachi and never known it. In my hurry to get from one place to another, I had made a few friends and a few enemies, but mostly I had just passed people on the road. *I think it is this way with too many people in this speed-of-light age*, I wrote. *We judge by surface impressions and sound bites, never considering what might be underneath. We too seldom really see the people who surround us. Sometimes it's good to get off the highway and putter along in the slow lane looking at faces and listening to voices. Sometimes the best thing that can happen is for your car to break down so that you have to rely on the kindness of a stranger.*

When it was finished, I sat staring at the words as the last amber light faded around me and the cabin grew dim. I wondered where Malachi was and whether he was finished at the grocery store. I pictured him climbing into his old car and driving into the brush-clad hills, the wind lifting the feathers on the roof, drifting in the window, thumbing through the pages of the old Bible.

The cottage was almost completely dark when I finally stood up and turned on the lights. The artificial glow made the darkness outside seem black and ominous, so I closed the windows, lowered the blinds, and locked the front door. Taking off my suit, I laid it on the bed, noticing the goat stains and realizing I had forgotten about them all day. I wondered what the people in the newspaper office and the grocery store must have thought of me. Glancing sideways at the long oval-shaped mirror on the dresser, I curled my lip at the bare facts of my situation. Three months of pizza and greasy Chinese food was showing up in all kinds of places. I looked pale and flabby, and generally awful. I needed to start some kind of exercise program.

Just the thought of that was enough to make me flip on the TV. I hated exercise—in any and all forms, no matter how exotic.

"Maybe I need a goat, after all," I muttered. Running with the goats was fun.

The television warmed up slowly, the picture crackling to life in the center first, then lazily spreading onto the screen until three cowboys with guitars stood in full color, and country music came blaring from the speakers. Jumping for the sound knob, I turned it to a tolerable level just as one of the performers started to yodel.

If there is something you want to watch, just call me on the phone, and I'll change the channel . . . Mrs. Hawthorne had said the night before. Ninety-nine channels, and we had to be tuned in to the Cowboy Channel, twenty-four hours—the logo in the bottom corner of the screen told me so.

Contemplatively, I looked at the phone, then walked to the window and peeked through the blinds to see if Mrs. H. was back from the hen session. The driveway was empty except for Jasper's old white pickup. Through the living room window of the main house I could see him in his chair, and I could barely make out the image on his TV screen of three yodeling cowboys in red bandannas.

Turning away from the window, I gave up the idea of asking him to change the station and just switched off the TV instead. Looking at the horseshoe-shaped clock on the wall, I shook my head at myself. Only nine-thirty, and I was ready to go to bed. In my old life, I would have just been winding up about now—headed out to dinner or the theater, to some D.C. soiree, or some political photo op. If I wasn't engaged in those activities, I would have been snooping around in unlikely places—watching for people of importance doing unseemly things. I would have been filled with adrenaline, my nose tingling with the scent of a good story, ready to go on for hours, maybe all night, just home for a shower, and back to the office in the morning. I would have been in that zone where the rush came like a drug—on top of my game, on top of the world.

In this new life, I was staring at a pile of notes filled with recipes, chitchat about historical architecture, and the six or so pages of emotional drivel about boats, and memories, and the old grocery clerk. There was no sparkle there, no excitement. The reality was that I couldn't even face the idea of starting on the *Southern Woman* article tonight.

The reality was that I couldn't face reality.

Turning off the lights, I left my notes on the table and climbed into bed. I lay in the darkness and thought about all the things I used to take for granted, and how much I missed them now. Brett was among those things. After six years of off-and-on living together, I assumed he would always be there. I got used to the feeling of someone's things being mixed with mine, of him being in bed beside me. It wasn't *him* I missed, really. Having learned the hard way who he actually was, it was difficult to find an ounce of tender sentiment for him. But I missed *someone* being there.

I missed it most at night . . . when the room was quiet and dark. I missed the warmth of skin, the sound of breathing, the touch of a hand on mine.

My mother had tried to tell me that Brett and I would someday part ways, and I would feel like this.

I laughed at her at the time. I told her that Brett and

I were happy with our relationship, that we were both very committed to our careers, that I was happy to have found someone who didn't resent my having my space and wasn't asking where I was all the time. That neither one of us felt the need to do the whole marriage-and-family thing right away. But Mom was right. If you go through years together, both fighting to maintain your separate identities—separate apartments, separate bank accounts, separate names—it's a sign that at least one of you isn't really in love, that you're holding out for something better.

Except if you hold out for too many years, it's too late for something better to come along.

Tears pricked my eyes, and I closed them wearily. I didn't want to do this anymore. I *wasn't* going to do this anymore. Sitting around crying was pointless. The only thing that would make me feel better would be to get on with life.

The phone rang just as my emotions were starting to spiral into that all-too-familiar pit. Pulling the chain on the reading light, I hurried to the kitchen counter and grabbed it, wiping my eyes impatiently. My voice quavered as I said hello, and I pretended to clear my throat.

There was an uncomfortable pause on the other end. "Hello, Collie?" Mrs. Hawthorne's voice, sounding concerned. Despite the peafowl on the pole outside, the connection was as clear as a bell. "Is everything all right?"

"Yes. Why?" I looked around the room, wondering if she could somehow see me, even though the blinds were closed. I didn't want *anyone* to know I was lying around in bed feeling sorry for myself, and I sure didn't want anyone asking questions. I needed to maintain the few shreds of dignity I had left.

"Well, I just drove by the grocery, and I saw your car parked there." Her words came in a breathless rush that I could barely decipher, like she had run ten miles to get to the phone. "The store is closed, of course, and the parking lot all dark. Well, it just gave me a terrible start. I was afraid something had happened to you."

Her concern made me smile. I considered reminding her that, after ten years in D.C., there probably wasn't much in San Saline I couldn't handle. "I'm fine. It's just that stupid car. It wouldn't start after I got groceries, and the old carryout guy drove me home."

"Oh, you mean Malachi," she said, but there was a strangely flat tone in her voice, and I wondered if she had a problem with Malachi because he was black—actually the only African-American face I had seen in town.

I suddenly felt I needed to defend the old man. "Yes. He was really nice about it. He saved me a long walk home, and then wouldn't even take a tip." I paused, but she didn't reply, so I went on about the car. "So, anyway, now I'm stuck. I called the rental-car company, and they want me to take the car to Copperas Cove to exchange it. I told them I'm not driving it that far, even if I can get it started tomorrow. Is there a place here in town that can look at it for me?"

"Hmmm." She paused for a long moment. Clearly it was not a simple question. "I'll tell you what. You just get a good night's sleep, and I'll make some calls first thing and get it worked out for you." She sounded overly eager, so much so that my intuition made me suspicious.

I reminded myself that she was trying to do me a favor, and that I needed to quit thinking the worst of everyone I met. "That would be so helpful." I looked at the pile of notes and the camera bag on the table and thought about the fact that I needed to spend the day tomorrow getting the first article written, not trying to get my rental car fixed. I didn't want to push deadline with Laura on my first project for her. "One thing I do need to do tomorrow is get my pictures developed and make sure they're going to be all right for the article. Is there a one-hour photo here in town?"

A long pause, and then, "A what?" As if I were asking in Russian.

"A one . . . hour photo," I said again, hopefully. "I need to get my pictures developed."

"No." She still sounded confused. "I just drop mine at the Ben Franklin, and they're back in four days."

Rubbing my eyes, I silently reminded myself that a place with no cellular service, no taxis, no rental-car station, and no real grocery store would, of course, not have a one-hour photo. "OK," I said. "Thanks for the information and the help with the car. Sorry I scared you."

"Oh, that's all right." She chuckled, and the sound made me feel warm and welcome. "You have a good night's rest, now."

Parting the blinds, I looked toward the house and saw

her in the tall kitchen window, leaning on the handle of a broom. "I will. Good night." I hung up the phone, but watched her a moment longer, thinking of our afternoon in the kitchen, and the story about the biscuits, and the way she laughed until her entire face turned red. I found myself smiling, too, and the last bits of my dark mood were whisked away like soot before the old straw broom.

As I turned off the light and slipped into bed, I had the strange feeling that everything would turn out all right. And not just with the car. But everything.

Closing my eyes, I thought about the day and all the strange and wonderful things that had composed it. . . .

My thoughts drifted to an image of wildflowers. I was floating like a bird overhead, gliding soundlessly on the breeze, and I fell slowly into a strange dream. I dreamed about Malachi walking among the goats, leading them through the blue flowers. Francis and Miss Grace were making jelly in a huge iron cauldron over an open fire. Peafowl were roosting outside the Sale Barn Café, and True the Tractor Man stood beneath his neon sign, yodeling in a red bandanna. . . .

I awoke in the gray hours of morning to the sound of snakes crawling on the roof, then the scream of a child crying desperately, "Mama, Mama, help!"

Jerking upright in the bed, I threw back the covers, jumped from the bed, and searched the floor for my shoes, crawling frantically around on my hands and knees. The combination of adrenaline and sleep cleared from my mind suddenly, and I stood up, looking around the darkened room, realizing where I was. Slapping a hand to my forehead, I fell onto the bed, groaning at myself and wondering if I would ever grow immune to the sound of peafowl waking the dawn.

The room was surprisingly cold, so I slipped beneath the covers again and lay looking at the ceiling, listening to the slithering sound that had panicked me the morning before. Knowing what it was, I could now hear the faint *click-click* of toenails on the tin roof. Even so, the sound was strange and eerie, and a person uninformed would never figure out what it was. . . .

Closing my eyes, I let myself drift into sleep again and didn't awaken until sunlight was streaming around the edges of the blinds, and the room was getting uncomfortably warm. A glance at the clock told me it was almost nine. I blinked at myself in the mirror. Sleeping from ten until nine was definitely a first for me, and not something I wanted to make a habit.

Swinging my legs over the side of the bed, I stood up with an unusually leaden feeling and slowly stretched my hands upward, my fingertips coming within a foot of the hand-hewn rafters. Staring at them, I thought about the Hawthorne ancestors, and how primitive the country must have seemed to them—filled with snakes, wild animals, and native peoples they couldn't understand. Devoid of civilization's conveniences, empty beyond comprehension.

"Hasn't changed much," I muttered, then mustered my pioneer spirit to turn on the TV and the coffeepot.

The coffeepot came on first, and the TV more slowly, like an old car with a crank, chugging to life. The picture spread lazily to full size, and the sound blared suddenly, making my sleepy senses lurch. Jumping for the volume knob, I wondered how the TV had managed to turn itself up overnight. The yodeling cowboys had been replaced by a John Wayne movie in faded Technicolor.

"Mornin', John," I said, pouring a cup of coffee and sitting down at the table to watch the Duke charge after a bunch of cattle-rustling bad guys. "Head 'em off at the pass. Your horse is faster than theirs."

The movie faded into a commercial just as the bad guys dashed into a canyon and took cover in the rocks, preparing to ambush the Duke. Left with no John Wayne to stare at, I was forced to look at the pile of notes and the laptop computer on the other side of the table. What I needed to do was get dressed and start working on the article, so I would still have time to do more research if additional material was required.

Instead, I picked up the Friday edition of the *San Saline Record,* which had come home from the grocery store mysteriously tucked in my sack. Unfolding it, I grimaced at the front page. Filled with poorly fit text, rivers of white space, and completely uninspired headlines, it was a journalist's nightmare. Becky's Little League photography in the center page wasn't much better. Half of the pictures were blurry and the other half mostly showed the shadowed backs of spectator's heads, with a smattering of the baseball game in the distance.

I couldn't keep from giving the paper an evil sneer, feeling vindicated for my encounter with Truitt McKitrick the day before. On my worst day, I could create a better newspaper than his.

Suddenly he was speaking to me from the television set. I blinked at the image, certain my conscience was punishing me for having evil thoughts. But there he was in full color, standing in a tractor showroom, talking about some newfangled, six-wheel-drive, one-zillion-horsepower tractor that was the newest thing in farm machinery, and how, even if you weren't gonna buy one, you ought to come on down to Friendly's Tractors just to lay hands on it and have a divine experience. He looked as giddy as an eight-year-old boy in a Hot Wheels factory, his blue eyes sparkling beneath his cowboy hat.

"So y'all come on down to Friendly's Tractors in San Saline, Lampasas, Llano, and the original store in Esther. We'll be a-waitin' for ya." He finished with that nauseating "Aren't I wonderful?" grin, and then there was a splice of an old man in overalls sitting on an ancient red tractor, saying, "Remember, *nobody* knows tractors like True the Tractor Man."

"Yes, well, it's a good thing you know tractors," I said, turning back to the newspaper, "because you're a lousy newspaper editor. Any first-year journalism student would know better than—"

A knock at the door stopped me, and I jumped at the sound—guilty conscience. It was probably Mrs. Hawthorne. I hoped she hadn't heard me through the door. I didn't want to get the lecture about unkind thoughts that she'd given to Becky the day before.

"Just a minute, Mrs. H.," I called, and folded the paper, tucking it underneath my computer so she wouldn't see I had looked at it. I didn't want her to ask what I thought. I had no idea what I would say. Blatant honesty had always been my credo, but recently that hadn't gotten me too far. Better that I just pretend I hadn't had time to read the newspaper. Reaching for the door handle, I realized I was still wandering around in my nightshirt, and it was probably nine-thirty by now, and that didn't look very professional. I started making excuses as I pulled the door open with a slow creak. "I'm sorry I'm not quite with it this morning. I stayed up late working last night." A blatant lie. "I had some . . ." I froze in the doorway, my mouth hanging open as I stared into the cowboy hat of True the Tractor Man.

The brim tipped slowly upward as he scanned my bare feet and legs, the Tweety Bird nightshirt, my mortified face, and finally the Medusa-like tangle of hair on my head. "Workin' hard this morning?" He had the nerve to give me that lopsided grin.

I flushed red from head to toe and all points between. "Well . . . I . . . yes . . . I . . ." Looking down at my legs, I determined that they badly needed an appointment with a razor. One more reason to blush. Reeling up my bottom lip, I looked sideways at him. "What are you doing here, anyway?" An ungracious comment, but at the moment I didn't care. I just wanted to wipe that annoying grin off his face.

Unfortunately, it didn't wound him in the least. "Mrs.

Hawthorne sent me. She said you had a problem with your car."

Great, on top of everything else, he's the town mechanic, too. The man is everywhere. Like fungus. "You fix cars, too?"

He shook his head, and I was relieved. "No, ma'am, but I *am* headed over to Copperas Cove with an empty flatbed trailer to pick up a load of bush hogs and a couple of cattle guards."

I blinked at him, unable to imagine what picking up a load of hogs had to do with me. "Oh," was all I could think to say.

Lowering an eyebrow, he tipped his hat back and scratched the dampened curls of sandy-brown hair on his forehead. "Mrs. Hawthorne asked if I'd help you take the car to Copperas Cove to trade it out." He spoke the words slowly, as if he were trying to explain nuclear physics to a ten-year-old, and it was giving him a headache. "I'll haul it over there on the flatbed, and you can drive the replacement back."

"Well . . . I was going to just have someone look at it here in town," I said, feeling out of place, and outnumbered, and vehemently wishing I had not involved Mrs. Hawthorne in the car business. "But it's really nice of you to offer." Nervous perspiration dripped down my back. I wasn't sure why, but I did know I wanted to end the conversation, close the door, and get dressed. "I don't want to cause you extra trouble. I'll just have it looked at here."

He shook his head, irritatingly sure of himself. "You won't find anyone here in town who can work on that little foreign job." Then that crooked grin, and a quick wink, like he knew he had me now. "Shoulda rented American."

For some stupid reason I smiled back, at least until his gaze drifted downward to where the dampened nightshirt was starting to cling to my chest. Then we both looked at each other and turned red like a couple of elementary school kids suddenly noticing the difference between boys and girls.

He cleared his throat, pulling the brim of his hat down, his eyes disappearing behind it. "So . . . I'll go on down to the grocery and load the car while you . . . get dressed, and . . ." He suddenly seemed to forget what he was going to say.

"All right." I gave my brain a quick shake as he turned away.

He stopped at the bottom of the steps and turned back. "Ummm . . ." He snapped his fingers beside his face, trying to think of something. "Oh, yeah . . . there's a one-hour photo in Copperas Cove, so you might want to take your film."

The remark made me wonder just how much he and Mrs. Hawthorne had been talking about me. "Thanks," I said, and stood watching him walk away before I closed the door and turned the dead bolt. "That was weird," I muttered to myself, crossing the room and lifting my suitcase onto the bed. "I need to have a talk with Mrs. Hawthorne." Just in case she really was getting some ideas about me and Truitt McKitrick. "Not gonna happen. No way. *Nada*." Of that much, I was sure. No romances. Not for me.

I stared at the suitcase for a few minutes before my mind finally stopped wondering about Mrs. H. and Truitt McKitrick, and came around to the issue of getting dressed. Remembering my experiences from the day before, I left my suits hanging in the garment bag and pulled out a plain white T-shirt and jeans—something nondescript, not flashy, and not the least bit flirty, which just showed how much the past months had changed me. In my former life, I would have been looking forward to a little harmless flirtation with a handsome stranger.

But I wasn't looking forward to spending half the day with True the Tractor Man. He wasn't easy to talk to, and I hadn't a clue what we might talk about, and I had lost all interest in and ability for aimless chitchat. I could give him a lesson on newspaper editing, but I didn't think he'd appreciate it much. He seemed the type who was supremely confident in his own brilliance—not one to take advice from a frizzy redheaded lady who spoke in Yankee.

Not wanting to be caught half-dressed again, I hurried through taking a bath and washing my hair, making the mental note that my next hotel room needed a shower, not a tiny claw-footed tub. The hair washing was an exercise in bathtub acrobatics, and when it was over, I felt like I'd been through a Tae-Bo class. Drying off, I slipped quickly into my jeans and shirt, pinned my hair up in a wet mass of curls, put on a little makeup, ate a banana, grabbed my shoes and my camera bag, and made my way to the porch in record time. Just in time to be waiting for my ride as if

I'd been there, sitting patiently for a half hour.

"What took you so long?" I asked, feeling a little more conversant now that I was dressed and looked like myself. A peacock fluffed his feathers in full display for one of the hens on the lawn, and I stopped to watch as True walked up from the driveway.

He gave me a peeved look, wiping greasy hands on his jeans. "That Japanese piece of sh . . . junk wouldn't start. I had to winch it onto the trailer."

"Doesn't surprise me." Taking out my camera, I finished the roll on the showy peacock. "Isn't he pretty? The colors are amazing."

I heard him scoff behind me. "If you like peacocks."

Tucking the camera in the bag, I looked sideways at him. I wondered if he always felt the need to throw cold water, or if it was just me he didn't like. "I don't, but they're still pretty." The peacock folded its tail as Truitt came closer, then squawked and dashed across the yard, sensing that the friendly tractor man was not in a nice mood. "Guess the peacocks don't like you, either."

He gave the observation an evil grin as we turned and walked toward the car. "Nice of you not to hold it against the peacocks about yesterday morning though." The words ended in a barely withheld chuckle.

Gritting my teeth, I willed myself not to blush. It only figured that he had heard about my snake-hunting adventure, like everyone else in town. *Wise is the man who can laugh at himself.* Chinese proverb. "I'm learning not to hold grudges. New Year's resolution."

He rolled his eyes downward and looked doubtfully at me from the corners. "Let me know how it works out." Opening the passenger door, he waited to close me in as if I couldn't figure it out for myself, then walked around the front to climb into the driver's seat. His mouth spread into a grin as he started the engine and we rolled down the driveway of Hawthorne House with the flatbed trailer and the demon-possessed car in tow. "So did you really go after rattlesnakes yesterday morning wielding a hair dryer and a red high-heeled shoe?"

"No," I bit out. Suddenly I felt the tickle of laughter in my throat as I thought of the ridiculous event, and how many wild versions of it were probably floating around town by now. "It was a paring knife and a fireplace poker. And I was *wearing* the red high-heeled shoes. . . ."

Chapter 5

IT took me the better part of a half hour to set him straight about the details of my snake-hunting adventure—from the first sounds of the snake crawling on the roof, to the last moment, when I was told the screaming child in danger was actually a peacock looking for a girlfriend. By the time it was over, we were laughing like two old friends as we wound slowly along the serpentine highway toward Lampasas.

Strangely, I didn't even care that the joke was on me, or that the story made me look like an idiot. The part of me that had always been so careful to maintain a certain image seemed to have stayed behind in D.C. Out here, I had no image.

It felt good to laugh, and to make someone else laugh. It made the day seem brighter and the situation with the rental car and the nonexistent recipe articles seem less ominous. True had a nice laugh—a warm, resonant, slightly out-of-control laugh that sounded like it should belong to someone with a good sense of humor. Which made me wonder why he was so humorless most of the time. I started thinking about what Becky and Mrs. Hawthorne had said the day before, and wondering about the awful event that had changed his personality.

He caught his breath and caught me looking. For just an instant, an unguarded glance passed between us; then both of us quickly looked at the road.

"So . . . what are those tall plants with the white flowers on top?" I asked, trying to think of something casual to say. "They're everywhere all of a sudden, but I swear they weren't there just a couple days ago when I drove down."

He looked out the window, unsure what I was talking about. "The ones with the big stalk up the middle?" I nodded, and he went on. "Yucca plants. They probably haven't started blooming north of here. These are just getting started. In a couple of weeks, these pastures will look like they have a low-flying cloud over them."

"Wow," I said, painting the image in my mind. "That must be beautiful."

"Yes, it is," he said as we topped a mountain and looked over miles of country below. Like an artist's canvas, it was painted with shades of sage green and azure, bright red and yellow, and dotted with pink and snowy white. "The tourists don't come here for nothing." But the look on his face said he'd prefer the tourists not come at all. I presumed that included me.

We sat in uncomfortable silence the rest of the way to Lampasas. Pulling into town, we passed Friendly's Tractors, and True honked and waved at the men sitting on the cement steps in front of the store.

"Glad to see my dad's got the crew working hard," he muttered, then looked at them in the side mirror and shook his head, his smile saying it really didn't matter. "So do you want a doughnut or a drink or anything? It's still about another twenty minutes to Copperas Cove."

"No. That's all right," I said, noticing how his mood seemed to liven up as soon as we passed the tractor lot. I took a chance on that being something he might want to talk about—a safe, neutral subject that didn't include tourists. "So do you have one of these tractor dealerships in every town? I keep running into them everywhere I go."

"Not every town," he answered as we passed through the main thoroughfare of Lampasas, past Pizza Hut, an ancient-looking hotel, and a tiny Wal-Mart that hadn't yet made Supercenter status and looked like it never would. "Dad has owned the ones in Esther and San Saline since before I was born. He came out of the army with some money saved and a lot of knowledge about fixing large equipment. He was originally a west-Texas boy, but he fell in love with the hill country when he was at Fort Hood in Killeen, so he came back here and started a business." His admiration for his father was evident in the way he spoke, his love made clear by the sudden softness in his face. He added, as an afterthought, "We just added the dealerships in Lampasas and Llano when I . . . uh . . . well, a few years ago."

I wondered if his hesitation had anything to do with Mrs. Hawthorne's big secret, but I didn't ask. Not directly, anyway, but years of newswriting had made me expert at ferreting out information. "Oh, I just assumed you had been in this business for years. That sign where my car broke down had your name on it, and it looked like it had been there a long time."

He suddenly seemed uncomfortable, maybe even embarrassed. He turned his gaze out the window instead of at me. "Well . . . it has." I couldn't quite tell in the shadow of the cowboy hat, but I thought he was blushing, and he quickly finished with, "It's . . . um . . . a long story."

Strike one. Silence fell over us again, and it was clear he had no intention of making small talk or anything else. I watched the scenery pass for a while, then tried another subject to see if I could get any farther. The changes in his demeanor only made me more interested in seeing what I could find out. Why I cared, I had no idea. Reporters' minds are like ravenous piranhas, always looking to feed on something. "Well . . . so how did you get into the newspaper business, anyway?"

He didn't seem the least bit suspicious, and the slight

change of subject made him conversant again. "The newspaper belonged to my granddad on my mother's side. She was working summers there when my dad opened the tractor dealership. She marched in there to sell him an ad, and he fell head over heels, and the rest is history."

A warm feeling went through me at the way he told the story—as if he recognized the significance of true love, and believed in the magic of it. "That's really sweet." My voice sounded surprisingly wistful, and I cleared my throat to make it stop. "So your mother comes from a newspaper family." I pictured old-time newspaper tycoons and small-town politics—scenes fit for a Western movie.

He answered with a noncommittal shrug. "Not really. My grandfather traded some cows for the paper when Mom was in high school. He ran it right up until he died last year. Mom and Dad are pretty much retired now, so it just sort of landed in my lap. I've been trying to talk Mom into selling it off."

I frowned at him, my grand vision of a newspaper dynasty shattered. His lack of enthusiasm for the business bothered me, though I couldn't imagine why. For some reason, I found it insulting. "It must keep you pretty busy putting together a newspaper on top of running the tractor dealerships."

"Not really." Again, a noncommittal shrug indicated that we were talking about something of absolutely no consequence. "You don't have to know much to run a newspaper. Just stick it all together and haul it over to the press in Copperas Cove. I spend more time delivering it than putting it together."

Yes, and it shows, you neophyte. I said the only constructive thing I could think of. "You know, if there's a college somewhere nearby, you could probably find a number of journalism students who would love to get some experience." *Any one of whom would be more enthusiastic and more skilled than you.* I could feel the rumblings of my temper awakening like a sleeping grizzly bear.

He glanced sideways at me as if my head had just popped off my body and landed on the floorboard. "Can't see the point in that. The paper doesn't make much profit as it is." He didn't seem to have any clue how irked I was, or that just *maybe* these were not the wisest things to be saying to a person whose profession was newswriting.

"I just meant that someone studying toward a journalism degree could probably give you some ideas about layout and design, editing, et cetera. It could be a mutually beneficial arrangement." I patted myself on the back for keeping the roaring bear in my throat.

He raised one brow and lowered the other like he didn't understand what I'd said, or couldn't believe it. "You mean they give *college degrees* in that stuff?"

Suddenly I lost all sight of the fact that I was a guest in his truck and that he was graciously driving me and my broken-down rental car halfway across Texas. The bear broke free and roared forth. "Occasionally," I bit out, wondering if he was really that stupid, or if he was just trying get on my nerves. "As a matter of fact, I have one. I have *two*. And it is pretty clear from looking at your paper that nobody there has *any* idea how to write an article, or take a photograph, or lay out a page. That is the *poorest* excuse for journalism I have *ever* seen, and, quite frankly, if you're not going to do any better than that, I can't imagine why you would keep the paper going *at all!*" The profile of his calm, slightly smirking face made me rage to the point of absolute insanity. "And I don't know what your personality problem is, but most of the time you are a complete *jerk!*"

Stopping at a traffic light, he turned his face slowly toward me, a sparkle in his blue eyes and that hint of a self-assured grin still on his lips. "Well, that's good to know," he said as calmly as if I'd just told him tomorrow's weather forecast. Pulling into the rental-car lot, he motioned toward the building, just a flicker of emotion cracking his polished exterior.

So I had gotten to him after all.

"Here's the rental-car lot," he said, climbing out of the truck.

Grabbing my purse and camera bag, I disembarked also. Gladly. Grateful for our trip to be ended.

He went on talking as he started lowering the ramps on the back of the trailer. The rapidness of his movements told me he was just as anxious to be away from me as I from him. "Next door in Wal-Mart is the one-hour photo. I'll have this car off the trailer in a minute and I'll go pick up my bush hogs."

Curse me, but watching him strain to loosen the rusty chain on the car made me feel guilty for being so ungrateful when he was doing me such a big favor.

"Well . . . uhhh . . ." I didn't know why I felt the need to end things on a better note. Conscience is often an inconvenient thing. "Thank you so much for helping me." He didn't reply, but kept working on the chains, grumbling at the car under his breath, the tanned muscles in his arms bulging with effort. I started feeling really bad for having been so nasty. "So . . . ummm . . ." I said the first stupid conversation maker that came into my mind. "How are you going to keep the bush hogs on the trailer, anyway?" It was nothing but a platform with no side rails or fences. I didn't know much about pigs, but I couldn't imagine that they would just stand there, riding down the highway, and wouldn't jump off. Still no answer from the other side of the trailer, so I tried one more time. "Do they come in a box or a cage or something?"

His eyes appeared over the edge of the trailer, and he looked at me like a confused version of Kilroy. "No. You just throw them up there and chain 'em down good and tight with the boom, just like the car. They'll stay."

The image in my mind was horrible, and it reaffirmed my notion of him as some kind of self-centered sadist. For certain, I did not want to know any more, so I said, "I think I'll go over to Wal-Mart and get my film turned in before I talk to them about the car. Thanks again for the ride and for hauling the car."

He disappeared behind the trailer again, and I wasn't sure if he heard me. Finally I just turned and started walking away.

"I'll stop back on my way out of town and make sure

you got your car all right," I heard him say, followed by an ungentlemanly string of expletives under his breath, concerning the make, model, and country of origin of the car.

"No need," I replied, not wanting to see him any longer, not wanting to struggle to make conversation with him any further, and definitely not wanting to see pigs cruelly chained to the trailer. "I'll be fine. As soon as my film is done, I'm going to head back. Thanks again."

Something crashed on the trailer, and he hollered, and I just ducked my head and kept on walking. By the time he got the car off the trailer, I'd be lucky if he didn't hunt me down and shoot me.

The tension started to drain from my body as I walked through the doors into Wal-Mart. The old man at the door greeted me, handing me a cart. Setting my camera bag inside, I walked slowly past a row of flowering plants and Bundt cakes on display, having the strange feeling of being back home. There is something about Wal-Mart that is universal and comforting. You can walk into one in any city, no matter how different or how far away, look around, and forget where you are. Every Wal-Mart looks like home.

After turning in my film, I found myself lingering over a rack of on-sale books and CDs. Then I remembered about the car, and anxiety crept back into my consciousness. I headed for the door, ready to take on the rental-car agent and demand justice.

Or at least a car that would run.

I got neither. The agent, who first had to waste a

great deal of time calling Dallas to see what the procedure should be, finally concluded by telling me, with very sincere regret, that she didn't have a car to give me. She was, that day, completely out.

I just stood there, all the blood draining down my body and out my feet until I was nothing but a ghost. "What?" I gasped, praying that my ears were deceiving me. "You've got to be kidding. They told me to bring it here." If she hadn't been so nice, and so bewildered herself, I would have been yelling. As it was I was more like . . . well . . . begging.

She checked her computer again, then winced, looking at me as if she were about to cry also. "I don't have anything coming in until tomorrow. There's a big graduation at Fort Hood, and everything in town's booked up with visitors through tonight. I'll save the first available unit for you tomorrow. It should be in about eleven in the morning."

"You don't understand," I replied. "I'm staying in a town an hour and a half from here. San Saline. Somebody dropped me and the car off. I don't have *a way home*." Panic rushed through me, and my mind sped like a mouse through a maze, bumping into obstacles, trying to find a way out. "What about those cars on the lot? Why can't I have one of them? I don't care what kind. I'll take *anything*."

She grimaced again. "Those aren't rentals. They belong to the used-car lot next door. They don't rent cars."

"Is there anybody else in town who does?" I was growing more desperate by the moment. I didn't care what it cost, or if the magazine would reimburse me for it or not. I just wanted a vehicle.

She shook her head, looking at the countertop, unable to face me any longer. "No, there's not. I'm sorry. L-let me get on the phone and see if I can get a car brought over from Killeen."

The offer glimmered like a candle in the darkness. "How long will that take?"

Leaning the phone on her shoulder, she tapped her pencil impatiently on the desk. "An hour or so . . . if they have a unit available." She tipped up the receiver and started talking. "Hello, April. I've got an emergency here. Do you have anything available? I've got a lady stranded." A hopeful pause, and then her face fell. "Oh, shoot. Well, do you think they've got any in Waco . . . ?"

I couldn't stand to listen anymore. Walking out the door, I stood on the sidewalk thinking about pulling out my hair strand by strand. Why, oh, why had I told Truitt McKitrick not to come back and check on me?

Pride goeth before a fall. I looked up and down the highway at the people passing. People with *cars,* capable of driving *anywhere* they wanted. People who would be able to make it home tonight, and . . .

The Friendly's Tractors truck came around the corner like a shimmering white knight, and I started running toward the road, waving my arms and screaming. People in passing cars glanced at me with looks of dismay as I made it to the edge of the parking lot and bolted through the ditch. At that moment I didn't care how stupid I looked, or how much of a scene I caused;

I was getting into the Friendly's truck if I had to jump in like Rambo at fifty miles per hour.

A sigh of relief went through me as the truck moved into the right lane and the blinker went on. True the Tractor Man passed me without looking, pulled into the rental-car lot, and went into the office. Panting back through the ditch and across the parking lot, I saw the agent point at me and True look over his shoulder with an expression of confusion, then step out the door.

"What are you doing out there?" he asked, as if he couldn't figure it out by looking.

"I was flagging you down." The expression on his face told me he hadn't even noticed me jumping up and down in the ditch like a madwoman. "They don't have any cars left. I thought I was going to be stranded here. Boy, am I glad you stopped." I had the horrible urge to throw myself forward and hug him, in spite of his views on journalism.

He may have sensed it, because he took a step back, shaking his head. "Well, calm down. I told you I'd stop back here."

"But I . . ." *I told you not to,* which was stupid. Instead I said, "Listen, I'm sorry to be so much trouble, but do you think you can give me a ride back to San Saline? If these people do manage to find a car, it will be hours before they can get it here. There's some kind of a graduation in town, and everything is rented out."

He scratched his chin thoughtfully, a hint of a wicked grin on his lips.

The agent stepped out the door before he could answer. "I'm sorry," she said, looking despondent.

"The best I can do is late this evening or tomorrow. If you can't come to pick it up, I'll have it delivered to San Saline for you. I'm really, really sorry for the inconvenience."

"That's all right," I told her. It all mattered much less, now that I had a way home. "I'm staying at the Hawthorne House Bed-and-Breakfast in San Saline. If you can bring the car there, that will be great."

The agent nodded, pleased to no longer have a desperate customer on her hands, and I sighed, pleased not to be spending my night walking the aisles of Wal-Mart, and Truitt McKitrick smiled, pleased to have been right in stopping to check on me. Or else he was flirting with the rental-car agent, who was definitely trying to flirt with him.

I offered them an opportunity to flirt in private by telling them I was going over to Wal-Mart to pick up my photographs and grab a candy bar. True apparently wasn't interested in hanging around, because he drove the truck to the Wal-Mart parking lot and waited for me there.

In short order, we were heading back to Lampasas, though True had informed me we would be taking the long way home, since he had to deliver the farm implements that were loaded on the trailer.

It suddenly occurred to me about the load of hogs, and I couldn't resist asking, "So where are the pigs?" I wondered if his plan hadn't worked so well, after all.

He looked at me like I'd grown a second head. "What pigs?" As if he had no idea what I was talking about.

I really wanted to know how the whole thing had turned out, so I tried again. "You know, the pigs." Still a look of noncomprehension, so I added, "The pigs . . . the bush hogs. You said you were going to chain them to the trailer and they would just stand there."

He squinted at me for a moment like he thought I was going to say, "April fools," then he snickered twice, pulled his hat off, and wiped his eyes with the back of his hand. "Good God, lady, where did you say you were from?" He hooted. "Bush hogs, as in bush hog mowers, like the ones on the trailer. You pull 'em behind a tractor? Don't they mow grass where you come from?"

Looking over my shoulder at the trailer full of farm implements, I slowly started to clue in. "Yes, they do." The whole thing felt far too much like the snake-hunting incident. Duped again. I did my best to defend myself. "And those are called *whirligigs*—whirligig mowers. The parks department uses them all the time, and I've never heard *anyone* call it a bush hog."

He laughed harder as the breeze fanned through the open window and lifted the damp curls of his hair. By the time he caught his breath, it was nearly dry. "Oh, Lord," he said finally. "I haven't laughed like that in . . . well . . . since this morning when you told me about the peacocks. What did you say you people call these mowers?"

"Whirligigs," I repeated slowly, as if maybe *he* didn't speak English. "Now you know the proper term for your next commercial." But I couldn't keep a serious expression, because the whole conversation suddenly seemed so funny.

He looked at me with a wicked twinkle in his eye, and a smile that could have charmed a nun. "Darlin', if I go on television around here and tell people to come over and look at my whirligigs, I'd be likely to get run out of town."

He laughed, and I laughed, and the afternoon breeze wafted through the window, laden with sweet floral scents. Suddenly the ride seemed very pleasant indeed.

Shaking his head, he squinted thoughtfully out the window for a while, then finally said, "Did you really think I was going to chain live hogs to a flatbed trailer and drive down the highway?"

Slapping a hand over my face, I nodded, feeling my cheeks redden. "It was a pretty strange picture."

"I'll bet." He chuckled, shaking his head and muttering, "Bush hogs," again, then laughing some more.

Rolling my eyes, I opened my candy bar and can of Coke, and started on lunch. "Stop doing that," I muttered, trying not to be infected again by his laughter. "You'll make me choke on my food."

He didn't stop, of course. Didn't even attempt to, so I finally did my best to ignore him, eat my lunch, and watch the scenery go by. We were pulling into the Friendly's Tractors lot in Lampasas before he sobered up. Stopping the truck in front of the building, he turned it off and climbed out.

"It'll take a few minutes to unload," he said. "Come on inside, where it's cool."

Setting my Coke on the floorboard, I followed him up the steps to the front loading dock, noticing that everyone in the garage was watching me. As we walked through the door, the girl behind the counter stopped in the middle of writing something and looked at me openmouthed.

"Mrs. McKitrick, True's here," she called toward the doorway of an adjacent office; then she turned to us again, said, "Hi, True," and looked at me with more than passing interest and something that might have been jealousy. "Who's this?"

"Hey, Amy." He ignored the question, glancing sideways as an attractive sixty-something woman in a denim skirt stepped from the office. "Hi, Mom."

"Well, hello, True." Mom McKitrick looked at me with the same intense interest, except Mom's smile was genuine, maybe even a little hopeful. "I see you've brought a friend along."

A gray-haired man in a cowboy hat and coveralls came in the side door from the garage before True could answer. "Afternoon, True." He stuck his hand out, and the two of them shook hands, as if they hadn't seen each other in a while, then he, too, looked at me. "I thought I saw someone in the truck with ya while ago when ya passed. So who's this pretty redheaded lady?"

All three of them looked at me, and I felt like a wax statue on display—a wax statue, blushing.

True looked as embarrassed as I felt, and he pretended to be busy writing an inventory slip on the counter. "This is Colleen Collins." He glanced privately at me and gave a quick wink. "She's a hitchhiker I picked up."

A shocked chuckle burst from my lips as I stuck my hand out in greeting. "Colleen Collins," I said again; then I felt compelled to straighten things out, so that no one would think we were on a date. "True did me a big favor today. I had a problem with my rental car, and I had to take it to Copperas Cove. He was kind enough to haul it there for me."

The three of them looked at me like I was speaking pig latin; then True's mother extended her hand and shook mine, and after her, the man, who I assumed was True's father. He and True had the same lopsided smile.

"Real nice to meet ya, Miss Collins," he said, looking curious, but maybe a little uncertain. No doubt it was my Yankee accent.

"It's nice to meet all of you," I returned, making my best attempt at being down-home. "But, please, people call me Collie."

He lowered both brows, moving his lips, chewing on a thought. "Collie, like the dog?"

"Bill!" True's mother gasped, looking mortified.

"Dad!" True glanced up from his form.

Only Amy didn't seem to care if I was insulted.

Dad raised his chin, scowling stubbornly at the two of them. "Aw, heck, I was just makin' sure I heard her right. Y'all don't have to whup me on the spot."

"It's all right," I said, having sympathy for Dad, who was clearly outnumbered and couldn't understand what the problem was anyway. "I get that all the time."

"See," he said to the others, looking vindicated. "She doesn't mind." And he reached out, patting me on the arm like he'd known me all my life, then stepped past me and headed for the door. "Problem is nobody around here's got a sense of humor. . . . I'll get those bush hogs off the trailer."

Chuckling, True shook his head and went back to filling out his forms. "Collie, do you need a fresh drink or anything? There are some chairs back in the office, if you want to sit down."

"All right," I said, and followed Mrs. McKitrick back to the office, while Amy perched her elbows on the counter and watched True write, as if it were an act of wonder.

"Amy, if you would dust those toys on the peg rack, that would be good," Mrs. McKitrick called over her shoulder as the two of us walked into the office. She rolled her eyes and added more quietly, "These young girls, these days."

Entering the office, I took the chair across from her, and we sat making pleasant chitchat for a few minutes about my reason for being in the area, and the newspaper business in general. I was pleased to find her more knowledgeable and enthusiastic on the subject than her son. She was an infinitely likable person, with a genuine smile and an oozingly friendly way of talking that reminded me of Mrs. Hawthorne. But there was an acute, intelligent look in Mom McKitrick's eyes that kept you on your toes.

I was careful with what I said, so as not to give her any wrong ideas. There was enough false information about me going around town already.

It was a few minutes before I noticed the row of framed Friendly's Tractors ads hanging on the wall beside me. They dated in chronology from black-and-white, 1960s genre, to modern ones that looked like they had just been taken out of a magazine. The old ones centered around the picture of a blond-haired little boy with laughing blue eyes, sitting on pedal tractors, or full-sized farm machinery, and even one on a pony. He looked vaguely familiar, and beneath him ran the caption *Home of True the Tractor Man*.

I quickly put two and two together. "So that's where True the Tractor Man comes from," I surmised. "You know, I asked him about that today, but he wouldn't tell me anything."

Giving me a conspiratorial look, she glanced out the door. "He's a little embarrassed about that." She looked at the pictures on the wall with a wistful sigh. "He was True the Tractor Man before he could walk and talk. That boy was just born liking machinery. When he was little, he did our advertisements and television commercials." She laughed. "Everybody just loved him. He was so good at it!"

Glancing up as her son stepped into the doorway, she gave him a sheepish shrug of her shoulders.

"Back then I was cute," he said, and looked at her with a wide, slow, adoring smile I had never seen before. When he smiled like that, he was something to behold.

She regarded him with the same devotion, and the scene was so sweet, a knot rose in my throat. There is nothing more touching than a full-grown man who still adores his mother.

He caught me watching and tipped his head down to hide behind the cowboy hat. "We'd better get on the road." He scratched a boot on the floor uncomfortably. "Gotta get back to San Saline. Collie's a busy woman." Just a sliver of a playful blue gaze caught me from beneath the hat brim. "Still have to stop in Llano and drop off five more whirligigs."

A chuckle pushed from me as I stood up. Mrs. McKitrick glanced questioningly from him to me, then shrugged her shoulders and followed us out.

"Collie, it was very nice to meet you," she said. "You stop by anytime."

The sound of that bothered me a little, so I reminded her, "Thank you, but I'll only be in town a few more days. It was nice to meet you, though."

"Well, enjoy your visit." And she gave me a look I recognized from my own mother—that contemplative, scheming, "maybe so" look that shows what's going on in a mother's mind.

True must have recognized it, because he gave her a tired glance and shook his head, then kissed her on the cheek. "See you sometime later in the week."

"All right, dear."

And we went out the door, practically husband and wife.

True shrugged apologetically as he waved at his Dad in the garage. " 'Bye, Dad. Don't work too hard."

"Be careful, son." Dad lifted his grease rag into the air in a gesture of farewell. "Nice to meet ya, young lady . . . uh . . . Collie." And then under his breath, shaking his head, "Just like the dog. I . . ."

Laughing, I climbed into the truck and shut the door.

True looked at me from the driver's seat and rolled his eyes. "Sorry about that," he said, nodding over his shoulder toward the dealership. "They don't get out much."

"That's OK," I told him. "I have a set of those, too."

He gave me a wry sideways glance. "I'll bet they're not farmers."

"Hardly." I chuckled. "We Collinses are pure Baltimore suburbanites. My dad owns an electrical-supply store and my mother is a high school journalism teacher."

True nodded, pausing to look down the road as we turned onto a different highway. "Well, that explains why you know so much about newspapers." He gave me a sideways look and raised a brow. "You an expert on electrical supplies, too?"

"Mm-hmm." For some reason, I blushed. "Ask me anything."

His eyes met mine for just an instant; then he looked at the road, grinning. "I wouldn't know where to begin."

I blushed again, feeling a strange combination of relief and disappointment as silence settled over us and the miles passed. As we crested a hill, a gigantic rock formation appeared in the distance, rising high above the tree-clad peaks like an overturned bowl with salad spilled around the sides.

"What in the world is that?" I asked, wondering if it

was natural or man-made.

"It's called Enchanted Rock, because it was an Indian holy place. The view from up top is really something." He paused and leaned forward to look at it out the window. "About the earliest memory I have is of hiking to the top with my folks and looking out over miles and miles of country. It's the kind of thing you don't forget." His eyes narrowed slightly, as if he were seeing it even now. "We used to do that every year. Of course, we can't anymore because the folks are too old to make the climb. Dad still sneaks up here with his buddies once in a while, though."

"I don't blame him," I said quietly, gazing at the enormous rock face as we passed, feeling awed by the size of it, picturing the little blond-haired boy from the tractor advertisements waving at me from the top. When I could no longer see him, or the rock, I looked at True and caught him watching me. I wondered what he was thinking.

"My mom's after my dad about his health, too," I said to bridge the silence. "She thinks he ought to get rid of his motorcycle, even though the only thing he uses it for anymore is to putter down to the bowling alley on Wednesday nights with his buddies."

True chuckled. "I guess that's just part of growing old. I guess you're lucky if you have someone who cares about you enough to tell you not to climb rocks and ride motorcycles to the bowling alley."

I nodded, looking out the window and feeling an unexpected twinge somewhere inside me. "You're probably right, but I don't think my dad would agree."

"Mine either," he said as the diesel engine quieted and we pulled into Llano. "Well, we're here. Time to set a few more bush hogs free."

The stop at the Llano tractor dealership went faster, so I waited in the truck, looking around at the historic town square, which was much like the one in San Saline. When the unloading was finished, we headed north out of town and into the vast, rolling countryside. The hills were covered with wildflowers and dotted with ancient-looking homesteads built in milk-colored stone. True pointed out the ranches along the way, telling me about the vintages and histories of the homesteads, the German origins of the settlements there, and the Comanches who fought bitterly to keep their lands. Listening to the steady, resonant sound of his voice, I gazed over miles of country, thinking about what it must have been like and how much fortitude it took to survive there. Even today, the people and the land were so much alike—solid, tough, yet vast in spirit and generous with simple pleasures.

By the time we reached San Saline and pulled up to Hawthorne House, I was mesmerized.

"Well . . ." For a moment I couldn't think what to say. I hovered in the doorway of the truck, not quite ready to say good-bye. "I can't thank you enough for the ride . . . and for hauling the car."

"Not a problem." His reply was unemotional at first. Then he looked at me, smiled, and added, "To tell you the truth, it was a pleasure."

I must have been a little addled, because I said, "So . . . I'll see you around town."

We stood there a moment longer, like a couple of awkward teenagers on a date. Finally he raised a finger and pointed at me. "You know, I've been thinking about what you said about my newspaper."

I winced.

"Do you really think it's all that bad?" he asked.

I winced again. "Yes. It is. Sorry."

I was grateful that he didn't seem upset or indifferent as he had been earlier—just interested in my opinion. He drummed his fingers thoughtfully on the steering wheel. "Well . . . I was thinking that if you have any time tomorrow afternoon, maybe you could come by the newspaper office and give me some pointers on the Monday edition." He smiled and gave me a quick wink. "Maybe help shape it up a little bit. Since you've got two college degrees, and all."

I tried not to reward him with a smile, but couldn't help it. "I'd be glad to." Closing the door of the truck, I stepped back. "I'll see you tomorrow afternoon."

"See ya then," he said, then put the truck in gear and started away.

Watching him drive into the amber sunset at the end of the driveway, I smiled to myself, thinking of how the day had started and how it had ended, and how it had been surprisingly . . . wonderful.

Chapter 6

PROCRASTINATION becomes an art form if you practice it long enough. With a little creative reasoning, I kept from starting the *Southern Woman* article Friday night, spending the evening, instead, sorting through my pictures and deciding which ones to send with the article I hadn't written. When that was finished, I fixed a turkey sandwich and watched part of the John Wayne marathon on the Cowboy Channel. Just as the movie was ending, I spotted Mrs. Hawthorne coming across the lawn, so I stepped out and met her on the porch, then sat on the cottage steps until after dark, telling her about my adventure with True the Tractor Man and the rental car. By the time the story was over, both of us were laughing, and the evening was spent.

As I closed the cabin door, that strange, warm feeling came over me, and I couldn't resist taking out my notepad and writing about the day—about demon-possessed rental cars and bush hogs chained to flatbed trailers, about delivering whirligigs and True's dad asking if I was named after a dog.

In the end, I wrote about friendship. *Sometimes it just happens to you all at once,* I wrote, *and you can't even say exactly when you stepped over the line. One minute you're just two people who are strangers to each other, and then suddenly there's a sense of understanding that wasn't there before. It's like the gust of a warm breeze, or the feathery feel of a bit of sunlight—*

just there all of a sudden, and not for any reason, but it lifts your heart, and you know you've gained something wonderful.

When I was finished, I set the pen down and flipped through the yellow sheets of notepaper flowing with a river of words and thoughts and feelings. Something strange was happening to me. I had lost the ability to write a simple magazine article, yet I could channel pages and pages of the sentimental meanderings of a warm-and-fuzzy alter-ego I didn't know I had.

The sound on the television ratcheted up suddenly, as if to save me from my self-examination, and the opening scene of *Rio Bravo* came on. Closing my notepad, I walked to the television, turned it down, then was drawn to the couch by some strange, magnetic pull. Something else was happening to me. I was becoming a fan of the Cowboy Channel. Me. A John Wayne junkie.

I watched until midnight, when the Duke marathon was over; then I turned off the lights and went to bed, feeling guilty for not working on the article, and determined to start tomorrow.

I dreamed about bush hogs, fleshy and pink, with short curly tails and long, smiling mouths, riding atop the flatbed trailer of True the Tractor Man, past the rental-car lot with the worried agent, past the tractor dealership with the men drinking coffee on the steps, past John Wayne on his favorite horse, slowly winding into the distance, disappearing down a ribbon of highway into the soft, violet hills below the setting sun.

The sound of snakes crawling on the roof and

someone calling for help outside my door woke me sometime early in the morning. Throwing back the covers, I swung my legs over the edge of the bed, then realized where I was and climbed under the covers again, pleased to have stopped short of searching for my shoes this time. Apparently it was possible to become accustomed to anything. . . .

When I awoke the second time, it was to the whispering of a guilty conscience, not peacocks. Lying in the bed, I stared at the bright streaks of dawn light pointing to the notes and photographs on the table. Today I had to get to work. It was Saturday already. Deadline on the first article was Wednesday—plenty of time still, but I wasn't even sure if I had enough research material to fill the length requirement. One way or another, I had to come up with a decent article. Now that I had wasted three days' worth of the magazine's time and money, I couldn't possibly back out of the contract.

"Not a problem," I muttered to myself as I climbed from the bed and went about getting dressed. "Breakfast at the café first, then straight to work. No distractions today."

Except that I had promised True the Tractor Man I would help him with his lousy newspaper. Why I had agreed to that, I couldn't imagine. I didn't have time, nor was I interested in the journalistic quality of the *San Saline Record.*

The whole touchy-feely scene of the day before seemed stupid now—me standing in the doorway of the truck looking like a doe-eyed adolescent, him grinning like an imp and asking if I wanted to come over and play newspaper tomorrow.

"Geez, Coll, what were you *thinking?*" I muttered, pulling my hair back and putting the clip in tight, so as to pinch off the circulation to the part of my brain that was writing sentimental stories and making friends with tractor-fixing newspaper editors. "Get a grip."

By the time I found my shoes and started out the door, I had my head on straight—almost. I was all the way to the driveway before I remembered I didn't have a car. Grumbling, I stood in the empty gravel drive, scratching my head and trying to decide whether it was worth walking the half mile to the café for breakfast, or whether I should just stay in the room and get to work.

It wasn't hard to talk myself out of that idea. I didn't have anything breakfastlike to eat in the room, and in the back of my mind I was wondering about something Mrs. Hawthorne had mentioned the night before about the cook at the café knowing a recipe for fried prickly pear pads and boiled mesquite beans—information that would surely help inspire me to get busy with the article.

With my guilt sufficiently banished, I tucked my notepad under my arm and started toward the café, following the faint, and now familiar, scent of the sale barn cattle corrals. As I came to the end of the driveway, I could hear the low rumble of idling semi trucks, and the nearly deafening racket of cows mooing, and the high-pitched whistles of drovers who sounded just like the ones on the Cowboy Channel. Walking slowly along the opposite side of the highway, I watched as a line of semi trucks and pickups with trailers moved through the covered portico of the sale barn, stopping one by one to deposit noisy, displeased bunches of cattle into the corrals, where cowboys on horseback chased them to smaller corrals and locked them in, which only made them angrier and louder.

In spite of the blowing dust and indescribable odor of the place, I couldn't resist stopping for a moment in front of the Friendly's Tractors lot and watch the goings-on. Behind me, a teenage boy with a long pole was carefully putting letters onto the bottom part of the Friendly's sign.

"Mornin', ma'am," he said, glancing at me from beneath the brim of a beaten-up straw cowboy hat. "Looks like it's gonna be a big one."

"Looks like it," I said, as if I knew what he was talking about. Something important was happening at the sale barn today, and it looked surprisingly interesting to me. Apparently I was not the only one, because the parking lot around the sale barn was full, and lines of parked cars, pickup trucks, and horse trailers were forming up and down the sides of the highway. Everywhere I looked, small groups of people were walking slowly toward the sale barn, or standing in small groups, or sitting on the tailgates of pickups and the fenders of horse trailers, eating breakfast and talking. Across the road from me, three elderly men in overalls were looking at the Friendly's Tractors sign, scratching their heads and trying to figure out the message.

The traffic on the highway broke for a moment, and

I dashed across the road to the café parking lot, then turned back to look at the sign myself.

New Shipment, it said in interchangeable black plastic letters. *Ask us about our w* . . . next letter. *Wh* . . . reload. *Whi* . . . reload. *Whir.* I was starting to get a sinking feeling. *Whirl* . . . I could feel my cheeks going red as the rest of the letters went up. *Ask us about our whirligigs.*

The old men beside me started to laugh. "Oh, Lordy," one of them hooted. "I'm gonna have to go across and find out what that's all about!"

Like an incognito celebrity, I ducked my head and hurried toward the café, my embarrassment quickly fading from my cheeks. I hated to admit it, but it was kind of nice to be recognized—even if it was for my own stupidity.

The old pink adobe building didn't seem as strange as it had on my first day in town—perhaps because I had time to adjust to the flamingolike color while standing outside the door waiting for a line of people to file out, or perhaps because I was remembering my first morning there. Looking at the building, I could hear the voices of the cactus-killing cowboy, Miss Grace and Francis, the lady with the beehive hairdo, and Mrs. Hawthorne. Each was part of the place—like the adobe blocks and the glass bricks, the wagon wheels and the pink paint. A strange mixture of generations, styles, and ideas that somehow fit together to create something strong and timeless.

This time, *Y'all come on in* felt like it applied to me also, and I didn't hesitate at the door, but stepped into the dimly lit interior, eager to see what I would find.

If anyone inside had anything to do with the Friendly's Tractors sign, or knew it was another joke on me, they didn't show it. Even though the place was packed, people hardly seemed to notice as I walked in. Maybe because there were already so many strangers in town.

Becky was sitting by herself in my booth by the kitchen door, and she raised a hand, waving me over.

"Good morning, Collie," she said, as if we were the best friends in the world. "How are you this morning?" She didn't seem to know about the whirligig sign.

I didn't tell her. "Just fine. So what's going on at the cattle barn today?"

"Big replacement-heifer sale, mostly." She didn't seem nearly as excited about the event as everyone else was. "First off, they'll sell some sheep and goats, then a few steers, bulls, and mama cows, but most of the crowd is here for replacement heifers."

"I see," I replied tentatively. After my experiences of the last few days, I had learned not to say too much before getting my facts straight. "What is a replacement heifer?"

She lowered a straw-colored eyebrow over one hazel eye, like she couldn't believe I was asking. "Well . . . a young cow that hasn't had a baby yet."

"I know what a heifer is." Thanks to four straight hours of John Wayne movies. "But what makes it a replacement heifer? I mean, a replacement for what?"

She chuckled at the question. "Old cows that can't

have any more calves."

"I see." I couldn't help smiling with her. Now I knew the rest of the story, as Paul Harvey would say.

Mrs. Hawthorne came by the table in a red-faced rush, poured a cup of coffee for me, and quickly told me what I should order for breakfast—huevos rancheros. So I did, and went back to talking to Becky, who didn't seem to be in a very good mood.

"So what's on your mind this morning?" I asked.

"Oh, nothing." Her lips pursed into a pout that made her look all of sixteen years old. "Jimmy and I had a fight. He wants to buy a new truck and I want to get a house, and we haven't got the money for anything because that ranch doesn't pay him squat, and I only get four-fifty an hour at the paper."

Not quite knowing what to say, and not in any hurry to get into a whining session with Becky, I just said, "Oh . . . that's too bad." And hoped the conversation would end there.

It didn't, of course. A complainer never fails to make good use of a sympathetic ear. "You'd think after nearly a year, I'd get some kind of raise," she went on. "I swear to God, True's lucky I don't just get sick of him and quit."

My parents instilled in me lack of patience with whiners, and besides, I was thinking of the obvious fact that her newspaper work didn't merit a raise, so I said, "Well, a business can only afford to pay employees as much as is profitable. Sometimes the best way to improve your standing is to help your employer turn a greater profit." That was a direct quote from my father, who had absolutely no patience with complainers.

Becky looked like it was Greek to her. "I don't see how I'm going to do that. True decides how everything's going to be with the paper. He hardly lets me do anything but book ads, make deliveries, and take pictures."

I pointed a finger at her, feeling myself getting strangely interested in the profitability of the *San Saline Record.* "But that's the important stuff," I said, feeling that old tingle of newspaper excitement trickle through me. "The ads are where the money comes from, and the subscribers reading the paper are the bread and butter for the ads. If you don't have people picking the paper up and using the ads, you won't have advertisers, and without advertisers you can't have a paper." I had a sudden moment of eureka, and looked her in the eye with an intensity that pushed her back in her seat. "You know, if you really want to keep working for newspapers, you ought to think about taking some college courses in journalism. There's so much to learn about photography, and layout . . . and marketing. It's really exciting once you get into it. You might really like it." The truth was, I didn't know whether she would or not, but I knew there wasn't much future in working part-time for four-fifty an hour, and Becky seemed far too quick-minded to be wasting away in such a job.

I realized suddenly that someone new was standing just behind me, and the someone was Truitt McKitrick, and he had heard at least the last of my commentary.

"See that, Beck," he said without looking at me. "Should have stayed in college. Aren't you supposed to be taking pictures of the sale this morning?"

Becky smirked at him in a siblinglike fashion, then laid her napkin on the table and pushed her plate away. "I guess I'd better get over there," she said loudly, glaring at True. To me, she added, "That's not a bad idea. I think I'll talk to Jimmy about it and see what he thinks. See you later." Then she grabbed her purse and scooted out of the booth.

"All right. 'Bye," I said as Mrs. H. rushed over and laid a plate of huevos rancheros in front of me. Huddling over the strange mixture of eggs, onions, cheddar cheese, and tomato salsa, I felt supremely embarrassed for having been caught running down True's paper once again, this time to his already disgruntled employee. I waited for him to say something about it, but he just gave me a sideways smile, shook his head, and proceeded to the bar, where Mrs. H. had laid out his breakfast.

I vacillated between going over there to apologize, and just staying where I was, ignoring the whole thing. Then I remembered the sign across the street, and decided he didn't merit an apology, under the circumstances.

The conversation between the two cowboys in the booth behind me got louder and perked my attention, so I sat a little straighter in my seat, listening. A good reporter can never resist the urge to eavesdrop.

I recognized the cactus-killing cowboy from the day before. ". . . well, they're kind of brownish blackish, and they have long, bony spines on the back, and big, long, tusklike things out the front, like this. They stand about three foot high, I think."

Turning my head slightly to the side, I looked out the corner of my eye to see what he was describing. I couldn't imagine what sort of a creature they were talking about. It sounded like a . . . miniature rhinoceros, but, of course, no such thing existed, so I listened some more, fascinated.

The man sitting directly behind me slapped his hands on the table and leaned forward intensely. For a moment I thought they were going to get in a fight. "But the truth is, you ain't never seen one in the wild."

"Well, no, I ain't," the younger man admitted. "But I seen what they can do to a pasture. Just one can shred a whole pasture to nothin', and not in very much time, neither. They'll leave it plumb mowed down."

The older man scooted to the corner of the booth, turned sideways in his seat, and gave me a quick wink. Clearly, he knew he had Cactus-killer corralled, and he wanted me to be a witness. At that point, I was so into the conversation, I wasn't even trying to hide the fact that I was listening.

"So," the old sage went on, "Yer' sayin' they don't need no special feed or nothin'."

"Not sure." The younger man shrugged, giving me a grave look, then glancing toward the bar. "You'd have to ask True, since he's the expert. Hey, True, do they need any special kind of pasture, or can you just let 'em hop off the trailer anywhere?" His partner at the table started to chuckle, but Cactus-killer went on with a sober expression. "I mean, what kind of food *does* a *bush hog* eat, anyway?"

In one decisive moment, I got the joke and realized I was the butt of it. Letting my head roll into my hand, I turned red and started laughing along with almost everyone else in the place.

The merriment went on for several minutes, then died as suddenly as it had started, and people headed for the door like someone had just announced a fire drill.

Mrs. H. stopped by my table to explain. "Almost time for the sale to start," she said, smiling at me with genuine fondness. "You ought to go over, at least for a little while. Anything newsworthy happens in town today, it'll happen over there." She glanced over her shoulder at the bar. "True, you take Collie on over to the sale and show her what's going on." Then she turned back to me, laying a hand on my arm as if she intended to pry me out of my seat and shove me into his arms. "You've got time, don't you, Collie? Lands! You can't miss your one and only chance to go to a real Texas livestock sale. There's just not anything else like it, anywhere."

"I guess." I reminded myself that I needed to sit Mrs. H. down and explain to her in no uncertain terms that I was *not* looking for love—not the tractor-fixing cowboy kind, or any other kind.

Mrs. H. grinned, looking frightfully pleased. "You're coming to supper tonight, aren't you, Collie? Vonda brought me a jar of those mesquite beans she puts up and sells to tourists, and I got the recipe. I thought we could try them with supper—just as a lark. I'm sure they taste pretty horrible, but you can call it research."

There was something about Mrs. H. that was just impossible to refuse, so I said, "Sure. What time?"

"Around five. We're going to eat early, then go watch the Little League game. You're welcome to come along. It's the *season opener*. They'll have fireworks and everything."

At the counter, True stood up, grinning. "Wouldn't want to miss that, D.C. It'll be practically as exciting as the cow sale. Bet ya don't get entertainment like this back home."

Slinging her dish towel, Mrs. H. popped him on the arm with surprising skill, cracking the towel like a whip. "Now, you just hush up with that, Truitt McKitrick, or I'll call your mama."

True gave her a sideways glance and a wicked grin, then made his way past her toward the door, motioning for me to follow. Over his shoulder, he said to Mrs. H., "You're buying my breakfast, aren't ya?"

"Not a chance," she grumbled back, shaking her head at him as I grabbed my things and hurried for the door. "I'll put it on your bill."

True was laughing under his breath as I caught up with him and we crossed the parking lot.

"You know, you shouldn't antagonize her so much," I said, thinking of how she had defended him to Becky, and how, in many ways, he didn't seem to deserve it. "She really thinks highly of you."

He looked down at me with a knowing twinkle in his blue eyes. "I'm not hurting her feelings." He seemed sure of it, and I suddenly felt that I should mind my own business. "She knows I like her, but one mother is all I can stand. She needs to quit hen-fussing over everyone. That's what's wrong with her son—she's been babying him all his life, and he doesn't know how to work for a living. She needs to cut the strings on him and Becky and let them grow up."

I didn't reply, but just stared ahead at the goings-on in the sale barn. I didn't want to get into a conversation about Becky, and what I had said to her in the café. I had a feeling he was lumping me in with Mrs. Hawthorne—nosy, too motherly, trying to iron out everyone's lives. Which was laughable, considering the wrinkled state of my own.

"So . . ." I said as we made our way past corrals filled with noisy, restless, smelly cattle, "are all these people really here *just* to buy cows? I mean, it doesn't seem like there could be this many people around who need a cow."

He chuckled at that, shaking his head. "Some are selling, a few buying. Truth is, cattle aren't a very profitable item unless you've got a big chunk of land that's not carrying a note. Most people are just here for something to do."

"Are you buying, or just watching?" I asked.

"Depends." He looked speculatively at the cattle milling around in the corrals. "I could use about a hundred heifers, but I'm not in any hurry about it."

I couldn't help thinking that a hundred cows must cost a lot of money, and wondering if the tractor business was really that profitable. I wondered where he kept a hundred cows, since Mrs. H. said he lived in an apartment above the newspaper office. "Oh," I said, following him to the main entrance of the building, two glass doors framed by an arched metal sign that grandly proclaimed the name of the place: *Monroe Livestock Auction, Bub and Dub Monroe, owners*.

True grinned at me, catching me looking up at the sign as he held the door open. "May not look like much from here," he said, "but wait until you see Bub and Dub in action."

I could hear the action starting in the main auction gallery as True and I made our way through the crowded hallway. Fascinated, I looked at the display of cattle memorabilia on the walls—county fair ribbons, 4-H trophies, photographs of championship cattle standing proudly with rings of flowers over their shoulders. Some dated as far back as the 1930s and 1940s. Some were as recent as last year—as if the pursuit of bovine perfection were a timeless torch, carried from one generation of Monroes to the next, proudly displayed for all to admire.

By the time we reached the door to the main gallery, the noise of the ongoing sale was deafening. The air was filled with the rattle of the auctioneer's voice, the sound of people yelling, the low murmur of dozens of conversations, and the bleating of disgruntled goats.

We paused for a moment just outside the room, waiting for a chance to thread our way through the bottleneck of bystanders in the door. Glancing up, I found myself eye-to-eye with two motionless, enormous, coiled rattlesnakes, hanging wired to the wall like something out of a taxidermist's nightmare. They were wearing tiny black cowboy hats, little blue bandannas, and had the names *Bub* and *Dub* hanging on cardboard signs around their scaly necks. Bub was wearing eye-glasses and holding a tiny walking cane in his coils.

Judging from the coating of dust and spiderwebs, Bub and Dub had been guarding the doorway for quite a while. They watched me with glassy raven eyes as I slipped through the crowd behind True, finally entering the main gallery, only to find that it, too, was packed to capacity. Standing on my toes, I surveyed the small dirt-floored sale ring, framed on one side by a raised auctioneer's stand with a swinging metal door on either end through which animals were being moved in and out. On the spectators' side of the ring was a high metal pipe fence, framed by a narrow walkway, then a row of old theater chairs, arranged into separate boxes for a privileged few. Beyond that were the commoners' seats—a semicircular row of steep, stair step–like bleachers, which were filled to overflowing with people. The whole thing had the look of an ancient jousting match, right down to the men in the ring, chasing goats around with sticks, like knights with long white lances.

True motioned to a box of empty theater seats with a Friendly's Tractors sign on the front, and I clued in to the fact that we were not doomed to stand in the doorway, or to try to squeeze into seats in the gallery. We were auction royalty. Like Sir Lancelot and Guinevere we crossed the room and regally slipped into the waiting box seats reserved for Friendly's Tractors.

The auctioneer looked up in the middle of selling a herd of shaggy white goats that reminded me of my friends in the bluebonnet pasture. "Forty-will-ya-forty-five-and-five-and— Hey, there's True the Tractor Man with a good-lookin' redheaded woman. Say True, how's yer whirligig this mornin'?"

Shaking his head, True smiled and waved him off, and the auctioneer continued on with the goats. "And will-ya-forty-five, come on they're just like Dub's girlfriends, they's cheap but they ain't free. Will-ya-forty-five . . ." A man at the edge of the ring in a yellow vest hollered, and the bid went up. "Forty-five-a-fifty-will-ya-give-a-fifty-dollar-bill-fer-'em. They's just like Dub's last wife, lotsa hair, not much brains, but they'll keep ya warm in the winter. Will-ya-go-fifty-times-twelve, there's twelve in the lot. Will-ya-fifty-fifty-fifty. Come on, True, the pretty redheaded lady likes goats, why don'tcha buy 'er a dozen?"

Another man in a yellow vest hollered at ringside, and the bid went up again. "Fifty-five-give-five-give-five-give-five . . ."

I leaned over and whispered to True, "Why are the men in the yellow vests the only ones buying?"

He gave me that rolling-eyed look I had come to recognize all too well, and leaned close to my ear. "Those are the bid spotters. If you want to get the bid, you nod at one of them and they call it out to the auctioneer."

"Oohhhhh." Now the whole thing made sense. After watching for a few minutes, I concluded that bid spotting was a bit of an art form in itself. When a bid spotter got a customer, he jumped in the air and hollered like he'd just won the lottery, adding to the excitement of the moment; then he watched his customer intensely, making all sorts of facial expressions and hand gestures to try to keep the bid going. All in all, it was a pretty interesting process to watch, but not nearly as interesting as listening to Bub and Dub.

Bub, a slender, stooped-over man who looked perhaps seventy years old and wore bottle-bottom eyeglasses, finished selling the herd of white goats and turned the microphone over to Dub, who appeared to be about ten years younger, wore a thick gray mustache, and looked like he could have once played linebacker for the Dallas Cowboys.

"All right, and look what we've got here," Dub began as a group of sheep were prodded through the door. "We've got a herd of fine spring ewes. Fine spring ewes with their whole lives ahead of 'em. Eighteen in the lot. It'll be yer money times eighteen. Whatda-ya-wanna-give-fer-'em? OK, thirty-five from Randal Pink, he's a cheap old fart, but we'll take his bid. Thirty-five-do-I-hear-forty-and-forty-and-I-have-forty-now-forty-five-now-fifty. C'mon now, eighteen ewes ready to go home and earn a livin'. They got Bub beat already, and they're only half as ugly. C'mon, Randal, you know you need these ewes. Now fifty-five-now-sixty . . ."

I lost track of the bidding for a while and just looked around the room, watching the crowd—men, women, teenagers, children, babies, old people, young people. All watching, talking, speculating, laughing, and looking very content to be crammed together on hard wooden benches in a hot, smelly building, watching herd after herd of sheep and goats come in one door and go out the other.

The odd thing was, I didn't mind it either. There was a strange mixture of stoicism and excitement in the room that was kind of nice—like standing on the edge of an ambling river, watching a whirlpool spin in the middle. I sat back in my seat, making a mental catalog of the average price of sheep and goats, for what reason, I couldn't say. It wasn't likely I would ever need that information in D.C.

True leaned close to me later as the first cattle were being prodded into the ring. "Let's go down and get some lunch now. I want to be back before they start the replacement heifers."

"All right." My legs were as stiff as ax handles when I stood up, and I realized I'd been sitting there longer than I'd realized. The clock on the wall said eleven-thirty. Half the day down the drain, already, and not one word written.

In spite of that fact, I followed True to the open-air barbecue stand beneath a grove of pecan trees outside the sale barn. The place was shady and cool and filled with the mouthwatering aroma of smoked meat.

Old Malachi was delivering a load of paper plates and bread from his car as we arrived at the start of the line.

"Mo-nin, Truitt," he said, then glanced at me with a look of recognition, and a wide, slow smile. "Well, hi, there, lady. I didn't expect to be seein' you here. You ever git that car to runnin'?"

"Traded it in," I said. "Can I help you carry those boxes from your car? I still owe you a favor, you know."

Ducking his head, he chuckled so that his whole chest shook beneath his oversize red plaid shirt. "No, ma'am. Them boxes are empty. This is the las' one. You'd best git in line for some food before the crowd gits here." Reaching out, he patted me on the arm, then moved me into position in front of True. "And if you want to do a favor for me, just mention my name to the Lawd tonight." He chuckled again. "I'm so old, I need all the help I can git."

I laughed, having the guilty feeling he knew I didn't say prayers at night.

Taking his empty box, he stood back for a moment, looking at me and True, thinking about something; then he turned and started slowly toward his car. "Y'all have a good lunch."

"See you later, Malachi," True said over his shoulder as we moved through the line, past the ladies scooping out potato salad and beans, to the man standing at the enormous black barbecue grill on wheels. He opened the pit and waited for the customers in front of us to choose their lunches, like cave men, right off the flame. I quickly figured out the unceremonious serving procedure—when you pointed at something, he gave you a quick sizing-up from the corner of his eye, then lowered a glistening knife, whacked off the amount he thought you needed, and deposited it on your plate.

I must have looked hungry, because my plate came

out with a huge slab of brisket on one side. "Wow," I said, gaping at it as I waited for True to get his meat. "Now, that's a Texas-sized lunch." But I was really thinking about how many fat calories had to be in something that size.

The pit chef grinned at me as he loaded True's plate. "You hadn't ever had barbecue like mine," he assured me. "It'll melt right off your plate."

"Right off my hips too?"

"That, too." He laughed, the long handlebars of his gray mustache making him look like the villain in a silent movie. Under his butcher's apron, he was dressed in an old-fashioned black brocade vest, black jeans, tall black-and-red cowboy boots worn outside his pants, and an enormous black cowboy hat, so he fit the part perfectly. The lettering on the side of the grill read, *The Barbecue Bandit.*

True pointed a finger at the chef as if he'd had a sudden thought. "You know, Collie, if you want real Texas recipes, Dandy's the man you ought to talk to. He's won the National Barbecue Cook-off fifteen times, cooked barbecue for seven state governors, two presidents, several Miss Texas pageants, and over a hundred Olympic athletes. You can't get any more Texan than that."

"That's a good idea." A tingle of interest tickled my nose, or maybe that was just the smell of barbecue. "I'd like to interview you when you get a minute."

Dandy set his tools on the side of the grill and wiped his hands on his butcher's apron. "Haven't got any customers right now," he said, following us to the nearest picnic table. When I had set down my plate, he stuck his hand out to shake mine. "Dandy Roads, pleased to meet ya." He nodded at the slab of barbecue on my plate. "Barbecue chefs are always pleased to *meat* folks."

I rolled my eyes at the lame chef humor, wondering what kind of parents would name their child something like Dandy Roads. "Colleen Collins. I'm doing a series of articles about Texas food for . . . a magazine."

"So what kin I tell ya?" he asked, sitting across from me and resting his elbows on the table.

Taking my notepad from under my arm, I folded back the sheets until I came to an empty one. "Well . . . tell me where you learned to cook Texas barbecue."

Dandy smiled, the expression in his eyes softening, and the lines of his leathery face tracing the contours of happy memories. "I learnt to cook barbecue from my daddy. For over forty years he was a ranch cook for the big Three C Ranch out in Menard country. Back in them days they drove cattle perdy regular from Menard, across the Pecos River, and to Alpine. Anyhow, you know, in them days, folks mostly ate game meat—rabbits, deer, turkey, and such, because the cattle was worth too much to butcher, and it was hard to use up a whole carcass before some if it went bad, in the summertime, anyway. Smoked meat lasted longer, and the mesquite smoke would take away the gamey taste of wild meat, so any good chef in them days knew how to barbecue meat. Of course, they always soaked it in brine solution for a day before cookin', so as to help take away the game taste, soften up the meat, and help preserve it also."

Some customers came to the pit, so Dandy hurried over to serve them. I caught up in my notes, then ate some of my lunch while he was gone.

True finished his meal just as Dandy was shelving his barbecue tools again. "I'm going to go back in the sale barn so I don't miss the heifers," he said. "If I know Dandy, you'll be here listening awhile."

"All right. Thanks for the introduction." I laid a napkin over the rest of my food and pushed it aside, more interested in the story than the lunch, even though both were good.

Dandy resumed his seat across from me, and I picked up my pen again. "So, anyhow, my mama died from consumption when I was four years old, in 1943. My daddy was an older man by then. He'd been a cowboy all his life and never married until he was near forty. Anyhow, after my mama died, he just took me with him, and that's how I learnt to serve up barbecue to folks. I never really wanted to do much else, maybe because I loved my daddy so much. I like havin' the chance to talk to folks. Daddy always believed in bein' the best at what he did. He'd been barbecue champion a time or two there in Tom Green County, so I guess I just had to see if I could do somethin' bigger. He and I built my first wagon, and I started goin' around to fairs and parties and such. Eventually won my first National Barbecue championship just before he passed on. He was a proud man that day, I'll tell ya."

Pausing in my notes, I glanced at him. He talked about winning the barbecue title as if it were the Super

Bowl, or an Olympic medal event, and I thought he might be putting on the dramatics just to tease me. Looking at him, I could see otherwise. There was a glitter of emotion in his eyes that said this was truly a life's quest, which seemed unbelievable to me.

We talked another twenty minutes about his experiences serving barbecue, then we discussed barbecue techniques, cuts of meat, and sauce ingredients—though real barbecue, he contended with a sneer of contempt, did not require sauce.

Finally a line started forming at the grill, and he left me to return to his throng of adoring fans.

Watching him laugh and talk, size people up and deftly flip portions of smoked meat onto their plates, I felt a new sense of admiration—not so much for the art of barbecue, but for the pursuit of perfection, in all its forms.

Turning my notebook to a blank sheet, I picked up my pen and started to write as a soft breeze rustled through the pecans overhead and happy customers settled into the tables around me, creating a low hum of conversation and laughter.

I wrote about the pursuit of excellence, the desire to climb to the peak of something that is in the heart of every champion. I wrote about Bub and Dub, the auctioneers, and the pictures and trophies on the wall of the sale barn—a testimony to the pursuit of bovine perfection. I wrote about Dandy Roads first learning the art of barbecue from his father, as a motherless boy on the vast, silent prairies of Texas. I wrote about him building his first wagon, traveling the state, and finally rising to the pinnacle of his field. I wrote about him in his black brocade vest and tall cowboy hat, serving barbecue to governors and presidents and Olympic champions—great men, who probably never realized they were in the presence of greatness.

Greatness, I concluded, *is achieved not only by those who become political leaders or wealthy men, or award winning athletes. It is found in people we look at every day, but never really see. It is in my father, who built a successful business from a borrowed thousand dollars. It is in my mother, who has convinced dozens of underprivileged children they are worthy of a college education. It is in my grandmother, who has played the church organ for thirty years and never missed a Sunday. Greatness is everywhere. It surrounds us every day, in everything we see. It hides in the accomplishments of ordinary people, passing unnoticed, in little things like barbecue.*

Chapter 7

I STAYED at the barbecue stand for a long time after I finished writing. What was left of my meal was cold, so I just enjoyed the dappled shade of the towering pecan trees, watching the customers come and go, and listening to Dandy tell jokes and make wisecracks as he served up meals. He seemed to know every person who passed through the line. I wondered if he really did, or if he just never met a stranger. No matter what the customers' moods when they came to his wagon, they walked away smiling, satisfied in more than just the need for food.

"Well, you look like you're deep in thought." True's voice startled me. He leaned against the corner of the picnic table like he didn't intend to be there long.

"No," I said. I had been thinking that, instead of shrinks, maybe what some of my D.C. coworkers needed was a good barbecue man. "I'm just too stuffed to walk."

True laughed—that same deep, warm sound that had made me feel at ease the night we met in the dark beneath the tractor sign. "Well, you missed the best heifers. There's nothing but junk coming in now."

"I wouldn't know the difference," I admitted. "So did you find any good cows?"

"Heifers," he corrected. "A female of the bovine persuasion doesn't get to be a cow until she has a calf."

I was quick to point out my newfound knowledge on the subject. "I know that." One does not watch hours and hours of the Cowboy Channel without learning something. "And when she can't have any more calves, some young, sexy replacement heifer comes along and takes over her spot."

True rolled his eyes, shaking his head. "Life ain't fair, is it?"

"Boy, that's the truth," I said, with a little more conviction than I meant to. True gave me an interested, sideways look.

I quickly changed the subject. "So . . . did you buy anything?"

His blue eyes narrowed slightly, and for just an instant I thought he was going to pin me to the wall on the subject of why life wasn't fair. Then he seemed to remember that he didn't have any reason to *care* why my life wasn't fair, and he shrugged it off. That hurt my feelings, though I couldn't imagine why.

He glanced toward the sale barn. "I picked up one lot of twenty-five heifers. There's nothing else here I'm interested in, so I'm going to load these out and get 'em to the pasture. You're welcome to use the seats if you want to watch the rest of the sale."

"No, that's all right." Standing up, I threw away what was left of my lunch, then tucked my notepad under my arm. "It just occurred to me that the new rental car may have shown up this morning, and I probably should have been there waiting. I guess the driver would leave the keys with Mr. Hawthorne. . . ." That strange urge to hover came over me again, as it had the day before, and I stood there feeling awkward and adolescent. "And I have to get started on this article. Deadline's midweek, so I have to get my act together."

Standing up, True slapped a fist against his thigh. "Aw, crap. You just reminded me about the Monday edition." He looked toward the sale barn, then toward the newspaper office, muttering in frustration, "It'll just have to wait till tonight, after the heifers are settled. That newspaper's a pain in the . . ." He glanced at me, as if he suddenly remembered I was there and really believed I might wither at the sound of an untoward word.

That made me chuckle. "Yesterday you said there was nothing to running a newspaper."

He gave me a snide, sideways sneer. "Yeah, well,

today it's a pain in the . . . uh . . . rear. I don't suppose you'd want to look at it after supper?" Then he seemed sorry he'd asked, and started to backtrack. "If you're busy, it's all right. This one's going to have to be kind of a rush job, anyway."

If the last one was carefully thought out, I'd hate to see a rush job, I thought, but I said, "No, that's fine. I'll just run by the newspaper office after supper." I could not imagine why I cared, or why I was volunteering when I had work of my own to do.

True nodded, standing there looking like he didn't know what else to say. "Well . . . I'd better get on the road. The longer the cattle mill around in these pens, the more weight they drop."

For just an instant I thought he was going to invite me to come along, and for just an instant I thought I'd say yes, then I got my head on straight.

"I'll let you get going," I said. "Thank you for showing me around the auction today."

"My pleasure. See you later."

He headed toward the auction barn, and I turned and headed toward Hawthorne House, hoping my rental car had arrived.

And indeed, my hopes crept up as I rounded the driveway. Actually, there were several new cars, and I wondered if Mrs. H. had some new borders, because it was the weekend. At the back of the line was a blue car with a rental-company sticker on the bumper.

"Oh, thank God," I muttered, thinking of the nervous rental agent and how much trouble she must have gone through to get a car all the way to San Saline for me. I regretted being so impatient with her, and . . .

As I came closer, something about the car sent a whisper of doubt through the back of my mind, creeping like a little black spider—inch by inch, step by step—as I walked past the dent on the back bumper, and the glue from a scratched-off decal in the bottom corner of the back window, and a discolored mark on the top of the backseat. . . .

The agent could not possibly have sent me . . .

"The same car." The half-eaten bag of soy nuts on the seat confirmed it. My gratitude flamed into rage. "They sent me the same car! I don't believe it!" Throwing my hands up, I paced back and forth on the driveway, ready to murder someone, anyone. "I don't believe it! I just don't believe it! The same car. This just can't be. . . ." But there were the soy nuts and a pencil engraved with my name. My mind stormed with a thunderous mixture of rage and desperation, crackling like lightning. Ramming my fingers into my hair, I considered pulling it out by the roots. "Ahhh! III'mmm going to *kill* somebody!"

"Everything all right, Miss Collins?" Jasper Hawthorne appeared on the porch and walked slowly down the steps, looking pleasant and unhurried, as if he couldn't see me throwing a fit on the driveway.

"No!" I shot back, trying to control myself. But I was too far over the edge—into the same kind of loose-lipped righteous rage that had helped end my newspaper career. "They sent me the same car! I can't believe it! After this thing stranded me *twice,* after I spent the *whole day* hauling it to Copperas Cove, they send me the same car!"

Jasper put his hands out in front of himself like he thought I might slug him. "Well, now, calm down. It's not as bad as all that. The boy said this was the only car they got, but they had it to the mechanic, and it's all fixed. You ought not have no more problems with it."

Gripping and ungripping my fists, I wondered what the odds were of that. "I hope they're right," I ground out, reminding myself that the whole thing wasn't Jasper's fault. I should have stayed at the cottage, so I would have been there to refuse delivery of the car and insist that they send another one. This mess was my fault for wandering off to the auction instead of working at home, as I should have.

The demon car and I were together once again, for better or worse. Probably worse.

I took a deep breath and mentally counted ten, then said, "Thanks for taking delivery of the car for me. I forgot all about it, or I would have been here myself."

"Aw, that's no trouble." Jasper smiled, a warm, genuine, paternal smile that reminded me of his wife's. "We've got other guests in tonight, and some into next week, so I hope the racket don't bother ya too much."

"I'll be all right." I felt bad for having acted so idiotic in front of him. "I'm going to lock myself in the cabin and get this article written before I go crazy worrying about it. If I don't get it in by Wednesday, I'm dead. I hope this car doesn't break down on me again. I have to go to the something-or-other festival in Llano next weekend. If I can't get there, I can't get my next story written." I felt the whole situation spinning out of control.

Jasper shook his head, making a *tsk-tsk* sound under his mustache. "Well, Wednesday's a long ways off, and so's next weekend, and the car's probably right as a cow in clover." His eyes met mine with the faintest twinkle of humor. "You know what we say around here. If ya drive along looking too far down the road, you're likely to hit a deer."

I stared at him in complete incomprehension, and my mind whizzed to a stop, thinking about a cow in clover and wondering if that was a positive assessment. *How right is a cow in clover, anyway? Depends on where the clover is . . .*

He leaned forward, illustrating with his hands as he explained. "If yer worryin' about what's way down the road, ya won't see a deer crossin' right in front of ya . . . and smack." He punched his fist into the palm of his hand, then gave me a sideways grin. "You get in a wreck."

"Oh, I see." I suddenly got the point and wondered if he knew me better than I thought. Worrying way down the road was my specialty. "Now that you mention it, I almost hit a deer that way the night I drove into town."

Jasper gave me a wry look. "Didn't learn anything, did ya?"

"I guess not," I admitted, chuckling as my morose mood seemed to fade like a puff of smoke. *Smile, and your heart is laughing . . .* "I'll try to keep my mind in the present."

"Good girl." He patted me on the arm, and I wondered what it was about these people that made everyone want to touch each other, as if the concept of personal space had never been invented in San Saline, Texas. Where I came from, the only people putting their hands all over everyone were political candidates, and everyone knew what they were after.

"I guess I'll get to work," I said. "But I'll remember your advice."

"Very fine. I just left yer keys in the car, case you want 'em. The missus is home to watch the place now, so I'm headed over to the sale to spit and whittle awhile." And he started toward his truck at the other end of the driveway, cussing at a trespassing peacock as he went. "Git the heck off my durned truck! Durned birds . . . crap all over the place. Git off my truck, or you're dinner!"

Laughing, I watched him run toward the truck with a bow-legged hobble. The peacock jumped into the air with a squawk and hopped to the driveway, leaving a rather large token of his affection on Jasper's windshield.

"That ought to stop you from looking too far down the road!" I hollered, laughing.

Jasper waved me off as he climbed into the truck and headed for the auction barn, grinding the gears in a strafing run at the peacock, who narrowly escaped with his life, leaving behind a section of his tail feathers on the driveway.

I walked over and picked them up, because they were too pretty to leave on the gravel for people to drive over. Twisting them back and forth in the midday sun like an Oriental fan, I watched the colors turn to molten metal, then to the soft, muted shades of the hills at sunset.

Jasper was right. No point looking too far down the road. While you're staring into the future, the present is passing by moment by moment, like fence posts along the highway, and you never know what might be between them unless you look. Sometimes it's best to focus on what is right in front of you. It might be something wonderful. Like the tail feathers of a peacock glinting in the sunlight of a warm spring afternoon.

With that newfound sense of hill country Zen I went to the cabin and began work on my article for *Southern Woman.* I didn't worry about having my byline on something so frivolous. I didn't worry about how I would move back into a serious newswriting job after having composed recipes and travel fluff for a women's magazine. I didn't even worry about whether the article was too emotional, or not emotional enough. I just wrote it, then sat on the porch rocker with my laptop computer and read it over. I pronounced it . . . not too bad. A little dry, but not bad for a first attempt.

It sounded reasonably similar to my other writing—not overly emotional like the stuff my alter-ego had handwritten on my notepad. This piece was something I could live with, though it didn't fill the length requirement Laura had given me. I'd have to add a little more background on the recipes, which was probably a good idea, since the article seemed to lack the *feel* of San Saline. I wasn't sure how to get that into the writing. I fiddled with adding bits and pieces from my notes, but I still didn't capture the feel I wanted. Laura would probably find the article acceptable. Never having been here, she wouldn't know what the story was missing.

But that didn't stop my vague sense of failure about the piece. There was a lot I wanted to say about these people and this place—the smell of the bluebonnets, the slow cadence of the language, the almost militant good cheer of the people, the way the live oak trees crouched above the pastures like crooked grandfathers shielding the grass with their arms, even the sound of peafowl first thing in the morning. I wanted to tell about Mrs. H. and Malachi, Bub and Dub, and Dandy Roads.

But they didn't seem to fit anywhere on the electronic pages. The piece was succinct and sterile, and they were not. It was black and white, like a newspaper, and they were Technicolor, like the Cowboy Channel.

But black and white was me. It was Colleen Collins, and I knew I wouldn't look at the article later and be embarrassed by its sentimental folly. So I printed it out and put it in an empty file folder, then went to the kitchen to plug in my computer and send the file to Laura by e-mail. I quickly discovered the old rotary phone was hard-wired into the wall, and there was no jack anywhere in the room, so I put the printed copy with my purse to take to the newspaper office for fax service, as Mrs. H. had originally suggested. Probably, I reasoned, if I *could* plug in the computer, the static on the line would just keep bumping me off the Net anyway. Score one more for the peacocks.

No cellular service, no rental cars, no theater, no deli, no e-mail . . .

I chuckled at the list as I turned on the TV and changed into a pair of navy slacks and a sky-blue silk tank top to go to dinner at Mrs. Hawthorne's. I was either going to have to start wearing suits or do some laundry, because my wardrobe of jeans and T-shirts was pretty well used up.

In the corner of the room, the television crackled to life like an old hound waking up from a nap, and began to howl at the top of its lungs. I rushed to turn it down just as a vinyl-siding salesman cut into the black-and-white movie and announced the beginning of Audie Murphy night, then offered to completely revamp the outside of my house for seventy-two easy payments. I stood watching him for a minute, thinking of True's tractor commercial, and for some strange reason, wishing it would come on so I could critique it again.

Then I shook my head at myself and finished getting ready. Mrs. H. had said dinner at five, and I didn't want to be late, though I had a sudden sense of not looking forward to it. I wondered who was going to be there and what we were going to talk about and why Mrs. H. had put such emphasis on making sure I remembered to come. It felt vaguely like another one of her well-intentioned traps, and I wondered if she would be bringing a parade of local eligible bachelors. Or perhaps just True the Tractor Man.

It seemed like a likely scenario, except for the fact

that he was busy with his heifers and his newspaper. I wondered if Mrs. H. knew that.

I finally quit wondering, turned off the television, and walked across the lawn to find out.

Jasper and his son, Jimmy, were leaning against the porch posts as I came to the steps.

Jimmy tipped his hat back and looked at me with a twinkle in his eyes and a grin that reminded me of his father's. "Kill any rattlesnakes lately?"

"Not today." I walked up the steps, getting the distinct sense he was flirting with me, though he was Becky's husband, and probably fifteen years younger than me. He was awfully young, in fact, to be Mrs. Hawthorne's son. Maybe that was why, as True had said, he was overmothered. She had told me her daughter lived a few hours away in San Antonio, so I guess that left her with little to focus on except Jimmy and his wife, Becky.

I felt a tickle of curiosity, like a sneeze working in the back of my nose, and I forced myself to ignore it. Mrs. Hawthorne's family history was absolutely none of my business.

Jasper pushed off the porch post as I crested the steps. Behind us, a copper-colored Lincoln glided into the drive. "Well, time fer us menfolk to hit the trail," he said. "The she-males are arrivin'. Pretty soon this place'll be full, and the hen-talkin' will begin."

Jimmy scoffed under his breath and threw his shoulders back as he followed his father down the steps, looking for all the world like a boy trying to act like a man, or like a rooster trying to impress the hens.

Except the hens were too geriatric to care, and they clucked little-boy greetings at him as he passed, telling him how cute his new hat looked and remarking how handsome he seemed with his new mustache and that it would surely fill in as he gained in years.

Jimmy quickly lowered his feathers and hurried after his father, like a surly young rooster just booted off the fence. The ladies started up the steps as the Hawthorne men roared out of the driveway seeking to wreak havoc on the strolling peacock population—a final protest, I presumed, against the bevy of females taking over their domain.

As another carload pulled up, I realized that I had, indeed, been duped into attending what True referred to as a hen session. I wasn't sure how I felt about that, but there was a measure of curiosity in the back of my mind as I followed the first group of ladies into the house. I was mildly surprised that no one seemed to think my presence there was unusual, or appeared to wonder who I was. Even women I had never met or seen around town greeted me like an old friend as we filed into the wide entry hall of Hawthorne House. The tall ceiling soon echoed with the high-pitched sound of female chatter, and the air was filled with that militant sense of goodwill, as if there were a collective determination to force a smile onto every face and a joyous song into every heart in the room.

It was clear that their pixie dust was not working on Becky, who was standing in the kitchen doorway with her arms crossed, looking like a little girl trapped at a grown-up party. Since she was the only other person under the age of sixty in the room, I walked over and stood next to her.

"You don't exactly look like you fit in here," I said.

Rolling her gaze toward me, she scoffed ruefully, "You, either. Matter of fact, it's your fault that I'm here. Mama Hawthorne said I had to come so you and me could talk about newspaper stuff. I haven't been to one of Mama Hawthorne's ladies' suppers since I got married. My mama used to bring me all the time when I was a kid, but all the kids and unmarried girls would just go out on the porch and goof around, not sit in here and listen to the ladies go on about church and other boring stuff."

"Oh," I said, not looking forward to the prospect of the evening. I wondered why Mrs. Hawthorne had invited me. "So this is some kind of a regular club?" A reporter always wants to know the details, even on the most bland of subjects.

Becky thought about that for a minute. "No," she said finally. "I mean, it doesn't have a name or anything. It's just been a once-a-month ladies' supper for as long as I can remember. Gosh, as long as anyone can remember, I guess. Jimmy's grandma used to host it back in the olden days. I think they've always had ladies' supper here at Hawthorne House. My mama's been comin' since she was first married. Ladies don't come to the dinner until they're married, or unless they get so old everyone knows they're not gonna get married. Back when my mama was young, it was a big deal to get to sit inside at the table."

My interest perked up like a cat sighting a rustle in

the grass on an aimless summer afternoon. Looking around the room, I sensed that the tradition had pretty well died out with Becky's generation. "So I guess not many young people come anymore."

Becky shrugged, as if she couldn't imagine why I cared. "The Little League opener is tonight, so some of the people dropping off kids for ball practice will be a little bit late, but they'll be here."

"That's nice," I said, feeling a sense of awe for a tradition that had apparently lasted through generations. Becky looked at me like I must be out of my mind, so I said, "I mean, it's nice that there's a tradition of women taking time to get together and talk. A lot of times it seems like women lose touch with their friends after they get married." I was thinking of a number of my friends who seemed to drop off the face of the Earth once they found a man. Even Laura and I don't keep in touch like we used to. Back in college, Laura, her sister Lindsey, and I were inseparable—a trio like the three musketeers. Somewhere in the world of work and live-in boyfriends, we'd lost that. But it wasn't the boyfriend who pulled me out of the pit when my life fell apart. It was Laura. "It's a shame—you know, that men make time for their friendships, and women don't."

Becky's eyes brightened with a look of discovery. "I never thought of it that way." She glanced thoughtfully around the room. "I guess that's why ladies' supper got started."

The lady with the beehive hairdo was wandering by as Becky spoke, and she stopped, turning to us with a pointed finger and an astute look in her faded brown eyes. "I can tell you how ladies' supper got started," she offered. "It began back in 1897. In those days, it was called the Daughters of the San Saba Valley Literary Society, and, just as now, it met the second Saturday afternoon of each month, while the men were occupied across the street at the swap meet." She moved closer to us with a conspiratorial look in her eye. "They called it a *literary society* so the men would think their wives were here talking about books, and knitting, and children, but the truth was this was a political group. Their first interest in those days was to secure the vote for Texas women. Mrs. Rebecca Glass Hawthorne was the founder of the group. She became aware that women in Wyoming had received the vote, and she was determined that Texas women had a right to the same, as well as property rights and rights to custody of their children in the event of divorce or marital abuse."

Fascinated, I pulled out my pad and folded back the sheets. From the corner of my eye, I noticed that several other women were regarding us with interest, as if they had never heard the saga before, either.

Our storyteller pulled her glasses from the end of her nose and let them hang on the chain around her neck, holding a dramatic pause that silenced the group and brought more curious onlookers. We stood before her like a class of fascinated elementary school children getting a first history lesson.

"Mrs. Glass Hawthorne was a considerable woman," she went on. "By that I mean she was intelligent, determined, and very educated for her day. Her father, Col. Nathaniel Glass, was well known as a judge, and then as a state senator, and when she married into the Hawthorne family, it was quite a political alliance. Her ladies' group started out with only a few forward-thinking women, but gradually those more timid, less educated, and more downtrodden came to see what sort of scandalous talk was going on." A light came into her eyes, and she threw back her head, smiling. I could feel ghosts crowding into the air around us.

"I never will forget my grandmother telling me about her first time to ladies' supper. There she was, a part-Choctaw girl, fifteen years old, just one week married, come to Texas to be the wife of a widow man her father picked for her. She came from a large, poor family in Oklahoma, and her father was not a very good man. He'd kept her out of school to work the farm because he thought a girl had no need of education. She could barely write her letters and could not read, and she had an Indian look to her features that often put folks off. Here she came, tiptoeing through that door, quiet as a mouse, wondering if she might be unwelcome. But she was so lonesome, and sad-hearted, and homesick that she came in anyway, even though she thought her husband might not like it and she was scared to death of what the ladies would think of her old brown sack-muslin dress."

Like a physical presence, the essence of the scared Choctaw girl drifted into the room, and we all glanced toward the door, envisioning her there. "Coming here was the first bold thing she'd ever done in her life."

The storyteller paused again, looking at me to make sure I was getting down every word. Her brown eyes were moist, like the centers of daisies on a dewy morning. I imagined they were like her grandmother's.

Looking down, I caught up on my notes and swallowed hard, a prickle of emotion in my throat. I could see that frightened fifteen-year-old girl standing, listening, hovering in the doorway of the dining room, uncertain whether to enter. I had the sensation of standing where she had once been, and, in a way, still remained.

"So there my grandmother was," she went on. By now the entire room, perhaps twenty women of all ages, had stopped to listen, spilling over into the doorways of the adjacent rooms and up the stairway. "Hovering right over there in the shadow of the staircase, when the most beautiful, elegant blond-haired woman floated across the room and stopped right in front of her. My little Choctaw grandmother was so terrified, she almost ran from the room like a sinner facing up to an angel, but then that woman smiled and took my grandmother's dark hand in her pale one, asked her name, and greeted her like fine company. Right then and there, my grandmother came to understand that she might be worth something. And, of course, the woman that she met that day was Rebecca Glass Hawthorne. Eventually she taught my grandmother to read and write, and opened her mind to a world of ideas. My grandmother was the last woman in our family who was not given a college education. And all of that was owed to Rebecca Glass, and the Daughters of the San Saba Valley Literary Society." Punctuating the story with a vigorous nod she gave me a small smile, then turned and walked into the dining room.

Murmurs of approval and general commentary circulated the crowd as we made our way into the room, where two long mahogany buffets waited with enough food to feed an army, and an enormous Queen Anne table had been set with crystal glasses, cloth napkins, and wildflower bouquets for centerpieces. Standing in line, I listened to the conversations of the people around me. The story about the Choctaw girl had brought back memories to everyone, and they talked about their experiences at ladies' supper as we waited in line.

"Ladies' supper almost died out during the Depression years," one elderly woman said. "There just wasn't enough folks left to hardly have a get-together, everyone heading for California, looking for work. The rest of us was just about too poor to do anything. My family stuck it out, though. My daddy was a member of the Bandera Last Man's Club, meaning they was committed not to leave Texas no matter what. At that time, we jokingly called this ladies' supper the San Saline Last Woman's Club."

The woman in front of her turned around, chuckling. "Remember how many of us there were during the Second World War?" There was the faintest hint of a German accent in her speech. "We had every woman from here to Llano coming. All of us women left alone on the farms—we were so glad to have a chance to get together and talk and take a little break from our work.

Remember that, Imogene?" Wrapping her arms under her ample breasts, she started to laugh, her face turning red. "Oh, Lordy, remember the time that bus full of soldiers broke down on the highway, and we fed them supper and got them here a-dancing?" Several older ladies in the crowd started to chuckle and flush behind their hands. "All of us and just ten of them. Oh, Lordy! We danced the legs right off those fellas. I bet they weren't much good to the army after that!"

Some of the ladies laughed, and some gasped, pretending to be scandalized, but there was also a light of amusement in their eyes.

A young woman who had come in late gave her grandmother a sideways glance. "You never told me about that, Nanny. Wonder what Grandpa would say."

Nanny gave her a warning look. "He ain't gonna know. That's been one of them good secrets for fifty-some years. There are certain things a man don't need to know."

The laughter of approval went up around the room; then Nanny went on. "And I still remember when all you young ladies started showin' up wearin' no brassieres and sayin' you'd got liberated. My lands! Oh, we old ladies thought that was terrible goin' around with no brassieres!" She slapped a hand over her chest, losing her breath to a gale of laughter. "Course, we older ladies didn't have the boobs for it, either!" The room split into a hurricane of gasps, squeals, and chuckles as she choked out a final sentence. "If we'd of liberated, we'd of knocked ourselves out trotting down the steps!"

The room descended into a torrent of uncontrolled giggles and affirmations as women moved through the buffet line.

Glancing at Becky, who was strawberry red under her blond hair, I laughed with them, juggling my plate, then finally taking a seat between Mrs. H. and Becky.

Becky leaned over to whisper to me, "I guess I'll have to start coming more often. You never know what'll happen at ladies' supper."

Chapter 8

THE ladies' supper was over more quickly than usual, because almost everyone was going to the Little League season opener at Mill Creek Park, east of town.

From listening to the conversations around me, I had gathered that the ladies' meetings often went late into the night. Over the years, the ladies had discussed presidential elections and politics, from McKinley through two Roosevelts, the Truman upset, the Kennedy assassination in nearby Dallas, and, most recently, the debate over the presidential election. Letters home from two world wars and several regional ones had been brought to the table, as well as most of the century's great issues.

Over potluck supper, the ladies had discussed the closing of free immigration, the annexation of the final states, women's suffrage, feminine liberation, civil rights, hippies, abortion, the Cold War, a man on the moon, women in the workplace, divorce, crime, day care, and dozens of other issues. The debate was, at times, more heated than others, and a few meetings had become the stuff of ladies'-supper legend. Members had come and gone over the years, left temporarily in anger, then returned when things cooled off. The group had helped to arrange marriages, repair relationships, encourage higher learning, gather money for charities, raise children, and bury loved ones. No male over the age of twelve had ever attended.

I was honored to be a part of it and a little sad when it was over. Standing on the porch with Mrs. Hawthorne as the guests departed to a chorus of "See you next time," I was vaguely aware that I wouldn't be there next time—that I would be back in D.C. Probably back at work. Probably back in my old life. Back to myself.

I wondered what I would be doing on the second Saturday of next month and whether it would be as magical as what I was doing now. Coming to ladies' supper was like opening a treasure chest filled with wonderful stories and endless possibilities.

Mrs. Hawthorne gave me a sideways look, trying to read my thoughts, and I quickly looked away, watching a peacock strut across the lawn.

"That was really a lot of fun," I said. "Thank you so much for inviting me."

She gave a sly nod. "I saw you were taking a lot of notes. Are you going to include our ladies' supper in your magazine?"

I couldn't help smiling at her assumption that the magazine was mine to do with as I pleased. "I already finished the first article—the one about your place. But

I was thinking I might see if the editor is interested in a stand-alone piece about the ladies supper."

The truth was that ladies' supper was worthy of more than just a magazine article—probably a book, but I didn't have the time or the inclination to write a book, so an article was the best I could do.

Mrs. H. said, "Well, that's good. That's good." She nodded, and together we watched a pair of peafowl copulate on the lawn. If she was embarrassed by the display, she didn't show it. Her mind seemed to be on something else. "Are you ready to go to the ballpark? Opening night is something to see. Did I tell you there will be fireworks and free homemade ice cream? *Everyone* will be there."

Everyone will be there. Everyone . . . I had a strange feeling she meant that a certain tractor man would be there. "I hate to pass up homemade ice cream, but I've got . . ." My mind slipped a cog just as I was about to tell her I was going to the newspaper office to help True. That was definitely information she didn't need to know. I didn't want to do anything to encourage her thinly disguised attempt at matchmaking. "I've got to get some work done."

"Oh, darn it all." She looked monumentally disappointed, and I instantly felt bad. "At least try to come out later for the fireworks. They won't start until about nine, after the last games are over and all the ice cream is served up."

I glanced at my watch. Six-forty-five. "I can probably do that." Surely two hours at the newspaper office would be enough. Probably more than I could stand.

After a couple hours trying to salvage the *San Saline Record,* I would be more than ready to watch something explode.

Mrs. H. clasped her hands together, looking overjoyed. "Very good. You know where Mill Creek Park is, right? You passed it on the way into town."

I nodded as the peafowl finished their open-air rendezvous, and trotted off looking happy. "Mm-hmm. Nine o'clock, right?"

"That's right. It's going to be a nice evening. The night air here can work wonders on a person. The hill country sky has stars in it you can't see anywhere else. I think that's because we're a little closer to heaven out here." She chuckled. "And a little farther from streetlights."

We ambled down the steps together, then parted ways on the rock path. I walked to my cabin carrying my file folder and notepad, then sat on the steps waiting for Mrs. Hawthorne to finish loading ice-cream freezers into her car and leave. The last thing I wanted was for her to see me going to the newspaper office to meet True.

While I was waiting, I pulled out my notepad and started to write. I wrote about ladies' supper, about how it felt to be part of it, how it went on through drought and famine, political upheaval and war, joy and sadness, hope and despair. I wrote about how it brought the generations together, how women sat around the table, learning where the people of San Saline had come from and where they had yet to go. I wrote about the busload of stranded war soldiers, rescued by the supper ladies and invited to dance. I wrote about hippies, and women's lib, and the shocking arrival of young ladies without bras. I wrote about all of the subjects the ladies had discussed over the years, and the feelings that had been shared, and the way the women clung together.

In the end, I wrote, *Members come and members go, but ladies' supper remains. So many faces, so many ages, so many experiences, so many different lives, all tied together by one small thread, reaching far into the past—as far as a tall, well-bred, golden-haired lady, and a lost, dark-eyed Choctaw girl, who couldn't read, but found her way to an open door.*

Folding the pad closed, I thought about the times the ladies of my family had gathered in my mother's kitchen. My grandmother had told stories about dancing with soldiers going away to war, and corresponding faithfully with them during the long years of battle, and thinking she would marry a young man who never returned, and then thinking she would never marry. I thought about my mother recounting that she gave up a college scholarship to marry young, then went back to college while raising three children and helping her husband run a business. I thought about my great-aunt Nan, who had a good heart, but a nose for gossip and an interest in politics that had once put her in the position of blowing the whistle on a crooked county commissioner. Thinking back now, I realized that those women gathered in my mother's kitchen had laid the foundation for everything I was, just as ladies' supper laid the foundation for the women of San Saline.

I put my notepad away as Mrs. Hawthorne climbed into her Oldsmobile and squealed onto the main road. I waited until she was out of sight before getting into the demon car and turning the key. It started with no hesitation, and I began to have confidence that the mechanic had indeed fixed the problem. Rolling down the driveway and through the nearly deserted streets of town, the car purred like a happy kitten, and I let out a long sigh, relieved that my transportation worries were finally over.

I even gave the dashboard a pat as I pulled up in front of the newspaper office and turned off the engine. "You're not so bad, after all," I told the car. "Just keep it up another couple of weeks; then you can break down all you want."

The car replied with a long, peaceful sigh and a harmless sounding *ping-ping* as the engine went silent. Listening absently, I looked over the curb into the newspaper office. Through the lettering on the glass, I could see True standing behind a light table, one hand braced on the tabletop, the other scratching the wheat-colored curls on his forehead. The look on his face didn't bode well for the progress of the Monday edition. He looked like me the one time I tried to cook Thanksgiving dinner for Brett's parents.

Like Wonder Woman sweeping in to rescue the helpless and downtrodden, I bounded up the steps and knocked on the door, then reached for the handle. As I came into the room, True looked up and lifted a hand filled with text clippings, headlines, and photos, as if I were the angel of newspaper deliverance.

"I was afraid you weren't going to show," he said, then looked at the mess in his hands with the defeated expression of a little boy just striking out in a baseball game. "You may wish you'd stayed away. This is a da . . . darned Chinese fire drill. I forgot Becky had that supper thing tonight. The articles weren't even printed and trimmed when I got here." He noticed a clipping of text stuck to the end of his rolled-up shirtsleeve and peeled it off, sticking it irritably to the table, muttering, "Hell," and then, "One of these days, I'm going to learn not to leave this until the last minute. I hate this damned newspaper."

Standing there temporarily mute, I concluded two things. True the Tractor Man was at the end of his rope, and cusswords in the presence of ladies were all right, as long as you muttered them under your breath.

I stepped silently around the table and stood beside him, trying not to laugh. The first thing I noticed, other than the fact that he was right about the disaster, was that the *San Saline Record* was put together the old-fashioned way—with typeset strips and wax glue. All the fitting and measuring, in a case like that, is done by hand. No computer to help you wiggle things around and count all the picas.

I wasn't sure I was at all prepared for that. I hadn't actually pasted up a newspaper since . . . college maybe, or high school. I wasn't sure. I was a woman born of the electronic age.

"Wow," I commented. "When you said paste up, you really meant it. From scratch."

True gave me a hopeful look, as if he thought I could snap my fingers like a genie and finish the job by magic. "There's another way? I'm open to ideas. *Any* ideas."

He sounded so desperate, I couldn't help chuckling. "I'm sorry. What I meant was, I'm used to the computer fitting the type and doing a lot of the calculations for pasteup. You don't have an electronic publishing unit hidden around here anywhere, do you?"

He let out a long sigh. "What do *you* think? This paper can't *afford* a new computer." Rubbing his forehead, he looked around the room, as if some solution might make itself apparent. "I've got to have this thing to the printer before midnight. Ads are already sold, so it's got to be delivered on time." His eyes darted back and forth, calculating. "Sh . . . shoot. It usually takes me half a day to get from this point to finished product. I don't know if I can make it over to Copperas Cove before they shut the press down." Glancing at me, he suddenly looked embarrassed for all the ranting. "I'm sorry, Collie. I thought I'd be finished by now and you could just look it over. I really didn't invite you over here to work. This could take half the night, and then it might not be done."

I shrugged, trying not to look too interested, but the truth was, it was all starting to look kind of . . . irresistible. A challenge and an act of mercy all in one. "Well, you know what they say. Never look too far down the road. You might hit a deer."

Pausing in his search for something on the table, he glanced sideways at me, his eyes sparkling sapphire blue in the reflected light from the table. "Say that up in D.C., do they?"

I grinned. "All the time. You ever hear it?"

"Mm-hmm. I think I told a redheaded lady that, one lonely moonless night."

"Huh." Glancing at the table, I tried to appear as if I didn't know who he was talking about. "Wonder if she made it to where she was going."

The weight of his gaze, or the closeness of his body to mine, or the quiet intimacy of the setting, made me look at him, and my heart lurched against my chest, then stopped. I couldn't speak.

"I'm not sure she knew where she was going." His voice was low, little more than a whisper. "I think she was lost."

My mind whirled with impulses that were strangely compelling. Admit that I was lost. Confess that I didn't feel lost now. Look away.

I looked at the table and so did he.

Nervously, he cleared his throat. I wondered what had just happened between us, and if he'd felt it, too. I wondered if it had caught him by surprise, or if he'd planned it. Or if I was imagining the whole thing. A trick of the late-evening quiet and the soft amber light drifting through the storefront window.

I decided it must have been that. Just a trick of the moment. Maybe a little indigestion from eating too many mesquite beans at supper. Nothing more.

"So . . ." My mind still insisted on floating around unfocused, like a butterfly in a field of flowers, uncertain of where to land. I gave it a kick and made myself start moving scraps of paper around on the table. "I think I can still remember how to do this. Do you have a pica pole and a proportion wheel?"

"A what?" I glanced up in time to catch a look as blank as the noonday San Saline sky.

"A ruler-looking thing with markings on it and a plastic wheel-shaped thing that reads percentages?" I couldn't imagine how he could have been pasting up a paper without such items. Even my mother's high school journalism kids knew how to use them.

"Oh, those." He walked to the desk and fumbled around for a while, then produced a yellowed plastic pica pole and a proportion wheel that looked like it had been printed in 1950. Bringing them back, he stood there bemused, as if he had no idea what to do with them. "I don't really use 'em."

Such a case was impossible for me to fathom, and I wondered if he might be joking. But he looked serious and completely unashamed of the fact that he didn't know how to use two of the most basic tools of newspaper layout.

"No wonder it takes you all day to lay out a paper," I said. *And no wonder it looks so bad when you get finished.* "How in the world do you figure out what percentage to print the pictures without a proportion wheel?"

He shrugged. "Algebra."

"Well, I'm no good at algebra." I snatched the wheel from his hand. "Let me see that wheel."

"Help yourself," he said, stepping back. Clearly, he didn't care what I did with his paper. "But you'd think a woman with two journalism degrees could handle some simple algebra."

Glancing up, I caught his grin, and I just smirked at him and went back to work. Things started to feel more normal and less like we were in the Twilight Zone. "You'd think a man who was desperate to get a newspaper out wouldn't insult the free help."

"Point taken." He chuckled. "Just steer me in the right direction, ma'am. I'm here to learn."

I wondered if that was true, but it really didn't matter. All I could do was tell him what I was doing and why, and hope some of it sank in. If it didn't, it really wasn't an issue to me. The *San Saline Record* could die a slow and painful death after its hundred-some-year history, and most of the world would never care. Back in D.C., I would never even know it was gone.

That idea lit in the back of my mind like a snowflake in June—out of place and hard to believe. Too cold for its surroundings. As at the ladies' supper, I felt a strange pang of regret.

I reminded myself again that I had been in San Saline only a few days and would remain only a few more. This wasn't home. I was feeling out of place because of the lawsuit, being fired from my job, and spending three months floundering in depression. This place was comfortable, like a child's closet hideout. But you couldn't do much in a closet. Eventually it ceased to be comforting and became confining, and you had to get out into the real world.

I sort of hoped that happened before it was time to leave San Saline—that I ran out of new experiences and got bored with the surroundings. Otherwise, it was going to be hard to go.

"So why are you fitting in the text first?" True's voice startled me from my thoughts, and I realized that I had been working for quite a while without explaining a thing. So I started talking, explaining as well as I could what six years of college and twelve years of working had taught me. The front page quickly began to take shape.

To my amazement, True seemed genuinely interested—mostly in the mathematical end of it.

"I'm thinking that you're a left-brainer," I said finally, when he was calculating measurements faster in his head than I could with the wheel and the stick. It occurred to me that it was a shame he wasn't an engineer. "Any chance you have a degree in advanced mathematics?"

For just an instant, he gave me a serious look that I couldn't read; then he shook it off and chuckled. "No chance." He reached around me to lay a headline on the page. The warmth of his arm brushed my waist and radiated through my blouse like a torch. My heart did that crazy leap again, and my skin prickled where he was touching it. If he was aware, it didn't show. He stared at the page like he had forgotten I was there.

"That's really . . ." He seemed to lose what he was going to say. Then he straightened, breaking the contact between us. He gazed at the page from a higher angle. "That looks really good. Professional, I mean. There aren't any gaps in it."

I swallowed that weird feeling in my stomach and stepped back also, adding distance between us. "Yes. That's the point. A newspaper is supposed to flow, like a river for the eye to follow. It isn't *supposed* to have gaps in it."

"In D.C., maybe." He rested one hand on the edge of the table, grinning at me. "But in San Saline, people need those blank spaces so they can jot down phone numbers off the bulletin board at the café. Those gaps are a public service."

The idea made me laugh. "I must have missed the public-service lecture in college."

Shaking his head, he laid the front page aside and replaced it with a blank grid sheet for the next page. "Trouble is, you went to some Yankee college where newspapers are just business. Down here, we believe in accommodating folks."

"I'll try to remember that," I said, and started laying out the text for the second page. The funny thing was, he was right. People's attitudes here were more casual—about everything. I couldn't quite imagine how they ever got any business done, and why they didn't go nuts from the inefficiency of it all. I tried to put a humorous light on it, saying, "Maybe we could just print some blank lines on the back page so people could keep all their phone numbers in one spot."

"Wouldn't be the same," he scoffed, handing me a headline. "Here, this one goes with the article about the sale last week. Becky's pictures were lousy." He grabbed a picture of the sale ring, taken from somewhere high in the stands, so that the herd of goats looked like white ants, and would look like bits of fluff in a newspaper reprint.

For some reason, I felt obliged to come to Becky's defense in spite of the fact that the picture really was bad. "Maybe she does a lousy job because you pick on her so much." I didn't look up to see his reaction, but just kept fitting the page together.

He laid the picture in place without answering, and I thought he was going to ignore my comment altogether.

Finally he made a thoughtful sound under his breath. "So you think Becky's not happy working here?"

"She doesn't seem to be." I felt better knowing that he was interested. I didn't want to believe he was really the heartless, underpaying tyrant that Becky made him out to be. "You're expecting her to do a job that should require a professional, and you're paying her less than most people make working at a fast-food restaurant. If I were her, that would make me want to go elsewhere." Glancing sideways, I saw him nod thoughtfully as he handed me more components for the page. My hopes crept up. My first attempt at labor negotiations, and I was making a success of it.

"Good. She should quit."

My hopes sank like a rock in a well, and for a moment I was flabbergasted. "But . . . I . . . wh . . ." I stopped what I was doing and looked at him. "That isn't very nice. Becky's a good kid. She deserves the chance to—"

"Becky needs to get her butt back in college." He cut me off, pointing out the window as if Becky were watching us from the courthouse lawn. "She graduated valedictorian of her high school class, got a scholarship, and was all determined to be a teacher, which she would probably be good at. Her first semester, she got a little homesick on the big campus at A-and-M, came home over Christmas break, and decided she was going to marry the first local boy she could get a net on. Poor old Jimmy Hawthorne didn't know what hit him. He wasn't any more ready to get married than your average twelve-year-old. He's still wandering around town thinking he's gonna be a rodeo star. The whole thing's a mess."

His sense of disgust with the matter was more than evident, and his voice was raised almost to the point of argument. I wondered why he was so emotionally involved in Becky's life, or if he hated the concept of marriage altogether. "Whether they're going to stay married or not, Becky needs to get back in college."

"Oh," I said, feeling stupid and meddlesome. "I didn't know all that." End of my career in labor negotiations. I was swearing off.

True let out a long sigh, shaking off the emotions. "Sorry." His control had returned. "I just get sick of Becky going around town bellyaching about how horsewhipped she is over here. I don't need any more bad press."

I didn't answer, but my curiosity perked its troublesome head, and I wondered what he meant by *I don't need any more bad press*. As far as I could tell, he was practically crown prince around this town. Now I wondered if there was something more I didn't know.

One glance at him stopped me from asking. There was a hard expression on his face that made him look unreachable—not like the laughing, joking charmer I'd been teasing with a few minutes before. I regretted bringing up the subject of Becky and made a note to mind my own business in the future. There was a lot more to True the Tractor Man than showed on the surface, that was for sure, but I had a feeling I wasn't going to find out what it was. I thought again about Mrs. Hawthorne's comment: *After everything that's happened, you can't expect him to be like he was before*. What did that mean?

It was more of a mystery than I could stand, so I forced myself to work in silence as we finished several more pages. I didn't speak until we were on the last page, and my urge to interrogate had faded away.

"Last page," I said, hoping to lighten the mood—to recapture the fun, cheerful interchange we'd had earlier. "I can leave out this list of garage-sale ads and keep a blank space for café phone numbers. Last chance."

He pretended to read the garage-sale ads and think about it, and I could tell he was in a better mood. "Nope. The ladies at the Methodist church will come after me with ropes and torches if I don't run this bit about the rummage sale. Better put it in. If anyone complains about the lack of writing room, I'll send them to you."

"Thanks." Smiling, I glanced sideways, and he grinned. His eyes were that sapphire blue again. A knot fluttered in my throat, and I turned back to finish the pasteup. Outside, the evening had faded, so that there was no light in the room except the glow from the layout table. Funny, I thought, that I hadn't even noticed darkness falling. Apparently, neither had he. Neither of us had turned on the overhead lights.

"Done," I said, and stepped back from the table, looking around his shoulder at the clock on the wall. "And only eight-thirty. Is that record time, or what?"

Shaking his head, he gazed at the pages with a look of awe. "Darlin', you have no idea. It's practically a miracle."

The praise actually made me blush a little. "Wow," I joked to cover my embarrassment. "I've never been accused of performing miracles before."

"I'm serious." He laid the pasteups carefully between the sheets of a large portfolio, so they could be easily carried. "You're good at what you do. You really have a talent."

"Thanks." Tears came out of nowhere and prickled in the corners of my eyes, and I turned away, pretending to look at the clock so he wouldn't see. After so many months of feeling worthless, it was good to hear praise. I didn't realize how much I'd missed it.

I swallowed hard, wondering what in the world was going on with my emotions. I changed the subject to something more neutral. "Well, now that the paper's done, I could use a pop."

"A *what?*" I turned around just in time to see him look at me as if I'd just sprouted horns.

I met his look with one of complete confusion. "A . . . pop." Still no response, only a look of shock, so I tried again. "A . . . pop . . . a drink . . . a cola . . . a caffeinated beverage of some sort."

The shocked look disappeared, and he rolled his eyes. "Good Lord, woman, where did you say you were from?" Shaking his head, he crossed the room and retrieved an old-fashioned bottled Coke from an ancient pop machine in the corner, then pried off the lid before coming back and handing it to me. "This is a *soda*. A *so-da*. Around here a pop is"—he actually blushed—"is . . . well, you just shouldn't go around this part of the world asking guys for a pop."

The wicked twinkle in his blue eyes gave me his meaning, and I blushed too, realizing my faux pas. "Oops. Thanks for the *so-da*."

"No problem." He grinned, clearly recovered. "But I can do better than a soda." He glanced at the clock. "The fireworks should be just about to start at the park. Buy ya a homemade ice cream?"

A smile tugged at the corners of my lips. "The ice cream is free."

He snapped his fingers in front of himself and shook his head. "Doggoneit, you found me out. Well, have pity on me, anyway. If I show up over there alone, those ladies will have me scooping out ice cream, and everyone knows that by the time the parents and the grandparents and the ballplayers get through the line, the scoopers usually wind up gettin' nothin'."

The smile, and the twinkle, were more than irresistible, plus there was the prospect of homemade ice cream and fireworks. "All right," I said. "But what about getting the newspaper to the press?"

He shrugged, the paper apparently of little matter compared with taking me to the ice-cream social. I suddenly felt very important. "I'll take it after. The press is open until midnight. They know I'm coming. They probably couldn't stand the shock if I showed up before eleven."

"Well, let's go, then," I said, grabbing my purse as he locked the front door, then ushered me to the Friendly's truck in the back alley. Opening the door, he waited for me to climb in, then closed the door after me, carefully, like I might break. In six years, I couldn't remember Brett ever doing something like that.

"Boy, it feels good to have the paper done," True said as he climbed into the driver's seat, and we roared off toward the park in a gravel-throwing hurry. "I'll tell you what, Collie, that was something else. I could have saved a lot of time all these months if I'd known what I was doing." There was a look of sincere admiration in his eye that made me blush again.

"Well . . . there is some science to it." I couldn't think of exactly what else to say. All the praise was more than my battle-scarred ego could handle.

"More art than science," he corrected, his eyes meeting mine with an intensity that drew me forward in my seat. "You're a wonder, Collie. Is there anything you're not good at?"

I just stared at him like a lovestruck teenager. I heard myself say, "Algebra . . . and . . . ummm . . . cooking." As if they were the breathy words of romance.

He grinned slightly, and I felt myself melting into a

pile of mush on the seat. "Well, then how did you end up in Texas writing cooking articles?"

The sordid story ran though my mind like a sobering blast of cold air, and I looked out the window, trying to push the past from my thoughts. "Twist of fate," I said, feeling his gaze on me, pulling me back.

I met his eyes, and he nodded silently, as if he knew I had some big secret I didn't want to tell, and that was all right. "Those twists of fate usually come along for a reason," he said quietly; then he looked at the road, and I sat there flustered and silent as we drove to Mill Creek Park and pulled into a parking space by the ball fields.

"Looks like the last game's just about to let out," True said, slapping the truck into park, climbing out in a rush, then trotting around to my door. "We can still get in line before the crowd."

His urgency made me laugh as I jumped out and he closed the door behind me, then opened the toolbox in the truck bed and pulled out a blue bundle of quilted cloth. He tucked it under his arm, then slipped his other hand under my elbow, seeming to think I was incapable of climbing the slope from the parking lot. His hand was warm against the surprising chill of the night breeze.

Laughter tickled my throat as we jogged across the park in a breathless hurry, as if we were going for the winning lottery ticket. "You're serious about this ice cream," I joked.

He winked as we slipped into line behind a dozen people who were already making the trip past the ice-cream servers, set up at a long picnic table filled with ice-cream freezers. "It's root, hog, or die around here," he said. "When the kids and the grannies get here, there's nothing left."

I laughed, and he laughed, and we gazed into each other's eyes. Just as we reached the front of the line, I saw Mrs. Hawthorne looking at us. True saw her too, and both of us stood at attention like a couple of schoolkids caught flirting in class.

I realized, with disgust, that this incident would hopelessly encourage her matchmaking efforts. She smiled like an adoring parent as we started through the line, holding our bowls out when we saw a flavor that looked interesting.

"Well, I'm glad to see you two made it." The words were innocent enough, but the meaning was clear. She gaped at the bundle under True's arm, and her mouth fell open. "True, you're not going to make her sit on a *horse* blanket, are you?" The ladies around her made *tsk-tsk* sounds and frowned at him as if he were a pariah.

True glanced at the bundle and then at Mrs. H., looking surprised and slightly offended. "It's clean."

Mrs. H. widened her eyes. "Oh, True, for heaven's sake. Look at her nice outfit. She can't sit on a dirty ol' horse blanket."

I stood there with my dripping bowl of ice cream, completely, utterly, and totally embarrassed. The line had stopped and everyone was noticing us there . . . together. Ducking my head, I started moving again.

True didn't look the least bit out of sorts. There was

a wicked gleam in his eye as he shrugged and started to follow me. "The blanket's mine." He glanced casually at me. "I guess Collie figured to sit on the grass."

Mrs. H. stood struck silent, crestfallen, and the other ladies stared at True with their mouths opening and closing mutely, like a bunch of surprised goldfish.

Biting my lip, I tried not to laugh as we finished going through the line and started toward a grassy slope where people were spreading blankets in the dim glow of the stadium lights, lighting lanterns and preparing to watch the fireworks.

"That wasn't very nice," I whispered, thinking of Mrs. Hawthorne's expression of monumental disappointment.

True glanced at me and shrugged. "She needs to mind her own business." Handing me his bowl, he spread the strange-looking blue nylon blanket on the grass on the far side of a shadowed grove of trees, where we could no longer see the ice-cream ladies, and the ice-cream ladies could no longer see us. I imagined them trying to gape around the brush, greatly frustrated.

The blanket looked like a gigantic blue ski vest with thick nylon straps and no armholes.

"Just been washed and mended," he assured me. "I have 'em cleaned every spring."

"So this is what the well-dressed horse wears in the winter?" I said, sitting down and turning up the corner so I could feel the wool lining underneath.

He reclaimed his bowl and dipped a spoon into his ice cream. "Only one *special* horse. This one's his favorite. But I'm sure he won't mind sharing."

"Tell him thanks for me." I chuckled, then started in on the huge pile of ice cream I had somehow acquired while moving through the line.

We sat silent for a while as the insects started to churr, and the stadium lights flickered out like dying fires, and the slope below us slowly filled with dancing lanterns, laughing shadows, and muted voices floating through the darkness.

Finishing my ice cream, I set the bowl aside and leaned back, bracing my hands behind me. It was as Mrs. Hawthorne had said. There were more stars in the hill-country sky than I had ever seen—so bright and clear it seemed as if I could reach out my hand and touch heaven.

Fireworks exploded in the air over the stadium, but I didn't look. My eyes were filled with the scattering of stars. I felt True brace his hands and lean back, his fingers just touching mine, minute points of warmth through which electricity started to flow.

"You're going to miss the show," he whispered low, a sound filled with uncharacteristic passion and longing. "Those stars are up there every night."

"Are they always this beautiful?" My question came in a whisper.

"No," he said under his breath, and I could feel him close beside me, drawing me in like a magnet to steel. "Tonight, they're more beautiful than usual."

I tipped my gaze slowly downward, following the Milky Way, which had once guided lost travelers home. It led me to a sea of deep, sapphire blue, sparkling with the reflections of a hundred ribbons of flame, slowly descending, fading, burning out just as I closed my eyes and his lips met mine. My heart bolted to the warm place where our bodies touched, hovering there like a butterfly in a ray of sunlight, and I kissed him. It was the most right thing I had ever done in my life.

Chapter 9

THE sky was afire with glowing amber sparks when his lips parted from mine and we opened our eyes again. Filled with a heady mixture of passion and rightness and something that felt like joy, I sat very still, my arm interlaced with his, our bodies close.

Somewhere in the deepest reaches of my logical self, I wondered why he had stopped the kiss. And why I hadn't. I wondered if he meant to kiss me, or if it just happened. I wondered if he planned it, or if he was drawn to me by something that couldn't be explained, just as I was to him. I wondered if his body felt warm on one side and cold on the other, like mine.

I wondered where all of this was leading and where it could.

"Wow," I said softly as the sky exploded in azure and crimson and blazing white. But I wasn't talking about the fireworks.

"Mm-hmm." I had a feeling he wasn't, either.

Neither of us said anything more, but, in unison, we lay back against the blanket, his body against mine, my head in the crook of his arm. My eyes drifted lazily from the fireworks, to the display of stars, to the nearby shadow of his profile. My mind painted the moment like a canvas. Something perfect that could only live on if artificially reproduced. I couldn't imagine it any other way, couldn't imagine it as the beginning of something larger. Such an image could not possibly fit into the frame of my life.

I wondered again what he was thinking.

The last of the fireworks burned out in the valley—a gigantic baseball and bat, which brought a cacophony of high-pitched squeals from the children running up and down the slope. When the last of the flame was gone, the hill was dark again except for the ghostly, lantern-lit images of people gathering their blankets, lawn chairs, and children, and moving toward their cars. Their voices were hushed, as if they too were reluctant to disturb the fragile perfection of the evening.

True and I lay very still as the last of the lanterns drifted from the hillside.

"See," he said quietly. "The stars are still there. But the fireworks only go on for a little while."

I wondered if he was comparing us to the stars or the fireworks, or if I was reading too much into the moment.

"I'm glad I didn't miss them." I sighed, trying to put all the questions out of my mind. *It's just a kiss, Collie. Get a grip.* "I guess we should go," I said, because I was starting to come back to earth and to feel embarrassed about the two of us lying there on the hillside like a couple of lovesick kids.

"Probably so." I thought I heard the faintest hint of regret, but he cleared his throat, and it was gone. "Better get the newspaper over to Copperas Cove before the press closes up."

The two of us sat up, then stood, and he rolled the horse blanket over his arm. Walking to the car, we moved slowly, both reluctant to leave, yet knowing we didn't have an excuse to stay.

"That water sounds nice going over the falls," I said, looking toward the mill pond, which was just beginning to reflect the light of the heavy orange moon drifting above the horizon.

"There was some discussion about filling in the pond a few years back." True sounded much more composed than I felt. "But the supper ladies took care of that. They pretty much run this town."

Thinking of the ladies' supper lightened my mood. I was glad to have something neutral to talk about. "That supper was quite an experience. There is some really interesting history there."

In the dim moonlight, I could see a hint of his smile as we reached the truck and he tucked the borrowed horse blanket in the back. "More to San Saline than meets the eye, hmm?"

I chuckled, thinking of my conversation with Laura Draper about the Texas project and about my morose feelings during the plane trip. "And to think I didn't want to come here."

"Good thing you did." His voice was low, and I thought he was going to say something romantic again. Instead he said, "Or I'd still be locked in the office working on a newspaper with gaps in it." And I knew the romantic interlude was over. I was strangely relieved.

He opened the car door and the glow from the interior lamp chased away the last ribbons of moonlight.

"Next time, I'll expect to see a more concise layout. No gaps," I said. *If I'm here for the next time.*

That devil-may-care look was on his face as he closed my door and walked around to his side. "What's life without gaps?" He slid into the driver's seat and started the rumbly diesel engine. "It's the gaps that keep things interesting. A block of text is just a block of text. Doesn't ever change. But a gap . . ." He paused, raising his finger with a look of melodrama. "A gap has infinite possibilities. It could be a grocery list, a little kid's drawing, a price for Bermuda hay, the starting time for the church potluck, a map to some land for sale . . . a phone number for a pretty girl. . . ." He winked, trying to flirt with me, and I wondered at the swift and infinite changes in his moods.

"So you stand in defense of the gap."

He shook his head, chuckling under his breath as we left the park and proceeded toward town. "No. I'm just making excuses for myself."

I laughed with him, and my anxieties flew out the window. "At least you're honest."

"Always." He pulled the truck into the parking space beside my car in front of the newspaper office. "With a name like True . . ." He left the sentence unfinished, scoffing under his breath as we disembarked the truck.

Glancing at him, I wondered if he really was as good

as his name. I suspected not. There was something under the surface that bobbed its head up every once in a while and then disappeared before I could recognize it. Something secret that he didn't want to discuss.

Turning to my car, I noticed the file folder with my *Southern Woman* article on the front seat, forgotten in my rush to save True from the evil newspaper gaps. "Oh, darn," I said, opening the door and grabbing the folder. "I meant to ask you earlier if you would fax this article for me. My cabin is not Web compatible, and Mrs. Hawthorne said I could fax things from here."

"Sure. I'll run it through while I'm grabbing the pasteups." True reached for the folder, and we stood for a moment, both holding it like a couple of one-year-olds afraid to let go of the coffee table and go our separate ways.

I spoke first, releasing the folder. "Well, thanks for the ice cream and the fireworks. It was a great time." No mention of the kiss.

"It was. Thanks for saving me from scooping with the ladies. . . ." He seemed to search for something else to say, but finally finished with, "And for helping with the newspaper. You probably saved my life." Saved his life, but no mention of the kiss.

"You're welcome. Good night."

"Good night, Collie."

The kiss, by silent mutual agreement, was swept into oblivion. Probably never to be mentioned again. He unlocked the door to the newspaper office, and I slipped into my car, and that was that. The end.

I sat in the car for just an instant, feeling regretful

and thinking of finding some excuse to go into the office after him.

But that would be stupid, I told myself. *What for?* I didn't have an answer, so I turned the key and the car roared to life, then wheezed. The gas gauge sank to empty, and the engine died an all-too-familiar death.

"Oh, no." I grumbled, turning the key and stepping on the gas again. A faint *click-click,* but nothing more. No promise that it would ever start again. Yanking the keys out, I slammed them against the dash. "Damn it!"

Sssshhhh, Malachi's voice came on the faint, dark breeze drifting through the window. *The Lawd is listenin' up there*.

"Well, apparently he doesn't work on cars," I muttered, grabbing my purse and climbing out. I was stranded again, forced to beg a ride.

I walked sheepishly to the newspaper office and stood in the doorway, the open door braced against my heel.

True looked up from the fax machine. "It's almost through. Did you need this back tonight?" An evil grin, and then, "You know, this is pretty good." As if he'd been reading my material. "No gaps, either."

"Very funny." I was too upset about the car to appreciate the joke. "My car won't start. Would you mind giving me a ride home?"

A wrinkle of consternation deepened just beneath the straw-colored curls on his forehead. "You're kind of hard on cars, aren't you? This is your second one."

But for my present state of complete disgust, I would have laughed at the observation. "They sent back the same one. They said the mechanic fixed it, but obviously not." With a sigh, I rubbed the developing ache in my forehead as I thought about trying to haul the car back to Copperas Cove again. "I think it's possessed."

True laughed, probably because *his* vehicle was working fine, and *he* wasn't stranded. "Hang on a minute. Let me finish your fax and get the lights turned out, and I'll drive you home."

"Thanks." Stepping into the room, I let the door close behind me and stood leaning wearily against the glass, trying not to think about the dead car behind me and all the inconvenience it represented. *Don't look too far down the road; you'll hit a deer.* Not much danger of that when you don't even have a car to drive.

True patted my shoulder sympathetically as he handed my folder to me and turned out the lights by the door. "Hang in there, Collie. It's just a car."

"I hate cars."

Opening the door and ushering me out, he flipped a latch at the top of the ancient oak door, then let it close behind us and followed me to the curb where the demon car sat with a squinty-eyed metal smirk.

True chuckled. "Want me to kick it for you?"

"Please."

He made the motion, but only hit the tire with his cowboy boot, which I didn't suppose would do any good. In silence, we climbed into the Friendly's truck and rumbled past the dollar store and around the darkened square.

I rubbed the bass drum pounding in my forehead, feeling defeated.

True seemed to find the situation amusing, probably because it hadn't occurred to him, as it was now dawning on me, that the whole town would see my car parked in front of the newspaper office, and True's upstairs apartment, when they went to church tomorrow morning. Between that and our appearance at the ice cream social, rumors would fly like lint in a whirlwind.

Things seemed to be taking on a life of their own.

Don't look too far down the road . . .

True turned off the headlights as he pulled into the driveway at Hawthorne House. I hoped the diesel engine was noisy enough that Mrs. Hawthorne would hear it and know I was home, not shacked up somewhere with True, as the presence of my car at the newspaper office would seem to suggest.

I was too embarrassed to mention the scenario to him. "Thanks for the ride," I said, noticing that the amber porch light made his eyes a dark, liquid blue.

"So I guess you won't be going anywhere tomorrow." He grinned, and I was caught between thinking how handsome he looked and indulging the urge to slug him.

"No," I grumbled.

"Want to take a ride out Brownwood way with me?" The question seemed almost rhetorical. He looked worried when I didn't answer right away, and he added a little more sugar to the mix. "I need to feed my cattle out that direction and look at a piece of river-bottom land. Not the most interesting stuff in the world, but it's a pretty drive." Tilting his head, he caught my gaze, and my stomach flipflopped. "Beats spending Sunday morning sitting around here. Can't call the rental-car office, anyway. It'll be closed until one."

"Sure," I heard myself say, sounding like I was about to swoon. The demon car left my mind completely. "That sounds like fun. What time?"

"How's nine-thirty?"

"Fine." Everything was fine and the world was a beautiful place. . . .

Jolting my brain to life, I opened the truck door and slipped my feet to solid ground.

True flashed his lopsided grin. "We'll be doing some walking." Leaning over, he glanced at my dress loafers. "You might want to wear your cowboy boots."

"I'll do my best." I chuckled, closing the door. "See you tomorrow." And I stood in the driveway, hugging my arms around myself and watching him drive away, amazed that I could have been so uptight a few moments ago and now felt as free as a leaf in the wind. I felt like dancing. And I wasn't a dancer.

I tried not to think too much about the meaning of it all as his taillights disappeared from the driveway and I went into the cabin. Tossing my clothes in a heap, I slipped into my pajamas, washed my face, and slid into bed, pulling up the covers to block out the nagging buzz of reality.

I dreamed about fireworks and laughing children with wooden pails of homemade ice cream. I dreamed about the Milky Way, bright and close like a trail dripped from one of the buckets—vanilla on a deep purple tablecloth. I dreamed about True's lips touching mine and the warmth of his body covering me like a blanket and stars raining down from heaven, just beyond my fingertips.

I dreamed about the two of us caught in each other's arms, waltzing, lighter than air, through a field of bluebonnets and blooming prickly pear. Just waltzing and laughing, not the least bit mindful of the thorns . . .

The feel of him was on my lips as my mind drifted to consciousness. Turning over, I stretched my hand to the empty side of the bed, almost expecting him to be there, as if I might have dreamed him into existence during the long night.

My grandmother always said, *If you dream about something three nights in a row, it will come to be.* I had dreamed about Truitt McKitrick for three nights. . . .

I realized the peafowl were in full symphony outside, and I hadn't even heard them. The sound of their screaming cleared the fog from my mind. I felt a sudden, painful jolt somewhere between my heart and my stomach, where loneliness likes to fester. For just an instant, I'd basked in the feeling of someone there, someone special, but it was a cruel trick of altered reality, like a mirage in the desert.

I knew that if I lay in that empty bed a moment longer, the whole disastrous mess would come closing in on me again—the lawsuit, unemployment, losing Brett, the lies to my parents. Mornings were always the worst, those first foggy moments of waking up and realizing anew how many things had changed and where reality now lay. Compared to this slow process of realization, waking up in a peacock-induced frenzy was actually merciful.

Throwing the covers aside, I walked over and turned on the TV, then moved to the kitchen to clean the coffeemaker and start a new batch. Across the room, the Cowboy Channel crackled to life, and there was True trying to sell me a tractor. He was wearing a ridiculous Mexican sombrero and riding a tame longhorn steer through the tractor lot, and I couldn't help laughing. My sense of gloom floated away and hid somewhere in the shadowed corners of the room.

On the television, the old farmer on the ancient tractor rolled across a screen of phone numbers, and I quoted the famous last line with him, "And remember, nobody knows tractors like True the Tractor Man."

I remembered that we had made plans for the morning, and my spirits perked up. Checking the clock, I realized I had slept later than usual. Eight-thirty. I had obviously missed the peacocks' first wakeup call.

Leaving the coffeemaker to fill at its usual slow pace, I hurried to the bathroom, went through the contortions of getting my hair washed in the claw-footed tub, then climbed out and slipped into jeans and a T-shirt. My last clean set of casual clothes, so I was going to have to get some laundry done.

Combing a generous helping of mousse through my hair, I poured some coffee and drank it while I was putting on makeup. Looking at my hair, I decided to leave the slightly damp ringlets. No Colleen Collins, businesswoman, today. Just plain old Curly Collie, who had been teased by countless schoolmates and relatives for the unruly mass of long Irish-red spirals—before the advent of hair mousse, which helped a great deal.

I was hunting for footwear when I heard the Friendly's truck rumble up the driveway. No cowboy boots, so I grabbed my short chucka hiking boots and slipped them on, threading the laces as True's footsteps crossed the wooden porch outside.

My stomach twisted like a rubber band tying itself into a knot as I tried to finish the last bow. "Just a minute," I called, and then, "I'm ready. I'm just getting my boots on." I turned off the TV on the way across the room.

True was looking at my feet as I opened the door. He gave my boots a hopeless frown, then raised his gaze and stopped for a moment when he reached my face, looking surprised, and . . . well . . . impressed.

I figured it was the hair, and I patted myself on the back for the burst of vanity that had convinced me to leave it down. For once, I had struck him silent.

But the truth was, he looked pretty good too, with his straw cowboy hat tipped slightly away from his eyes, and his blue polo shirt neatly tucked into the waist of his jeans, showing off a well-used belt buckle that sported a picture of a rider roping a steer, and said *Bandera Annual Steer Roping, Won by Truitt McKitrick.*

I looked up when I realized he'd caught me staring. "And I thought you spent all your time selling tractors," I said, to cover the fact that I had been ogling him. "I didn't know you were a rodeo star."

True ducked his head, seeming a little embarrassed. "Not recently," he said. "I'm too busy, and the horse is too old."

"Oh, too bad." I walked with him to the truck. "Can't you get another horse?"

He shrugged. "Wouldn't be the same. I've had that horse since I was a kid. He hasn't roped in years and neither have I." He gave me an overly dramatic look as he opened the passenger door. I knew he was toying with me. "Both just ready to be put out to pasture to nibble on dried-up bluestem and mesquite beans."

"Well, that *is* sad."

"Yes, ma'am, it is." He sounded like Audie Murphy on the Cowboy Channel.

I shook my head as he started the engine and we rumbled out the driveway. This time I hoped the engine was quiet enough that Mrs. Hawthorne wouldn't hear and know I was off on another junket with True the Tractor Man.

I needn't have worried. Everyone in town was standing outside either the Baptist church, the Methodist church, or the Church of Christ, and we rumbled past all three at slow speed. True stuck his hand out the window and waved, not the least bit ashamed to be heading down the highway instead of into a church parking lot. I ducked my head in proper Christian guilt. Even though I wasn't a church regular in D.C., I never would have gone past the house of worship in my hometown on a Sunday morning and gleefully waved at the faithful. I would have either gone to church or sneaked around the back road.

But that was me. True obviously didn't care what anyone thought. I wished I had that self-assured attitude. Life would have been easier.

As we left town behind and moved onto the highway leading north, he sang with the radio—proof that he didn't care what anyone thought. He was badly tone-deaf.

After a while, he glanced at me and stopped singing, as if he'd read my thoughts or perhaps the expression of suffering on my face.

"Sorry," he said.

"It's all right. So how far are we going?"

"Another six miles." He pointed into the distance. "If you look way over there in the valley, you'll see the Colorado River. That's where we're headed. I planned to look at that piece of property for sale first."

"What a view." Shading my eyes, I squinted into the distance just as the truck made a rapid right and almost threw me onto the floor.

"Sorry," True said. "This is where we hit the county road."

"This is a road?" I shouted over the rumbling of the engine, the grinding of the tires on the gravel, and the rattling of the truck over the washboardlike surface. It looked more like a cowpath than a public road. I had the strange sensation of finally having found the edge of the civilized world. Mile after mile of gravel road passed and the only evidence of people were weathered barbed-wire fences interlaced with thick cedar bushes.

The scenery was beautiful. The road wound lazily

through low valleys where clear-water creeks trickled over timeworn white stones, the water glittering like liquid silver. The creek banks and the open pastures were crowded with wildflowers, like so much confetti strewn from heaven in haphazard patterns of blue and yellow, pink and crimson. Here and there, we passed cattle grazing in the creek bottoms or on hillsides as we wound slowly upward, out of the dense vegetation, where the cedars grew lower and more sparse, and finally not at all. The views from the boulder-strewn hilltops were unblocked and went on for miles, showing an endless range of jagged hills and lifeless volcanic cones that had once stood at the bottom of a primordial sea.

"This is incredible," I whispered, feeling that we were winding back in time. "It's just . . ." There wasn't a word grand enough, so I whispered, "incredible," again.

True's eyes smiled, the same color as the vast sky overhead. "It's a perfect spot." The tone of his voice said he understood what I was feeling, and I experienced an unfamiliar sense of oneness—of having my thoughts read. "I'm hoping to buy this land across the river from mine for a house site. There's a high granite bluff that rises two hundred feet above the river. From there, you can practically see tomorrow coming."

"It sounds amazing," I said under my breath, imagining waking up in a house so close to the sky you could stand at the window and see tomorrow. And you weren't afraid of it coming.

The brakes squealed as we pulled into a gateway

with a rusty *For Sale* sign nearly obscured by cedar bushes. Putting the truck in park, True started to climb out.

"I'll get the gate," I offered, welcoming the chance to stretch my legs and clear my head. I didn't wait for him to answer, but slipped out and closed the door behind myself. He said something just as it slammed shut, but the words were lost in the noise.

Taking a breath of the thick, earthy scent of cedar, I skirted the truck, then did a high-wire act crossing the row of metal pipes that covered what looked like a huge, damp trench beneath the gate. Balancing on the narrow pipes as I fiddled with the chain on the gate, I tried not to look into the trench below. I could picture my feet slipping through the gaps and me hanging on the pipes like a gymnast caught on the parallel bars. And True laughing.

Something moved in the corner of my vision just as I unhooked the chain—something as long as my leg and as big around as my forearm, brown and slithery, and about six inches from my foot.

"Holy crap!" I heard myself scream. Flinging the gate open, I danced across the pipes with the grace of a ballerina and clambered onto the hood of the truck on all fours like a cat.

True faced me through the window with eyes wide and mouth open.

It didn't occur to me to be embarrassed. "A sn-sn-sn-snake!" I hollered as he rolled down the driver's side window and leaned out. "Geez, there's a big snake over there!"

True's look of alarm suddenly paralleled mine, and he reached behind the seat, pulling out a glimmering rifle. "What kind of snake?"

A puff of disgust forced itself past my throat, and I climbed a little higher onto the hood, clinging to the windshield wiper and wondering if a snake could jump onto the hood of a pickup. *Did you know a diamond-back can propel himself as far as five feet when he strikes? Five feet? Five feet?*

"I don't know! The scary kind!" I hollered in horror and disgust because he still wasn't aiming the rifle and I was trapped in mortal danger.

To my relief, he sighted the rifle, and I closed my eyes, waiting for the blast that would free me. Instead I heard True laughing, and I opened my eyes to see him putting the rifle behind the seat, unfired.

"It's just a little bull snake," he informed me, grinning. "Not more than a foot long. They're good snakes. They eat rodents and other vermin."

Unwilling to accept the concept of a "good snake," I remained where I was. "Well, you'd better get it out of there, because I'm not coming down."

He stepped out, tilting his head as if I were a lunatic. "They don't bite, Collie. He's more afraid of you than you are of him."

"Not *likely*!" As my white-knuckled grasp on the windshield wiper could attest. "I'm *not* coming down."

"Oh, good Lord, woman." He scooped me off the hood in one swift motion, carried me around the truck in a sniveling ball, opened the door, and deposited me on the seat. "You act like you've never seen a snake before."

Which was pretty much true, but I didn't say so. Smoothing back my hair, I regained my composure as we drove through the gate and bounced along a path that led through a maze of overgrown cedar brush, where a million snakes could hide.

"Well, that was exciting," I said finally, then changed the subject. "So why do people around here dig those ditches under the gates and then lay pipes across them?"

He crooked a brow at me. "That keeps the cattle from crossing if the gate's open. They see the ditch and they're afraid to walk across the pipes."

"Oh." *And I know just how they feel.* "I thought maybe those were speed bumps."

True rolled his eyes and snickered. "Don't they teach you anything important in Yankee journalism school? Those are cattle guards."

"Ooohhh, cattle guards." I recognized the term, though I had been defining it incorrectly. "I thought a cattle guard was a person who kept the cattle from being stolen."

He shook his head and chuckled ruefully, and I chuckled with him, because now it seemed rather funny.

Slowly, the truck dipped and bumped its way along the path like a tank moving over a rutted battlefield.

True looked around the unkempt pasture and made a disgusted sound under his breath. "This place will take a lot of work. It's really been let go."

He continued to survey the land critically as we drove out of the nest of cedar brush and into a wide expanse of wispy sage-green grass, covered with wildflowers. I could see that the trail was leading us up a tall hill to a grove of ancient-looking trees standing high on the ridge like the chieftains of battle.

As we came closer, it was evident how ancient the trees really were. The largest of them had trunks perhaps three feet in diameter and branches so wide and thick they shaded the ground so that no underbrush could grow beneath. I imagined that they had sheltered homesteaders, and Spanish explorers, and Comanches before white men had ever set foot in the hill country.

An uneven pair of ropes and a rotted wooden swing hanging from a branch testified to the fact that someone had been there before us.

I gripped the dashboard as the truck lurched up the rocky cap of the flat-topped butte and finally came to a rest beneath the shade of the ancient trees. True turned off the engine and looked at me, and the world was silent, breathless with expectation.

Chapter 10

THERE was a strange sense of anticipation in me also, but not the racy, tingly kind I always got when following a good story. This was the feeling of being about to discover something wonderful, like knowing there's a rainbow overhead, even before you look up and see it.

"We're here," True said quietly, then opened his

door. The click of the latch and the squeak of the hinges seemed deafening against the silence, threatening to shatter the picturesque scene like a glass menagerie.

I opened my door and slipped out, my feet sinking into the carpet of dry leaves. Overhead, a spring breeze whispered quietly through the canopy of live oaks. Proof that the world was still moving, after all.

True took a few steps from the front of the truck, then stopped and looked over his shoulder, reaching out his hand and motioning me forward, raising one finger to his lips to signal quiet. There was a look of discovery in his eyes that told me he'd found something.

I tiptoed forward and slipped my hand into his without thinking. It felt right. His fingers closed around mine as if he felt it too, and he pulled me forward, close against his side, then pointed through a gap in the trees. Leaning down, he whispered in a warm breath against my ear, "Over there."

Peering through the trees, I saw an abandoned native-stone building with a wide front porch supported by pillars of stacked stone. Two arched windows watched us like wise old eyes, glimmering with tears of dusty, broken glass.

A movement in front of the building caught my attention, and I noticed a doe grazing calmly in a sunlit patch of grass, unaware that we had invaded her sanctuary. Nearby, a pair of spotted fawns jumped and twisted, bolting in playful circles like two tiny unicorns frolicking near the ruins of some enchanted castle. Holding my breath, I watched them, amazed at the serenity of the scene. It was as if every detail of the place and the moment were perfect.

The breeze stirred again and a bird called loudly in the branches above us. Raising her head, the doe gave a low sound of alarm, calling the fawns, then turned and bolted with them into the cover of the trees.

True glanced sideways at me and smiled, and we moved forward, ducking under the low branches, my hand intertwined with his. We stopped in the clearing where the doe had been, and stood looking at the old building, which must have once been a school or church. Built of milk-colored native stone, it was large, with a tall, peaked roof, the sagging rafters partially covered with tattered tin. On one end, a high stone chimney rose starkly above the roofline, and on the other was a bell tower, solid and soundless like the kinsmen of Sleeping Beauty, frozen in place year upon year, waiting to be awakened. Looking at the brass bell, I wondered how long it had hung there in silence.

I followed True up the stone steps to the porch. The old boards whispered in soft voices, and the water-scented breeze stirred the nearby trees and rattled the surviving windowpanes. A hawk cried overhead, circled, then glided away to the place where earth met sky, perhaps only twenty feet from where we stood. My breath caught in my throat as I walked to the edge of the porch, gazing over the river bluff, down to the silver ribbon of water two hundred feet below. I looked outward over miles and miles of vast, silent country painted in every shade nature could create, stretching into the distance, the hills fading to muted gray, reaching toward the horizon. . . .

True was right. You could almost see tomorrow coming.

I heard him draw a long breath, felt the warmth of his body just behind mine. A current began to flow between us, and my thoughts swirled like a leaf caught in the breeze.

"This is it," he said, then paused, seeming to wonder about my thoughts.

"It's perfect," I whispered.

I heard the long, deep sound of his sigh, as if my approval were a relief. "I was thinking of building a new house here."

"Oh, I wouldn't." The words rushed from me with a sense of desperation. My heart already held the perfect picture. "I would refurbish the old building. It has such a wonderful feeling to it. I think it would be a shame to tear it down."

I heard the boards creak as he turned to look at the building. "You may be right. The stone looks solid. Everything else would have to be redone. This was one of the first schools along this part of the Colorado River, built around 1870, I think. Guess they built it to last."

I turned from the endless view and leaned against the cool stone pillar, watching him as he stepped forward and gazed into the tumbledown structure. The floors had been removed at some point, so that the doorstep was nothing but a stone precipice overlooking a tangle of boards lying on the dirt.

My gaze drifted lazily down his body, and my mind flashed to a picture of the building restored, a home created, the trees whispering just as they were now, the sky just this shade of blue . . . True standing in the doorway, looking at me.

And then he *was* looking at me, and the vision melded with reality, like metal sculptures melting together, until it was hard to tell where the dream ended and reality began. And even harder to care. His eyes were as blue and compelling as the sky on the far horizon. Looking into them, I thought I could see tomorrow coming. . . .

He crossed the distance between us, and I slipped my hands over his chest, around his neck, into his soft, damp hair as his lips met mine. He kissed me deeply, fully—not a kiss from a stranger, but a kiss from someone who knew everything about me, all I thought and all I felt, every stroke of the unlikely, impractical dream my mind had painted, every ounce of the need I felt for him and for the dream.

In that instant, I knew he felt it, too—the need and the dream. The words passed between us in the silence, in the kiss, in thoughts unspoken, but shared. Something strange and wonderful was happening. Something that was meant to be.

When his lips parted from mine, he stood for a long moment looking into my eyes, smiling just a little—warmly, as if he understood.

A thousand questions swirled through my mind, but never reached my lips. Instead I heard myself say, "Nothing like this has ever happened to me."

"Me either," he confessed, then pulled me into his arms, against his chest, encircling me, keeping out the rest of the world. "Some things just happen."

"I guess so." *But not to me. In my life, things happen because I plan them. . . .*

"Planning is overrated." I wondered if he'd read my thoughts, or already knew me so well.

"You're right," I agreed, and it was the truth.

We stood for a long time, wrapped in the dream, in each other, gazing into the distance, looking for tomorrow.

But it seemed to move farther and farther away, until it was impossible to glimpse. Finally we parted and walked silently to the edge of the bluff. The view was breathtaking, but I knew the moment was lost.

True pointed to a group of brown and white cattle grazing like giant ants in the lush green pasture far below on the other side of the river. "The girls look hungry," he said. "I guess we should go."

I nodded, following him away from the edge. "I guess we should." But I didn't want to. I wanted to stay and pretend, like a little girl in a playhouse.

But the grown-up world marches on, and you have to march with it, so I climbed into the truck with True, and we left the enchanted castle behind, winding slowly down the hill again and into the crush of cedar growing like a tangle of vines around Sleeping Beauty's hiding place. I wondered if I would ever come there again.

The rattle of the tires crossing the cattle guard brought me back to reality.

True stopped the truck on the other side of the gateway and looked sideways at me. The intensity was gone from his face, replaced by a hint of a smile, and I wondered anew at the rapid changes in his moods.

He shrugged over his shoulder toward the open gate, and I followed his line of vision.

"No way," I said, crossing my arms over myself.

"Passenger always gets the gate." He gave me that wicked grin and I felt the temperature in the truck rise by ten degrees.

"Who says?" Picturing the snake incident, I became more determined to stay where I was.

"It's an old cowboy rule."

I leaned sideways, almost close enough to kiss him. For a fraction of a second, I thought about it, but regained my senses, and said, "Well, I'm not an old cowboy, so you're out of luck."

He laughed and actually reached out and tweaked me on the end of the nose, which no one had done since I was a child. It was kind of . . . sweet.

"Good thing"—he chuckled—"or all of this sparkin' would look pretty darned stupid." Getting out of the truck, he walked across the cattle guard as if he hadn't a care in the world.

I laughed and blushed at the same time, because it was the first time either of us had mentioned our romantic encounters in a sober moment. Then I sat there watching him wrestle with the rusty gate and thinking about how good he looked doing it. He really was . . . something . . . totally different.

I couldn't imagine why he wasn't happily married

and living in his house on the bluff with someone. Tending cows. Selling tractors. Raising kids.

That nagging investigative urge buzzed through my thoughts like a bee looking for a place to land, and I closed my eyes for a moment to try to make it go away. But the first question was out before he was all the way into the truck.

"So have you lived in San Saline all your life? You seem to know everything about the area."

He gave me an enigmatic, sideways look, then put the truck in drive and started down the road. "Well . . ." Some hesitation, during which my hopes crept up, then, "Mostly. More or less. Why?"

"I just wondered." I could tell he wasn't going to be an easy mark. "I thought you must have learned all that advanced algebra somewhere else. . . ."

He didn't look at me, and for a moment I had a feeling he wouldn't answer at all. Finally he said, "Math is just one of those things you're either good at or you're not."

An evasive answer, if I'd ever heard one. Shades of my past life, interviewing politicians . . .

Was it my imagination or was the truck careening down the dirt road at a dangerous rate of speed—as if the driver couldn't wait to get to the next pasture and end the conversation? We bumped across the Colorado River bridge so quickly I barely saw the water go by.

"So you always knew you wanted to stay here and run the family tractor business?"

"Well . . . things work out the way they're supposed

to." The facade cracked, and he added, "When you're young, you don't always know what you want." His gaze caught mine for just an instant, and I saw something black and deep, like the opening to a well, filled with emotions and experiences I could only guess at, murky with torment.

Then we skidded into a gateway like stuntmen in a rodeo movie, and the conversation was over. He didn't even ask me to open the gate, but jumped out of the truck as if it were on fire and took care of the gate himself.

I thought about the look in his eyes and wondered if I wanted to know more. If he turned out to be something other than True the Tractor Man, jovial conversationalist, rescuer of lost women, occasional romantic, and lousy newspaper editor, how would I feel about him?

And how would he feel about me if he knew all that was in my past? Was it worse than what was in his? Not as bad? Did it matter?

Don't look too far down the road . . . I thought. *Just enjoy the day, Collie. Stop trying to map everything out.*

True seemed more relaxed as he climbed into the truck again. I tried to relax, too, and let go of all the questions.

He stopped the truck just inside the gate and looked toward the herd of cattle on the other side of the pasture. "So do you want to pour feed or drive the truck?"

"Pour feed," I said, like I knew what he was talking about.

He lowered a skeptical brow, and I wondered what I was in for. “All right,” he said. “Come around the back of the truck and I’ll get you set up.”

“OK.” Opening my door, I checked for snakes, then slipped out, hurried quickly around the pickup, and climbed into the bed of the truck beside him. “What do I do?”

“The idea is to spread the cubes out in a line on the ground, so all the cattle get some.” He illustrated with his hands as if we were discussing rocket science. “When they come trotting around behind the truck, you just pull the strings on these sacks one by one.” He motioned to the row of sacks hanging off the tailgate. “Most of the cubes will spill out on their own. Just dump out what’s left and throw the sack into the front of the bed.” Jumping down, he paused and looked at me. “You sure you wouldn’t rather drive?”

“I’m sure.”

I wasn’t sure at all. The cattle had spotted us and were running across the pasture in a noisy, jostling herd. I was starting to wonder what would happen to me if I couldn’t get the sacks open. I had visions of my run-in with the goats.

“All right.” True gave me that sly smirk that told me I was in for an experience. “Hang on. Here come the cows.” And he trotted back to the cab, leaving me there to dump feed or die trying.

I was still wrestling with the first sack when the herd overtook the slow-moving truck and began battering the sides, licking the bumper with long pink tongues, and making a cacophony of noise that would have put the peafowl to shame. Finally the sack gave way, and small green cubes spilled onto the ground. Some of the cattle stopped to eat, and some jostled after the truck, begging for the next sack and the next, until all were gone, and all the cattle had stopped, except for one large red-brown cow, who practically climbed into my lap as the truck stopped. I scrambled backward, and she reached up and cow-licked the entire length of my arm.

"Aaahhh! Go away!" I squealed, and she blinked her long red eyelashes at me, looking wounded.

True exited the truck and came around to the back, then reached out and scratched the cow on the forehead like it was a gigantic dog. "This is Biscuit."

"We've met," I said, wiping the goo off my arm with an empty sack. "She's a man-eater."

True laughed. "She's a little spoiled. I raised her on a bottle." He grabbed a bucket of grain and dumped it on the ground. "She's not too sure she's supposed to be a cow."

Biscuit ignored the feed and looked at True with dark, soulful eyes, then stretched out her neck and uttered a long, mournful sound.

"I think she's in love," I joked. "Maybe I should sit in the truck so you two can be alone."

He jumped into the bed of the truck and stood on the edge, counting the cows. "I have that effect on females. Eighteen . . . twenty . . . twenty-two . . . Especially redheads."

That deserved a reprisal, so I stepped forward and gave him a shove. He lost his balance and his arms flailed wildly, catching the tail of my shirt, and the next thing I knew we were tumbling from the truck. We landed with a thud in the grass, like a couple of kittens at play, and True rolled on top of me, giving me an evil look.

"You're in trouble now, aren't ya?"

I tried to look coy, because I supposed he was going to kiss me. "That depends on what you've got in mind."

The words turned his eyes steamy, and he smiled wickedly at me, leaning closer. I closed my eyes just before his lips touched mine and . . . and Biscuit kissed us both. On the mouth.

"Biscuit!" True hollered, jumping up and chasing my rival away.

"Eeeewww!" I groaned, sitting in the grass and wiping the gooey smell of fermented vegetables off my face. "Oh, yuck. I need a towel." Climbing to my feet, I stumbled to the cab of the truck with one eye glued shut, in search of a rag.

By the time True joined me there, I was wiping off the last of the mess on a stack of leftover Dairy Queen napkins.

True winced, watching as I looked in the rearview mirror and tried to comb a strand of slime out of my hair. "Sorry," he said, taking a napkin and wiping his face, which hadn't taken nearly as bad a hit as mine. Not fair, considering it was his cow.

The smell of cow breath started to fade, and laughter tickled in my throat. "That was the worst kiss I've ever had."

True gave me a wounded look. "Sorry, but I'm just a country boy."

Outside, Biscuit wailed, and the two of us fell into laughter as we headed for the gate.

We kept laughing until we had left the pasture behind and driven several miles down the county road to the paved highway.

True paused at the stop sign and pulled his hat off, wiping his eyes and catching his breath. "I've got one more pasture to check, but I can take you home first if you've had enough."

"I'm all right," I said, even though I knew I should probably go back and try to find some solution to the rental car problem. "In fact, I can't remember the last time I've had this much fun."

True shook his head, looking at me with genuine admiration. I had a feeling I had passed some kind of test. "Let's go, then." He turned the truck away from San Saline and pulled onto the blacktop.

Relaxing in my seat, I looked out the window with a mixture of fascination and anticipation, like a sailor setting out on an unknown sea, wondering what I would find.

We drove for a while in silence, the kind of silence that happens between two people who are comfortable together. I had lost the urge to pry details out of him. Things felt good the way they were, and I didn't want to spoil it.

We passed through a small settlement that was little more than a few old houses, an abandoned railroad building, and a gas station. On the outskirts, a flurry of bright colors and human activity caught my eye, and I surveyed with mild interest the peaceful scene of an old white clapboard church beneath a grove of ancient live oaks. The lawn was filled with brightly clothed tables, ladies in billowing dresses, men in suits, and children running like puppies in the grass. I noticed a familiar old car with a tattered cream-colored roof, and I pointed, looking at the sign on the front of the church that read, *Riverbend Free Baptist Church. Catfish Fry Today.*

"That's Malachi's church!" I said, searching for him in the crowd of African-American faces moving among the tables.

True glanced sideways, seeming perplexed. "Mm-hmm. Malachi's been preaching there since services were held in the old log freedman's school out back. You can see the porch of the old log building still standing, and that bucket hanging upside down from the post used to be the school bell. If it weren't for Malachi, I don't think there would have been a real church building here." Slowing down, he pointed out Malachi, clothed in a white apron, standing behind a huge fish fryer. "Looks like he's frying fish today." True honked the horn, and old Malachi looked up and waved.

"Oh, can we stop?" I blurted, turning to look back as we passed, and the building hid the fish-fry scene from view.

True slowed the truck, glancing at me from beneath lashes lowered incredulously. "Collie, you do realize that's a *black* church? We'd probably be the only white faces there."

I wondered what he meant by that and whether he had a problem with the idea, but I decided to press on. "I don't care. I promised Malachi I'd put a donation in his collection basket, and I may not get another chance. We don't have to stay long."

"If we stop, we're staying for catfish." His eyes were bright with anticipation. "Darlin, you haven't experienced Texas until you've been to a Bible-thumpin', brimstone-throwin', tent-preachin', fried-taters-catfish-'n'-caramel-pie Sunday social."

I suddenly felt a little unsure of what I was getting myself into, but I said, "Well, let's go then."

So he wheeled the truck around, and we drifted into the parking lot, stopping just below the sign on the front of the building. If you looked hard enough, you could see the ghost of the original name, *Riverbend Negro Baptist Church*. I wondered when it had changed, and how people had felt about it before, and after. I wondered if the children running nearby in the grass could even see the shadows of the old letters, and if they understood, or even cared. I wondered, after Malachi and his generation were gone, if anyone would remember.

The people around the tables regarded us with curiosity and surprise as we stepped from the truck, and I questioned the wisdom of my decision. We were, indeed, the only white faces in the crowd, and the crowd seemed transfixed by that fact. Where I came from, race was not such a big issue, but things were different in the South.

If True was the least bit uncomfortable, he didn't show it. Leaving his hat in the truck, he combed through his hair with his fingers, then walked around to escort me to the fish fry.

A white-haired woman hobbled around the end of one of the tables and barred our path, squinting up at True through bottle-bottom glasses. "Well, it's True the Tractor Man!" she said, as if he were Robert De Niro. "How are you doin', you fine-lookin' hunk a' man?" Grabbing him by the shoulders, she shook him with surprising strength, considering that she was stooped over, and looked perhaps a hundred years old.

True grinned flirtatiously. "How's that new lawn mower working out, Miss Martha?"

Miss Martha smiled. "Oh, it's very fine. My grandson just mows that lawn so nice." Peeking over her glasses, she winked suggestively. "But if *you* wanted to come make a service call at my house . . . well, that'd be fine too."

"Miss Martha, you're a married woman." True took her hand in his and patted it fondly, and I got the feeling they'd known each other for a long time. "I'm afraid of what would happen to me if I made a service call at your house."

Miss Martha giggled behind her hand, then fanned herself as if she were steaming up. "Oh, Buster's harmless. He's getting old, you know. I may be lookin' again soon."

"Well, you let me know." True grinned, and Miss Martha beamed like a twenty-year-old. I could see that his charm worked as well on old ladies as it did on

Yankee redheads and lonely cows.

"Miss Martha!" I recognized Malachi's voice. "You better git back to servin' that pie and leave them young folks alone. Can't you see that boy's got him a pretty lady on his arm?"

Miss Martha reached up and pinched True on the cheek, then went back to her serving place. True and I proceeded to the catfish table, where Malachi was hard at work.

"You out workin' this Sunday mo'nin', Truitt?" he asked, and there was just a hint of preacherly reproach in his tone.

True looked toward the table filled with salads in brightly colored bowls. "Had cattle to feed."

Malachi nodded, smiling at me. "Well, the Lawd is in the pasture, too." He paused to serve steaming-hot catfish to a passerby. "But we're proud to see you made it to His little catfish fry. We're gone to have a preachin' session here in a minute. Hope you'll take a plate and stay awhile."

True stepped to the end of the table and grabbed two plates and some silverware, handing one set to me. "Wouldn't miss it," he said, then nodded at me. "Collie's here to make a donation."

Malachi shifted his attention to me as he piled a steaming helping of catfish on my plate. "Well, I knowed she would. She's got a little angel in her, this gal. I can see it in them blue, blue eyes." He smiled, and I felt warm and welcome, like I belonged there. "We're proud to have ya with us today, Miss Lady. Mighty proud."

"Thank you, Malachi," I said, and smiled once more into those age-yellowed eyes before moving down the line. If there was an angel there, I knew it wasn't me, but him.

I watched True work the crowd as we made our way past the food tables and into the shade of a grove of live oaks, where most of the people were already sitting with their plates on lawn chairs, quilts, and hay bales.

True really did have the makings of a politician. His rapport with people was amazing. He remembered names and children born, illnesses and tractors bought from one to twenty years ago. He asked people about themselves and thus managed to say very little about himself. Just as he did with me.

Still, he seemed relieved when the conversations ended, and Malachi took the podium on what had once been the porch of the old log freedman's school.

A hush fell over the crowd, and Malachi stood for a moment looking down at his tattered Bible—the one I had seen on the dashboard of his car.

Finally he drew in a long breath, and everyone waited, knowing something profound was coming.

"I want to talk to you today about . . . *love!*" His voice rose to a crescendo on the last word. "Not love like you see in the movies, or love like you say, 'I *love* pie, but I don' *love* mustard greens.' Not *love* like I see on my granddaughter's school papers, 'I *love* Billy,' and then it's crossed out nex' week. I want to talk to you about *real love*. The kind of *love* that can't be crossed out. The kind of *love* that won't fade away. The kind of *love* that don' depend on how somethin' looks or smells or tastes, or how someone acts. The kind of *love* a brother ought have for a brother, and a father ought have for a son, and a mother ought have for a child, a neighbor for a neighbor, and a man for a woman. Love that comes from praisin' the Lawd and lovin' all his creatures. *Amen?*"

Around us, the crowd raised its voice into a fervent chorus of "Amen!" True glanced at me with a secret smile as Malachi grew louder and even the trees seemed to shudder in response.

"I want to tell you what the Lawd says about love. The Lawd says, 'Love one another as I have *loved you!*' Love all the flaws. Love all the weaknesses. Love all the disappointments. Love as Jesus loved, *Amen!*"

Voices raised into a fever of affirmation and hands flew into the air, fingers outstretched, twittering like the wings of birds.

I listened as the message continued, a lesson about agape love, service and devotion to others, about forgiveness and unconditional acceptance. I could barely hear the preaching above the cheering, muttering, and affirmations. For a girl raised as a straitlaced Presbyterian, it was an otherworldly experience.

Malachi pointed an accusing finger, seeming to single out people in the crowd. "If you love someone because they are strong, what happens when they are weak? If you love someone because they are beautiful, what happens when they aren't beautiful anymore? If you love someone because they are young, what happens when they are old? If you love someone because they are rich, what happens when they are poor? If you love someone because they are faithful, what happens when they are unfaithful?"

He paused, leaning against the podium, bowing his head as if God were whispering in his ear. The crowd grew silent, and the hush was powerful.

Malachi surveyed the audience, his eyes intense, his voice little more than the whispering of the breeze among the leaves. "When you look at your brethren, look with your heart and not your mind. Love with your heart and not your mind. The mind changes like a river, but the heart is lastin' like the sea. God is in your heart."

He paused and the parishioners answered with a murmur of "Amen," and a silent chorus of twittering hands.

Malachi scanned the crowd; then his gaze halted on us, on True, and the sermon quietly went on. True shifted forward in his seat, as if drawn by the power of the old man's gaze. "Love is in your heart like a great, great *ocean* of wat-ah. But you have to let the ti-ide flow out, flow out and cov-ah the world around you or your life will be dry, dri-ah like a desert, brother."

Then Malachi looked at me, just at me, and I felt the crowd fall away as if he and I were connected through a long tunnel. "The Lawd is leadin' you like a horse to wat-ah, but he cain't make you drink, sister. He's callin'. You listen. He's wakin' up your heart and all the lastin' things are in there . . . if you look . . . if you trust . . . if you believe. It's there inside. If you listen hard enough, it will lead you home."

A flush of emotion washed through my body and I found myself nodding into Malachi's soft, silent gaze, my mind and body filled with a will other than my own.

Malachi nodded in return, slowly, his eyelids drifting downward with a look of satisfaction; then he bowed his head and closed his eyes, leaning on the podium, exhausted of all his strength.

The crowd remained silent for a long moment, as if he had stirred every heart beneath the shade of the trees that warm spring day. In quiet reverence, the parishioners began to pass the collection plate as two teenage boys helped Malachi descend the steps of the podium. Reaching into my purse, I took a hundred-dollar bill out of my emergency fund and folded it into a piece of paper. Just before the basket came to me, I wrote *For Malachi's baptistery* on the outside, then slipped it beneath the other donations.

When I glanced up, Malachi was looking at me, and smiling.

Chapter 11

THAT image of Malachi stayed in my thoughts as True and I said our good-byes and left the church. Something was on True's mind, too. He was quiet as we drove to a nearby pasture to check another herd of cattle. It wasn't until we had finished putting out feed that he seemed to return to himself, and even then, there was something slightly reserved about his manner.

I wondered if he might be thinking about what Malachi said, or if he was just embarrassed by all the talk about love. I wondered if it was possible to be in love with a person and a place you'd only known for a few days. Had it really been only a few days, less than a week? D.C. seemed like a lifetime ago.

True rested his arm on the open window, giving me a long, contemplative look as we pulled onto the highway and headed toward San Saline again. "So what's on your mind?" he said, as if I were the only one in the car who hadn't had much to say for the last half hour.

"Oh . . . nothing. I was thinking about . . ." *falling in love, having a family, becoming a cowgirl* . . . ". . . work. Why?"

He shrugged, but I had the feeling his interest was more than casual. He was staring out the window with an intense expression. "I just wondered. You haven't had much to say since we left the catfish fry. I thought maybe you'd been struck by the Holy Ghost or something."

I chuckled. "No. But Malachi is something else, isn't he? He knows how to capture a crowd. I wonder why, in all these years, he hasn't moved up to a bigger church."

True glanced at me, frowning, seeming . . . disappointed. "Not everybody is looking to make the bigtime."

"I suppose not." I felt a little stung, because I had a

feeling the retort was aimed at me. Or maybe I was being oversensitive. "I just meant that Malachi has a lot of talent, that's all. That was some sermon. He had the whole crowd in the palm of his hand." What I really wanted to know was whether the sermon had affected True the way it had me. Whether it had started him thinking.

"That he did," True agreed, still looking out the window at the road. "Sorry about all the matchmaking, though. Matchmakers are like stray cats around here; they're everywhere, and they're always on the prowl."

Nervous laughter pushed past my throat, because I could feel us getting closer to the heart of the matter. Something unintended rushed from my mouth. "I'm starting to wonder if they know something we don't."

He just nodded. Clearly, he'd already thought about it. "Maybe they do. Mrs. Hawthorne is probably dancing on air, after seeing us together last night and today."

"She probably is." I couldn't help smiling at the picture of Mrs. Hawthorne gleefully plotting her next move.

True gave me that devil-may-care grin, and the knot in my stomach melted. "Doesn't really matter at this point. You've already borrowed my horse's favorite blanket and kissed my best cow. Around here, that's serious."

"Oh, really?" I felt my sense of reality going foggy again and my mind getting giddy. "So once you've kissed a fella's best cow, then what's next?"

He kept his eyes trained on the road, but I could see

the smoldering look. "I was thinking of a trip to San Antonio. I have to go Tuesday and Wednesday to look at some tractors. If you come with me, Mrs. Hawthorne and Malachi will probably dance in the street together."

"So after you kiss a guy's best cow, then the next thing is a trip to San Antonio to look at tractors?"

"Usually."

"Well, I'd hate to break with tradition." A faint, practical thought crossed my mind about hotel arrangements and separate rooms, but instead of making it clear that I wasn't looking to jump in bed with anyone, I said, "San Antonio sounds great. I'm supposed to do a couple of articles about the food there."

"Good." True looked frightfully pleased, and I felt a ridiculous sense of joyous anticipation. I couldn't imagine why, when what I probably should have been doing was kicking myself back to sanity, wherever that was.

What I should have done was ask what was in his mind, and where he saw all this leading, and whether he realized that I would be heading back to D.C. in a few weeks. Probably I should have been asking myself the same questions, but instead I made small talk about San Antonio and restaurants, and the Bluebonnet Festival in Burnet next weekend, where I was supposed to do an article on the chili cook-off. True asked me if I wanted to help set up his tractor booth before the big event in Burnet on Friday, and like a ninny, I said yes.

By the time we reached Hawthorne House, we had

planned something for almost every day of the week, but we hadn't talked about any of the things that really mattered.

True seemed to realize it, too. There was a deep, thoughtful look in his eyes as we stood together on the porch of my cabin. In some corner of my mind, I wondered whether Mrs. Hawthorne was watching us. True reached out and stroked his fingers along my arm, and I decided I didn't care. I looked into his eyes, and I was lost.

"It's been a good day," he said quietly.

"Yes, it has." I wanted him to stop talking and kiss me. I didn't want to get into all the questions, and the details, and the talk about me going home in a few weeks. "It's been a perfect day."

He looked at the peafowl strutting in the afternoon sun on the other side of the lawn. "You think it's possible for something to be meant to be?"

"I don't know." My mind was screaming *yes*. "Do you?"

His lips curved into the faintest hint of a smile. "I'm starting to wonder."

"Me too."

His fingers caressed the side of my face, featherlight, and then he leaned down and kissed me, and my heart answered his question.

Yes, it is possible that some things are meant to be.

The screen door slammed on the main house and our lips parted. True stood gazing at me with his fingers twined into my hair.

"Meet me for breakfast in the morning?" His words

were hoarse and passionate, intimate sounding.

"Sure." A breathless whisper. All that was left in me.

He smiled, an expression filled with all the things I had ever dreamed of in a man. "You'd better get inside and call the rental-car company before they close. Let me know if you need me to take the car to Copperas Cove for you again tomorrow."

"I will." And I almost wished I would need him to, just so we would have an excuse to spend the day together. "Good-bye."

"See you in the morning, Collie." Then he turned and strode across the lawn, with the same confident, relaxed stride I had noticed that first night at the tractor lot—as if he had no reason to hurry and no reason to care what anyone thought.

I stood gazing after him until the Friendly's truck disappeared from the driveway. When I looked up, I noticed Becky watching me from the front porch of the house. Blushing, I wondered how much she had seen and what she was thinking. I heard Mrs. Hawthorne call her from inside, and she turned and walked back.

After she was gone, I went into my cabin. It was past four, so I hurried to call the rental-car agent in Copperas Cove before they closed. There were no peafowl on the phone, so I could hear her clearly as she apologized profusely, promising to drive over personally in the morning and exchange the car for a new one, and to take the demon-car days off my rental-car bill.

"It's parked downtown in front of the newspaper office," I told her. "I left the keys in it." Something that I never would have considered doing back home in

D.C. "If you would deliver the new car to Hawthorne House for me, I would appreciate it."

"Yes, ma'am, I surely will. I'm really so, so sorry about all this. Our mechanic was sure he had that car fixed."

Fortunately for her, I was still in the grips of a warm, fuzzy, and generous mood, because that car and their service were really sore subjects for me. "I don't think that car *can* be fixed. But as long as I never see it again, I'll be happy."

"I don't blame you. Thank you for being so patient about it."

"You're welcome." Me? Patient? My hill-country alter-ego must have been affecting me more than I thought. "Good-bye."

"Good-bye, Miss Collins."

And that, I hoped, was the end of the saga of Curly Collie and the demon-possessed rental car. Sitting at the kitchen table, I stared out the window and thought about the car and about everything that had happened because of its quirky personality—good things, if I really thought about them. The car brought me together with True and Malachi. If not for True having to drive me home after the fireworks, he wouldn't have invited me to go with him for a Sunday drive, and I wouldn't have been to my first Sunday catfish fry, or had my first cow kiss, or seen what tomorrow looked like from the enchanted schoolhouse on the river bluff. If not for the whims of the demon car, I would have missed the most wonderful things about my visit to the hill country. I would be just another busy outsider, buzzing in and out of town, getting my work done, but never really getting to know the place or the people.

Maybe God was trying to tell me something. Or maybe it was all a coincidence. Hard to say. It depended on how you looked at it, and how much you believed in divine intervention.

Reaching for my notepad, I turned to an empty sheet and began to write. The words that flowed through me were about the day—the old schoolhouse on the bluff above the river, built over a hundred years ago by the work-weary hands of pioneers. I wrote about the way the wind fluttered through the live oaks, like the soft voices of whispering children, and how the shreds of broken glass clinked in the windowpanes like the *tap-tap* of a teacher's chalk against slate.

I wrote about how, just down the road, the children of former slaves gathered to learn things that had been forbidden to their parents only a generation before, and how their parents and grandparents came together to raise up a tiny, windowless building hewn from the carcasses of live oak trees. I wrote about how different those two places were—one on the hill, one in the valley; one of stone, one of rough-hewn logs, without even the adornment of windows; one with a fine brass bell, one with only a bucket turned over and hung on a string.

Different places, the words ended, *both teaching lessons of sacrifice and hope. Both built so that generations could look out and see tomorrow.*

Closing the pad, I gazed out the window and saw Becky stepping onto the front porch of the cabin. Setting my papers aside, I stood up and opened the front door.

She entered without really being invited, holding up a plate of cookies like a passport. "Mama Hawthorne and I just finished making some cookies for the old-folks' home. I thought you might like some."

"Thanks, Becky," I said, but I didn't feel especially thankful. The truth was that her presence there was driving away that soft, sweet sense of altered reality I had come to like. I could tell she had something to say, and that I wasn't going to like it. The feeling was in the air, like the change in barometric pressure before a rainstorm. From somewhere far away, I thought I heard the sound of thunder, and then a peacock cried out, making me jump.

"I was just getting some work done." I nodded toward my laptop and pad on the table, hoping she would leave.

Instead, she set the cookies on the end table and sat against the back of the small sofa, looking at the plate of cookies, and then at me. "So there's kind of a thing going on between you and True." Her pale hazel eyes gave me a look that said, *Don't deny it, I saw you on the porch. . . .*

"I guess so," I muttered, then felt compelled to add, "We're just enjoying a little time together. It's no big deal."

She gave me a suspicious look, then said, "I'm glad." A pause, during which she studied the cookies, then, "Because if you're thinking about anything serious with True, you're making a mistake."

My heart sank to my shoes. *Plunk,* like a stone into a pool of murky water. I couldn't think of anything to say.

Becky looked up from the platter at me, then past me to an old picture of a Conestoga wagon on the wall. "True's been back here for five years, and he has a few dates with somebody, and then that's it. You're not the first one, Collie. He's probably had a dozen girls on the string at one time or other, but he hasn't gotten serious with anyone since his divorce. He's sort of known as a, well . . . a . . . heartbreaker around here now." She looked at me again, intense, trying to read my thoughts. "I just don't want to see you get your feelings hurt, because you're a nice person and you've been sort of a friend."

"True's divorced?" I heard myself mutter, and the words rattled around the empty shell of my consciousness.

"He hasn't even told you that?" She flashed a look of pity, then sympathy.

"I didn't ask . . . really." *I tried asking, but he wouldn't tell.*

"Did he tell you anything about what happened before he came back to San Saline?"

"No." *I never even knew he left.*

"Did he tell you he used to be a lawyer in Dallas? He and another guy had their own law firm and they made lots of money at it?"

I felt myself sink back into a chair, like a prizefighter stunned by a left hook.

Becky went on, watching me intently, gauging my

reaction. "He was, like, the biggest success this town ever saw. He hardly ever used to come back and visit, so it was kind of a shock when he came back and got married to a girl from here. But she was real pretty and she'd been back and forth to Dallas trying to be a fashion model, so it kind of fit, you know?"

I nodded, staring at her, openmouthed.

Becky paused, fiddling with a string on her shorts. "They never came home much, so I guess they liked it up there. Kendra was into all that society stuff. Everyone says they had a big house and all. They had a baby girl. I saw her one Christmas when they came back and Kendra was taking her around showing her off. True was crazy about that baby; I know that."

My mind spun and spun, like a compact disc player gone crazy, flashing pictures of a big house, wife, law school, baby, Dallas. None of which I could equate with True. Or maybe I just didn't want to.

Becky continued to look at her lap. "I don't know exactly what happened, but I think some shady things were going on with True's lawyer partner, and True didn't like it. Anyhow, all of a sudden, he wanted to give it up and move back here, but Kendra didn't want to. I heard she started fooling around with his lawyer friend. I think she didn't want to be with True if he wasn't going to be a rich lawyer. Anyhow, they were going to get a divorce, and when they were moving out of the house, the baby wandered out and drowned in the swimming pool."

"Oh, my God," I murmured, my stomach twisting into a knot, bile churning into my throat.

Becky looked at me and nodded, a hint of moisture in the corners of her eyes. "Well . . . I just didn't want you to get your feelings hurt, that's all. Mama Hawthorne shouldn't be trying to push you two together. I don't think True's ever gonna get over all that. He isn't the same person anymore at all."

"Who would be?" I didn't know what else to say. I was caught between anger and sympathy, self-defense and pity. I was ashamed of myself for being glad that Becky had told me True's history behind his back. I was ashamed that I had sat there listening like a gossiping teenager, but I was also glad I now knew.

Becky stood up, her duty now done. "I'm sorry, Collie." She looked at me as if the depths of my disappointment were visible in my face. "I've been trying and trying to tell Mama Hawthorne to quit pushing you and True, but she doesn't think I'm right. If I were you, I'd just stay away from True, unless . . . well, unless you're just looking for something kind of . . . casual." She stood up, and I walked her to the door.

"Thanks, Becky."

"You're not gonna tell anyone I told you all of this? Mama Hawthorne would kill me."

"No. I won't."

"I just thought you ought to know."

"I know," I answered, wishing she had never come. "Good-bye."

"Bye, Collie." And then she was gone. I stood leaning against the closed door, looking over the wreckage of her short visit. The wreckage of a foolhardy dream I had always known was way too far from reality.

So what was I so upset about? I *was* really just looking for something casual, wasn't I? I was just having a sort of . . . vacation fling, like one of those island things, only not on an island.

So why did I feel like a used grapefruit—cut in half, hollowed-out in the middle, and shriveling on the outside? Why did I feel more lost and deeply hurt than I had when Brett and I broke up after six years together?

It didn't make sense. But it was the truth.

Taking my notepad, I sat on the couch, looking over the stories and trying to decide how I had come to this point. How I had left behind a successful, practical, sane self and become so lost that I was hanging on the whims of people I'd known for only a few days.

A rainstorm blew in with surprising fury, and I locked the door and pulled the shades, trying to close out the clatter, but it was in my head as much as outside. It whipped me into a torrent of nightmares as I slept—painful dreams about a beautiful fashion model, and a big house, and a baby girl with True's blue eyes. Floating in a pool of crystal-blue water. Limp in his strong arms. Bathed in tears.

The salt of sorrow was on my tongue when I awoke. I thought about True's baby daughter. I wondered where she rested now and if he ever went there.

Outside, the dawn light was gray and bleak. The peafowl were silent. There was nothing but the soft drumming of rain.

Standing up, I walked to the window and raised the shade, then sat at the table and looked out into the morning gloom. I thought about True and tried to imagine all the emotions inside him that I had never guessed—the secret self I had glimpsed once or twice. Was Becky right that he would never leave it behind, never be ready to move forward?

Resting my head in my hands, I struggled to smooth the thoughts away. I reminded myself for the hundredth time that I was going to be leaving Texas in a few weeks, and True's future and mine would be two separate paths.

Glancing at the clock on the wall, I realized it was probably time for breakfast at the café. True would be waiting for me there, having no idea of what Becky had told me. I wondered what I would say to him. And how he would react if I told him I knew.

Part of me wanted to get it all into the open, to confront him for having led me to believe in a picture of him that wasn't accurate. Part of me wanted to leave things as they were and say nothing at all.

The urges fought like angel and devil as I bathed and dressed, combed my hair, and stepped onto the porch. The rain had ended, and I started toward the café, my feet sloshing in the leftover puddles on the gravel driveway. In the trees, the peafowl still sat with backs bowed and heads tucked, as if the day were not worth waking for.

The highway was nearly deserted as I walked up the shoulder. The town square ahead looked empty and silent. I had the sense of the wonder being spoiled, the glitter gone, the magic lost, the town a mere shell.

Coming closer to the café, I saw that there were only two cars in the parking lot. The Friendly's truck was not one of them. I wondered if Becky had gone to True and told him that I knew everything.

Crossing the highway, I stepped in a puddle and the water seeped through my loafers—cold reality bringing me back, making me see how foolish I had been to have created San Saline as some sort of utopia in my mind. Why I had expected that the normal human problems didn't exist here, I couldn't say. Birth, death, marriage, divorce. Lies, truth. Those things went on everywhere.

"Get a grip, Collie," I muttered as I reached the café parking lot. "This isn't somewhere over the rainbow. It's just Texas."

And True wasn't at the café. I considered not going in. I wasn't in the mood to face Mrs. Hawthorne and more of her well-meaning matchmaking.

Why did everyone here think it was a good idea for True and me to be together, if what Becky had told me was accurate? If he wasn't interested in more than a few dates with anyone else, why did Mrs. Hawthorne think he would be interested in something different with me?

He's sort of known as a heartbreaker around here. What in the world was I doing?

The familiar rumble of a diesel engine interrupted my thoughts, and I looked up to see the Friendly's truck coasting into the parking lot. The fragile threads of my good sense floated away like spiderwebs in a gale as the truck came to a stop beside me.

The passenger window lowered and True leaned across the seat. "I have to run over to Lampasas for a tractor part. Want to ride along and have breakfast over there?"

It seemed strange that he would be smiling. But then again, he didn't know. . . .

"All right," I heard myself say. I climbed into the truck and we headed toward the sun, which was just climbing above a bank of deep blue clouds.

True seemed to be in a good mood. He whistled as we drove out of town. When we had reached the open highway and started up the hill that led out of the San Saba valley, he glanced sideways at me.

"Something wrong this morning?" he asked. "Did you get everything straightened out with your rental car?"

I nodded, feeling queasy and wondering if I wanted to start a confrontation or just go on talking about things that didn't matter. "They're supposed to bring me a new one this morning."

"That's good."

"Mm-hmm."

We drove in silence for a while longer. I looked out the window, thinking that the bluebonnets were even thicker and more beautiful than the week before when I had arrived, or maybe I had grown fonder of them.

True finally took off his hat, set it on the seat, and looked hard at me, brows drawn together beneath a fallen wisp of hair. "All right, so whatever it is, just come out with it. No point sitting there staring out the window. Maybe I can help."

"Maybe you can," I said, but I couldn't look at him. I knew I was lighting a fuse with no idea what was on the other end, where it might explode, or how much damage might be done. "You're the problem."

True sat a little straighter in his seat, looking confused. "All right . . . but you'll have to give me a few more details." His mouth quirked, as if he were hoping to make light of it.

I felt my temper start to rear its ugly head. I didn't want another double-talking session with him, so I came right to the point. "Well, it's just that all this 'Aw, shucks, ma'am, I ain't never been out of the county and I'm just a poor ignorant country boy' stuff is pretty much a load of crap, isn't it? Why didn't you tell me you were a lawyer from Dallas?"

For an instant he looked shocked; then his expression cooled noticeably. "That doesn't really apply anymore. It's in the past."

The frosty nature of the response twisted a knife somewhere deep inside me. "True, you know what I mean. I'm trying to figure out who you are."

His eyes met mine and I fell in like a person diving into a pool without any idea of how deep it might be. "No, Collie, you're trying to figure out who I *was*. I don't see why it matters."

It matters because I think I'm falling . . . "I just want to know . . . where we are."

True let out a long, slow sigh, disappointed in me, frustrated by the question. "Somewhere between San Saline and Lampasas. That's about all I know for sure."

There were tears in my eyes, so I looked away. I had a feeling Becky was right. This was probably the point at which he excused himself from a relationship and rode into the sunset. Right now he was probably wishing he hadn't invited me to breakfast.

The thought was like a thousand pounds pressing on me. I felt crushed beneath the weight of it without understanding why.

The truck moved to the side of the highway and stopped beneath the shade of an overhanging live oak. I wondered if he was going to turn around and go back to San Saline. I couldn't even look at him. I blinked the moisture from my eyes, trying to build a wall of anger, but all I felt was hurt.

"Collie." His voice was tender and compelling. I turned to him without wanting to. His gaze met mine and I fell in again. "I don't have any answers. We're in uncharted territory here. You're not like anybody I've ever met. You make me laugh. I haven't laughed like this since . . . well . . . in years. It feels good. I don't care about the past. Your past. My past. Any of it. What do you say we just leave it at that and go on?"

I don't think True's ever gonna get over all that . . . I could hear Becky's voice drumming in my ear. *He's sort of a . . . heartbreaker around here now.* Was I setting myself up for more pain than I could bear?

The Lawd is leadin' you like a horse to water, but he cain't make you drink, sister. He's callin'. You listen. . . .

A sense of peace washed over me, as it had that day in the field outside the old freedman's school. I intertwined my fingers with True's and took a leap of faith.

"All right," I said. "We'll just leave it at that and go on."

And that was the end of it. True put the truck in drive and we sped along the glistening ribbon of hill-country highway, trying to leave the past behind.

Except in the back of my mind, I knew that the past is like a relentless bloodhound. It keeps tracking your every move, and sooner or later when you slow down, it overtakes you.

Chapter 12

TRUE'S parents were at the café in Lampasas when we arrived. For a flickering moment, I wondered if the meeting was contrived, but they were obviously surprised to see us there. True's mom looked shocked to see us together at all.

"Well, my goodness . . ." I could tell she was searching for my name, and then, ". . . Collie. You're not having to take your car over to Copperas Cove again, are you?"

True's dad stood up, pulled out a chair, then patted the backrest, smiling at me. I had a feeling everyone at the table was very interested in finding out what we were doing there together.

I did my best to look casual. "No, I'm just along for breakfast this morning."

Mom McKitrick's eyes sparkled with sudden enthusiasm, and she sat a little straighter in her seat, giving me that *maybe so* look. "Well, isn't that nice?"

I didn't quite know how to answer, so I sat in the seat

beside True's dad and glanced across the table as True leaned over to give his mom a kiss on the cheek, then sat in the chair across from me. I noticed he was blushing a little. It was cute.

We sat in silence for a moment, staring at each other like chess players, all trying to decide what the next move should be. Mom McKitrick was looking from me to True, and True to me, slowly sizing things up with that wise look in her blue eyes.

Mercifully, the waitress came by and took our breakfast order, breaking the stalemate. When she was gone, True's mother pulled the Monday *San Saline Record* from under her place mat and unfolded it halfway, laying it on the table. "I was just looking at today's edition, and it looks wonderful. Did you get some new help over there?"

"Collie worked on it with me." True took a swallow of his coffee, glancing at me with a twinkle in his eye. "She has *two* degrees in journalism."

Mom grinned broadly, looking almost ready to reach across the table and welcome me to the family. "Well, how wonderful! Things surely needed some shaping up at the *Record*."

True shrugged. The poor performance review didn't phase him at all. He studied the paper upside down. "It does look good, doesn't it? Collie has a real talent for it."

I rolled my eyes at True, feeling embarrassed by all the sappy dialogue. "It's more science than art. Now that you know how to use a proportion wheel and a pica pole, you'll have a talent for it, too."

True looked at me sardonically from beneath lowered brows.

"Not in this lifetime."

Wide-eyed, Mom McKitrick turned to True. "Truitt Heath, do you mean you've been doing that paper all this time without using a pica pole and a proportion wheel? No wonder it has so many gaps in it."

I bit my lip to hold back a snicker.

True's dad reached out and turned the paper around, looking at it and then at me. "Heck, sounds like we could solve the problem if she'd just stick around and do the paper with him from now on. How 'bout it . . . uh . . . Collie?"

"Bill!" Mom was aghast.

"Dad!" True choked on a swallow of coffee.

Dad McKitrick ducked his head and grumbled into his coffee cup. "Well, I was just statin' the obvious." He gave me a sliver of a glance and a quick, conspiratorial wink. It reminded me of True, and at that moment I fell in love with Dad McKitrick, too. Mom McKitrick might still be trying to size up the relationship between True and me, but Dad had it solidly figured out. He was ready to move things on down the road to the next junction.

The waitress was merciful again and brought our food before anything more could be said.

The food gave us an excuse to talk about something more neutral, like eggs, bacon, and whether hash browns ought to be cut in chunks or shredded on a cheese grater. Mom McKitrick was generally in favor of the food that morning, but Dad was certain the quality had declined under new management, and that they should start eating at the café down the road.

True and I sat watching the point and counterpoint fly. Momentarily, it looked like the discussion might lead to an all-out McKitrick feud, but then it ended over grape jelly and we started on a conversation about the upcoming bluebonnet festival in Llano and what equipment should be transported over for the Friendly's Tractors display.

Mom McKitrick offered to come and help True hang the banners and decorate the booth, because, as she nicely put it, that wasn't really his area of talent.

True shook his head. "No need. I've got help lined up." And he winked across the table at me.

Mom caught it, and Dad caught it, and I winced inwardly. Having True's parents in on the seedling relationship just made the stakes higher if things didn't work out. And I still didn't see how they could. D.C. to Texas was a little too far for a long-distance relationship.

As we finished breakfast, I was thinking about the story Becky had told me, and wondering how True's parents felt about their fashion-model ex-daughter-in-law. It was hard to picture them with someone like that. Of course, it was hard to picture True with someone like that, too.

It wasn't hard to picture them being crazy about their granddaughter, as my parents were about my brother's twins. I couldn't imagine how my family would survive it if something happened to the children. We would never be the same, and I supposed True's family wasn't either. That kind of heartbreak never goes away. I guess you just learn to live with it as best you can.

While True and his dad argued over the check, his mother and I walked out the front door and stood waiting in the gathering sunshine of a bright hill-country day.

Mom McKitrick gave me a pointed look. "So I recall you said you were only here for a little while doing some magazine articles."

I nodded, glancing over my shoulder and wishing the men would come out. I knew what she was getting at and I didn't have a good answer. "A few weeks probably. It's a freelance job, so I'll be here as long as it takes."

She chewed her lip thoughtfully, that quick look in her eyes. I had a feeling she was doing some advanced algebra in her head, and right now she was adding a few things up. "So you're somewhat self-employed, then."

"Yes." *For now, anyway.*

"How wonderful." She looked pleased. "I'll bet that opens up so many possibilities for you."

I knew what she meant, and she knew I knew. There was a silent conversation of insinuation going on between us. "I suppose," I said. "This is my first time freelancing, so"—I used True's words—"I'm sort of in uncharted territory."

Reaching across the space between us, she patted me on the arm as the men came out the door. "Oh, well, you'll find your way. Don't worry. Things have a way of working out."

We smiled at each other as True and his dad came out the door; then we said our good-byes. Jumping into the truck, True and I hurried to the Friendly's Tractors lot, grabbed some boxes, and scooted out of there before the old folks could show up. That, I could tell, was by design. True's design. He'd had enough prodding for one morning.

"Sorry about all that," he apologized as we headed out of town. "I thought they would have come and gone from the café by this time of the morning."

"That's all right," I assured him, as I had after our last meeting with his parents. "If my parents were here, they would have been the same way, except my Mom isn't quite as circumspect as yours. She's pretty much to-the-point on everything." The image of my parents in the Lampasas café made me chuckle, and I added, "Come to think of it, if my parents were here, they would be so far out of their element, there's no telling what they might do."

True cut a quick sideways look at me. "Guess they don't get out in the country much."

"Only twice a year. Once in the fall to do their traditional drive through the countryside looking at the fall color, and once in the summer, when all of the clan converges on a guest farm in Maryland." The memories made me laugh. For as long as I could remember, my family had been going to the summer family reunion at Ten Maples Farm. It had been the backdrop for dozens of outrageous stories that were still repeated around the family. Suddenly I regretted not having gone in the last few years.

True glanced at me, waiting for the rest of the story, so I went on. "I think the farmer dreads our reunion all year long. The last time I went, my grandmother's seven redheaded brothers came from all over the country, and oh, my gosh, was that a wild time. . . ." I went on to tell about the zany things that happened that summer, and other years during the summer family reunion—everything from horseback-riding disasters to cow-milking contests, all of which were pretty funny when performed by a bunch of urbanites.

True didn't talk much about his family, but I did gather that he was an only child, but he'd once had a brother who died very young. That and the death of True's daughter seemed like too much misery for one family. I didn't blame him for not wanting to talk about it.

The demon car was gone from the newspaper office when we pulled into San Saline. As we stopped in front of the building, True mentioned starting work on the Wednesday edition, so I went inside to help him for a while. Once again, I was in the mood to linger.

Becky looked surprised to see us together. I couldn't tell if True realized she was the one who told me about his background. Maybe he didn't want to give her the satisfaction of reacting.

"You get the extra Mondays delivered yet?" he asked.

Becky, for her part, wasn't doing a very good job of covering her guilt. She looked at the papers on her desk, her face beet red. "No. I've been taking down classifieds this morning. We had a lot of calls."

True seemed perfectly unconcerned about her strange behavior. "Well, I'll watch the phone now," he said. "Go ahead and deliver the rest of the leftover Mondays. You can go home when you're done. There won't be much to do this afternoon. When you go by the lot, tell Tim he can come by here and get these parts out of the truck whenever he's ready for them."

"All right," Becky said, and scooted out the door like she had a pit bull on her tail.

I pretended not to notice and started looking at the scraps for the Wednesday edition. I had, after all, promised I wouldn't tell True she was the one gossiping about him.

True stepped forward and pushed the door closed behind her. I could feel him looking at me, but I kept my eyes on the newspaper.

"In the future," he said flatly, "don't believe everything Becky tells you. She's got a big mouth and a nineteen-year-old brain."

"Point taken."

And that was the end of the discussion. He never asked what Becky said, or how much she had told me, or why. I admired him for letting go of it so easily.

As we worked, we slipped into an easy rhythm, and the uncertainty of the morning fell away. Things started to feel right again as I put together a couple of articles for him about an award-winning pig and elementary school kids on the honor roll.

"You know," I said, after I finished printing the articles at the computer, "there are so many good stories around here, you ought to put some historical stuff in the paper. Human-interest pieces about some of these old homesteads, and ladies' supper, and whatnot."

True looked thoughtfully at me from the light table. "That's not a bad idea. Maybe I could get some of the church ladies to write up some things."

Drumming my fingers on the keyboard, I tried to decide how to tell him that wasn't what I had in mind. "Well, I meant real feature stories. You know, go out and do interviews, research the history, take some good pictures."

True scoffed, pulling out a grid sheet and laying it on the table. "Don't have time for all that. Mostly I just take what people send in and what Becky comes up with, rewrite it a little, and slap it in the paper. Best I can do." The end sounded deliberately wistful, and I had a feeling he was trying to seem inept, so I would help him. Brett used to do that in the kitchen. I was familiar with the strategy.

I came over and stood beside True as he moved a couple of headlines around on the grid sheet, looking uninspired.

"Text first," I reminded him, pulling the headlines out of his fingers. "Then you can see how it fits and decide whether it gets a two-column headline or a three-column headline. Didn't you learn anything the other night?"

He chuckled under his breath and I felt the heat of it on the back of my neck. "I tried not to."

"You need to learn this stuff." I pretended not to notice the change in the temperature of the room, but my journalistic integrity was turning to mush.

He braced his hands on the light table on either side of me and I felt his body press against mine. "I like my dad's idea better. You stay here and do it for me."

You stay here . . . I wondered if he meant for today, or forever. I swiveled in his arms and my head began to spin. "All right, but just . . . this once."

Then we kissed, and passion rushed over us like a riptide. His fingers twined into my hair and my hands slipped around his body, pulling him closer. The tide surged, pulling us under, making me forget who I was and where I was, and all the things I had been worrying about. There was no sound, no light, only the two of us and a sense of destiny that was overpowering.

We parted and his gaze met mine. I saw a mirror of my thoughts. I knew, without being told, that he had never felt anything like it before. Neither had I.

Dimly, I heard the phone ring. True didn't seem to realize it until it sounded a second time, and a third. Finally he shook off the fog and stepped to the desk to answer.

"*San Saline Record* . . ." He cleared the deep, passionate sound from his throat, then wiped the moisture from his forehead with the back of his sleeve. "All right. Tell me what tractor they want and what they're offering." He picked up a pen and sat down in Becky's chair, writing figures on a pad. I could tell it was going to take a while, so I turned back to the pasteup, rubbing the palm of my hand over my racing heart. One more kiss like that, and we were likely to end up in a broom closet somewhere.

Fifteen minutes later he was still on the line, directly

with the customer now. "Listen, Clarence. This is the best I can do. . . ." A pause, during which I could hear a low, raspy voice reverberating through the line. "No, I'm not pulling your leg. It's been twenty years since you bought that John Deere 4020 from Dad. Tractors have gone up since then. . . ."

I glanced over my shoulder and he rolled his eyes, pointing at the phone and giving me a helpless look. "No, it won't help if you go over and talk to Dad. Clarence, you know he's not nearly as nice as I am."

The bell on the front door chimed, and I glanced up to see Mrs. Hawthorne coming in. She looked at True and then at me with a self-satisfied expression.

"I thought maybe I would find you here," she said, standing on the other side of the light table.

"You're looking for me?" I couldn't imagine why she would be. "Is something wrong?"

"No," she said, but there was a vague air of concern about her, like a shadow. "You've got a phone message from that Laura Draper who booked your room. She said she tried you on your cellular and in the cabin, but she couldn't reach you. I explained to her that we don't have good cellular here in the valley . . . and about the peafowl."

I rubbed a hand across my lips to hide my amusement. I could imagine what Laura was thinking right now. "It's probably about the article." I felt a pang of concern. I hoped Laura wasn't going to tell me the article stank and it wouldn't do. Deadline was Wednesday, and I didn't have time to start over. I had already mailed the photographs and the hard copy.

Mrs. Hawthorne glanced at True, who had his back to us and was still arguing with Clarence on the phone. "Would you like to come back to the house and call her since the phone's tied up here? I can give you a ride. She said it was *very* important."

A note of disquiet went through me. Laura wasn't the type to light fires without a reason. "I guess I'd better." I glanced at the unfinished newspaper layout, and then at True. "Let me tell True I'm leaving."

"Very good." Mrs. H. stepped toward the door, leaving us discretely alone.

Turning around, I walked to the desk and waved a hand in front of True.

"Clarence, can you hold on a minute? Clarence, can . . . Clarence . . ." He finally held the phone away from his ear as the old man's ranting went on.

"Sorry about all this," he whispered, but he didn't seem too sorry. I had a feeling he'd rather be talking about tractors than pasting up the paper. "You get the paper done?"

"No." I leaned close and spoke quietly, so I wouldn't be heard on the phone. "I have to go back to Hawthorne House and return a call from my editor. I guess you're on your own, big guy."

He rolled his eyes upward like a lazy hound begging to be scratched. "But you're coming back, right?"

Gathering all of my resolve, I leaned near to his ear and whispered, "I don't want you to get spoiled."

He grabbed the front of my shirt, pulled me closer, and kissed me good-bye as Clarence droned on about tractors on the phone.

Then he let go of my shirt and gave me that irresistible grin. "Spoil me. Come back later."

"I'll try." Straightening my shirt, I stood up and saw Mrs. Hawthorne watching us from the doorway, smiling ear to ear. I wanted to wave my magic wand and disappear.

Instead I grabbed my things and followed her to the car.

We were barely past the dollar store when she drew a long breath and said, "So it looks like things are getting serious between you and our Truitt McKitrick."

I felt like a thirteen-year-old being dragged into a sex talk with Mom. "I wouldn't say that." *Lie, lie, lie.* "We've only known each other a few days."

Mrs. Hawthorne looked very wise and very sure of herself. "Sometimes that's all it takes. When things are right, they're right. Sometimes you just know something's meant to be. I'm never wrong about these things. I don't play Cupid very often, but when I do, I'm sure of it. I can promise you that." She paused, concentrating on the oncoming traffic as she waited for a chance to pull onto the highway, then squealed into a space between cars. "I don't play Cupid unless I know what I'm doing."

I sighed and looked sideways at her, regretting having gotten in the car in the first place. A walk would have been less stressful, and quieter. The truth slipped past my lips. "Please don't play Cupid with me, Mrs. Hawthorne. I know you mean well, but I have to go back to D.C. in a few weeks."

Her shoulders slumped, and she looked crushed. I

instantly felt bad. But it was the truth.

She drew a long breath, straightening her body as the air came in, like a puffer fish blowing up for a confrontation. "Is there somebody waiting for you back there?"

"Well, no, but—"

"Can't you write your magazine articles from anyplace?"

"Well, yes, but—"

"Then the problem is really just in your mind."

I shook my head, relieved that we were pulling into the driveway of Hawthorne House and I would be able to end the conversation. "There's more to it than that."

Slipping the car into park behind what appeared to be my new rental car, Mrs. H. looked at me and gave a slow, knowing smile. I caught a glimpse of thoughts I couldn't quite read. "Oh, of course. There always is."

I wondered what was behind the hooded expression in her eyes as we exited the car. I thanked her for the ride and started toward my cottage.

"Feel free to come use the phone in my office, if you have trouble with the one out there," she called, bracing her hands on her hips and looking at the phone line overhead. "Looks like there's a squirrel on the pole. . . ."

Shaking my head, I went inside and gathered my notes, trying to get myself in the right frame of mind for a conference with Laura. But my mind didn't want to travel into that frame. My mind wanted to stay in San Saline, not whiz through a phone line at the speed of light, into the real world.

A finger of dread scratched up my back as I picked up the phone and dialed Laura's number. Sorting through my notes, I listened to the directions of the electronic operator at Landerhaus Publishing Company, then typed in Laura's extension number.

The line clicked and she answered, "This is Laura Draper." My stomach knotted up. "You have reached my voice mail. I'm out of the office. Please leave a message and I will return your call."

Relief melted through me. "Hi, Laura. This is Collie returning your call at"—I glanced at the clock—"twelve o'clock Texas time. I guess you're still at lunch. I'll try you back in a half hour or so, or you can call me." Then I hung up and went outside to check my new rental car.

To my great relief, the car was white. When I glanced inside, there were only three thousand miles on the odometer, so I figured chances were fair that it was in good working order.

Mrs. Hawthorne stepped onto the porch of the main house with a tray in her hands. "Come on up and have some lunch with me, Collie. I've fixed some nice chicken salad and apple-ring pickles." She set the tray on a small wicker table in the corner of the porch. "Did you finish your call already?"

"No," I answered, walking reluctantly up the steps. I didn't want to continue our earlier conversation. "Laura must have been at lunch. I'm sort of waiting for her to call me back."

Mrs. H. glanced toward my cabin. "Well, the screen's open. You can hear it ring from here. Have some chicken salad. The tea is fresh-brewed."

I crossed the porch and sat at the table with her. My stomach was still knotted up, and I didn't feel much like eating.

"Laura didn't say what she wanted?" I asked.

Mrs. H. twisted her lips to one side, looking down to wipe a spot of mayonnaise off her flowered T-shirt. "No. She didn't seem to want to tell me. I asked, of course." As if it were the most natural thing in the world for her to be nosing into my business calls.

I pictured Laura trying to dodge Mrs. Hawthorne's determination, and I tried not to laugh. "Don't worry about it. I'll find out soon enough. It's probably just some editorial stuff about the article I sent in." I was trying to convince myself more than her, trying to forget that Laura's message had come with *very important* attached to it. And that wasn't like Laura at all.

We sat eating in silence, watching the birds wander around on the lawn looking for worms.

Finally Mrs. H. leaned away from her plate and crossed her arms over her chest, sighing. "You know, I haven't always lived in San Saline. Oh, I've been here for thirty-some years and now it seems like I never lived anywhere else, but I grew up in California."

I set down my tea and relaxed in my chair, relieved to be talking about her and not me. "I didn't know that. You seem so at home here. I thought you were from San Saline."

She giggled, her weight making the old wicker chair rustle and squeal. "Oh, heavens, no. I wasn't always who I am now." Her chin tilted upward and her eyes drifted partway closed. She gazed across the yard, into the past. "Once upon a time I was a little tiny lady with big dreams." Looking down, she smoothed her oversize shirt and shook her head. "I didn't gain all this weight until I hit the change of life, you know." She raised a finger, with a sudden thought, then stood up and pointed at me. "Just a minute. I have something I want to show you." And she disappeared into the house in a hurry, then returned a few moments later with an old black leather-bound scrapbook in her hands. Laying it on the table, she opened to a black-and-white picture of a tiny young woman in jockey's silks, posed atop a sleek black racehorse.

"I was going to be the first woman jockey to win the Kentucky Derby," she said, sinking into her chair and tilting her head so she could see the picture, too. "Oh, Lordy, wasn't I a sight? My daddy was a trainer out in California, so I'd been riding racehorses for as long as I could remember. I was good at it too, as good as any man in my day. Only problem was, I wasn't born a man. Back then, women really couldn't get the work, except at bush-league tracks and as exercise riders."

Shaking her head, she looked at me and smiled, stroking her fingers over the picture. I smiled back, because I understood what she was saying. My mind rushed to paint a new picture of her, and I was amazed at how much I had wrongly assumed.

She turned to a page with a faded racing program and a picture of a photo finish. "This is me winning on a long shot. I was a good rider. I knew those horses like the back of my own hand. I could feel everything they had in them and bring it out. Women have a feel for horses that men don't have." She chuckled softly. "But you couldn't convince any of the owners of that back then. But times were changing, and I knew if I just kept racing long enough, I'd get my chance at a real racetrack. My daddy believed I could do it, too." She pointed to one of the pictures. "That's him. Lord, he was good to me. He believed I was one of the best riders ever. . . ."

She paused for a moment, and I carefully turned the pages of the book, looking at a tiny female jockey whose smile I now recognized and whose dreams I understood.

Mrs. Hawthorne went on, and I could hear the young woman in the pictures speaking. "I always thought that would be my life, especially after I was past thirty, ancient for a gal in my days, and all my old girlfriends were married with babies, and I was still riding horses." She stroked her fingers over another of the pictures, one of men in cowboy hats roping and branding calves. I recognized the young jockey woman there, too, except she was wearing a cowboy hat and holding a rope, her dark hair flying in the breeze beneath the brim of her hat. "And then I came to San Antonio to exercise horses on a winter farm there. I met Jasper, and as soon as he brought me home to this place, I felt something. By the time the winter was over, the racetrack was so far from my mind, I could hardly imagine it anymore. Then spring came, and the races were in the newspaper, and I started thinking about it again."

The intensity of her gaze drew me away from the book, and I looked into the sparkling eyes of the girl who once wanted to win the Kentucky Derby. "I sat right here on this porch, right where you are now, and I thought about which dream I wanted to give up and which one I wanted to keep. I thought about whether I was too old to marry a man and start a family. Finally I just made my choice, and I've never been sorry. If I'd gone back to the horses, I'd probably be an old, fat, lonely lady with some pictures and faded ribbons on my wall. I wouldn't have my Jasper and my Jennifer and my Jimmy, and Becky, such as she is." Her head inclined to one side, and she smiled slightly. She knew I understood. "The things that glitter the most in life aren't the things that last. Oh, that glitter lights your path for a while, but then it burns out, and if you're not careful, you find you've let the real things pass you by in the meanwhile. Sometimes your chances don't come around but once."

The afternoon breeze stirred the pages of the photo album, lifting the corners of the pictures, carrying the musty scent of aging paper, of time passing, of something real drifting by. I stared at the face of the young jockey in the pictures and wondered who she would have been if she had made the other choice. I wondered if I could do as she had done, leave one life behind and step into another without looking back. I wondered if, maybe, it wasn't too late, after all.

Sometimes your chances don't come around but once. . . .

The phone rang in my cabin, and both of us jumped,

startled by the unnatural sound cutting through the quiet hill-country afternoon.

"That's my call," I said, and jumped up, hurrying to catch the phone before Laura hung up.

I was breathless when I picked up the receiver and said hello.

"Collie?" Laura's voice.

"Hi, Laura," I took a swallow of water from a glass on the counter, trying to catch my breath. "I'm sorry; I had to run for the phone. What's up?"

"Collie, where have you been?" The tone of Laura's voice sent a mad rush of adrenaline through my body. "I've been trying to reach you since Friday."

"Sorry. I've been a little out of touch. What's going on?" A sense of dread descended over me like heavy black smoke, choking out the brightness of the day. I knew, without being told, that everything was about to change.

Chapter 13

"FOR heaven's sake, Collie, don't you watch the news?" Laura sounded frustrated and uncharacteristically emotional. "It's been all over the place."

Don't you watch the news? My mind raced to make some sense of it, to understand what the news could possibly have to do with me in San Saline, Texas. "I'm sorry, Laura." Maybe there had been a big fire in D.C. Maybe my apartment had burned to the ground. Maybe the newspaper office had been vaporized. "You're going to have to fill me in. I don't have a clue what you're talking about. I haven't seen anything but the Cowboy Channel for a week now."

Laura didn't laugh. I knew something was very wrong.

"The whole thing at your newspaper has blown wide open," she went on. "It's all over the news. Your boss has been brought up on *federal* charges . . . blackmail, bribing a public official, embezzling, you name it."

I stood there with the phone buzzing in my ear, staring at the plastic wagon-wheel clock on the wall and feeling it drift farther and farther away, as if I were passing into a long tunnel. *Tick. Tick. Tick* . . .

"Collie, are you still there?" Laura's voice came from somewhere outside the tunnel. "Hello? That little Williams libel suit you testified in was just the tip of the iceberg. Your ex-boss, Ross Bennett, was into all kinds of crap. He had a little black book of senators and House members. They say he was *blackmailing* people to get them to give huge government contracts to businesses he was invested in. Senators and House members were rolling over for him because they didn't want him exposing their secrets in the *Business Daily.* Over the years, he had managed to uncover a lot of dirt about a lot of important people. He used the newspaper to slaughter anybody who wouldn't go along with him and his cronies. That's why he put out that article about Senator Williams last year before the election. He knew if Williams got in office again, he was going to oppose a big government housing contract to one of Bennett's businesses. Bennett wanted to make sure Senator Williams didn't get re-elected, so he printed that article about how Senator Williams took illegal campaign contributions. The only problem was that this time Bennett's sources weren't good, and Senator Williams took him to court for libel."

"Oh, my God," I muttered. My mind jolted into action, and the room around me came into focus again. All the events of the past months became clear. Crystal clear. "That's why he rolled over on me in the lawsuit. That's why he made it look like I was the one who wrote the article about Senator Williams, when really it was his article. All I did was edit it and touch it up."

My thoughts were clicking like a train rushing down the fast track. "He didn't want the information to be traced back to him, because he was afraid someone would find out about all of the things he was into. That's why he was so desperate to have me lie on the witness stand and say I wrote the story. He said the paper would protect me, and that the case would go better if I took responsibility as author of the article and refused to reveal my sources for the information in it. He almost had me convinced to do it, too. But then when I got on the witness stand, I couldn't do it. I told the truth."

The train slammed headlong into a brick wall, and I stood looking over the wreckage of my life, putting the pieces together like a puzzle. "This is huge. I was right in the middle of it all, and I didn't have a clue what was happening." I was blinded like a rabbit in the headlights of an oncoming truck. The legal case had gone by so fast, I never knew what hit me. The paper lost the case, paid damages to Senator Williams. To everyone on the outside, it looked like I was the cause of it all. It looked like my sloppy reporting had cost my employer millions. I was fired the day after the case was over, and suddenly I was a pariah to every employer in town.

Laura let out a long breath on the other end of the phone. "Well, it's all out in the open now. Bennett is going to be toast by the time federal prosecutors get through with him. Turns out they've had him under investigation for a couple of months now, and they've got a file on him a foot thick. You're lucky you got out of there when you did. Word is, they think some of the higher-ups at the paper might be involved with him."

"Amazing." I felt numb, confused, a little scared. "I'm not going to end up in court again, am I?"

"No," she answered. "The case seems to be focused only on events in the last few months. You're lucky you got out of there."

"No kidding," I said, breathing a long sigh of relief. "You don't know how glad I am that I'm not involved in this."

Laura chuckled under her breath. "Oh, but you are. *Everyone* in D.C. is looking for you, girlfriend." Her words rushed with excitement. "Everyone wants to interview you, since you were in the middle of a related case, but you haven't been called to testify in this one, so you're not under a court gag order. Everyone wants to hear what you've got to say—to see if you have any inside information. And I mean *everyone*. The TV stations, the papers. The evening news wants to make you a special consultant. *Network TV*. The biggest of the big! Can you believe it?"

"You're kidding," I whispered, hardly able to catch my breath. "Where did you hear all this?"

There was a pause, during which I had the eerie feeling my friend was hiding something. "It's your big chance, Coll. You've got to get on a plane and get back to D.C."

"Well . . . but . . ." *But I have to go to San Antonio tomorrow with True the Tractor Man.* My mind struggled to process the idea of jumping back into the lion's den in D.C. "I . . . haven't finished this article series yet."

"What are you, *nuts?*" The volume of Laura's voice reverberated through the old black phone and into the room. "Hel-lo . . . Collie . . . are you high on mesquite beans or something? We're talking about *network* TV here. Forget the articles. The first one's fine. I'll get someone else for the rest. Get your butt on a plane and get back to D.C. This is your big break, Coll. I'm going to try to clear a few days on my schedule and fly up. I've got to see all this for myself." She caught her breath, and I could hear a twitter of excitement. "Get on a plane. Tonight."

Get on a plane. Tonight. I stared out the window at Mrs. Hawthorne, still sipping iced tea and looking at her memory book, unaware that a bomb had exploded not thirty feet from her. Suddenly she seemed very far away, as if she and Hawthorne House and the entire town of San Saline were shrinking with each tick of the clock.

Get on a plane. Tick . . . tick. Tonight. Tick . . .

"It'll have to be tomorrow." My stomach felt queasy.

"I can't get to the airport tonight. I'm out in the middle of nowhere." *And I have to explain this to True, and Mrs. Hawthorne, and . . .*

Laura huffed an irritated sigh. "All right. Tomorrow, then. Let me know when you're flying in. Be ready when you get there. The scavengers are looking for you. Reporters are camped out everywhere. By the way, don't give your story away for free. Make sure you field all your offers before you make any deals."

"I will." I stumbled a few feet to the table and sank into a chair, rubbing my eyes, my head spinning. "Laura, who told you all of this?"

There was another long pause, then finally she said, "Brett called me. He said his phone had been ringing off the hook with people looking for you. He thought I might know where you were."

The spinning grew faster, more sickening, like a merry-go-round out of control. "Why would he think that?" Brett had met my old college roommate, Laura, a few times when she visited me, but he would have no way of knowing I was doing articles for her.

Another pause, during which I could feel Laura squirming as if the phone line were twisting into a noose. "Well . . . Coll . . . he was the one who called and asked me to give you this Texas job in the first place."

I drew in a quick, infuriated gasp of air, and she quickly went on. "Now, Collie, don't get all in a fit. Brett was just worried about you. He said you'd been lying around in the apartment for months, and you wouldn't talk to anybody, and you hadn't even been home to see your parents. He was worried about you."

"Oh, I'll bet," I bit out, blood flaming into my face. I had sunk so low as to be a mercy case even to my shmuck of an ex-boyfriend. The man who dumped me the minute the legal trouble began because he was worried about losing his job as marketing VP for the paper, and worried about having a smear on his name that might affect his eventual political aspirations. Six years together meant practically nothing to him. "This gets worse and worse! He was probably trying to get me out of D.C. so I wouldn't sue the paper for firing me. Bennett probably told him to get me out of town."

"Give the guy a break," Laura soothed, and I could tell Brett had worked his public relations magic on her. "I really think he was trying to do something decent. He feels pretty bad about the way things turned out. Anyway, it doesn't matter now. You're back on top, Coll."

"I guess so." Then why did I feel myself sinking into the pit again?

"Let me know when you're flying in."

"I will."

And we said good-bye. I hung up the phone and sat staring out the window, thinking about D.C. and clamoring newspaper reporters, network TV deals and political blackmail, about Brett calling Laura and about revenge against the people who had destroyed my life.

A peacock raised its feathers on the lawn just beyond the cottage and turned slowly in circles, glinting in and out of the afternoon sun. A day ago, I would have stopped to watch, but suddenly the world outside my window seemed a million miles away.

Taking a quick look around the stone cottage, I calculated the time it would take to get my things packed and ready to go. Then I went outside and told Mrs. Hawthorne I would be leaving in the morning, and why. I told her that a big story had broken, and I was going to cover it. I didn't tell her I *was* part of the story.

She looked unconcerned at first. Then she seemed to realize I was leaving and not coming back. A hollow expression came over her, followed by a look of deep disappointment. She sat shaking her head, speechless for what seemed like an eternity.

"Oh, Collie, I just hate to see you go." She stood up and stepped forward, her hands suspended between us, as if she wanted to hold me there. "I just . . ." A fictional life filled the air between us, and I knew what she was thinking. *I just thought you were going to stay in San Saline, marry True the Tractor Man and start attending ladies' suppers.* She shook her head, sighed, then said, "We're just going to miss you around here."

Get on a plane. Tonight. "I'll be back." Would I? *It's your big chance, Coll.* "This opportunity is just . . ." *You're back on top.* "I'd be crazy to pass it up."

Mrs. Hawthorne shook her head, knowing better, seeing herself, a young woman standing at the crossroads, making the other decision. She reached out slowly, took my hand in both of hers, and gazed deeply at me. I saw the slender, pretty girl astride the sleek racehorse.

"You take care of yourself." Her voice was hoarse

and deep with emotion. "Do what is going to make you happy in the long run." The final words were in the air, but never spoken. *Sometimes your chances don't come around but once.*

And that was where the conversation ended. I didn't want to stand with her anymore, in the spot where I had come so close to another life.

I told her I had to get busy packing. She nodded, pretending to focus on gathering the dishes onto her lunch tray; then she started toward the house. Halfway through the doorway, she stopped to ask if I needed her to do my laundry.

"No, but thank you. I'll get it done when I get back to D.C." The trembling of my own voice made my eyes burn. Shaking it off, I turned and headed toward the cabin.

Get a grip, Collie. Get a grip. What was wrong with me, anyway? This was the opportunity of a lifetime. Everything I'd ever worked toward and could probably never have achieved, handed to me on a silver platter. No more clawing my way up. Just fielding offers, and taking the best of them. What could be better than that?

I called my apartment and checked the messages on my machine. It was just as Laura had said. The tape was full—reporters calling for interviews; newspaper and magazine editors who a month ago wouldn't have given me the time of day, now offering me jobs; two calls from TV stations and one from a network. The Bennett story was huge, as Laura had said, and everyone wanted an inside track. Why wasn't I excited?

"Geez, Collie, you've gone soft," I muttered to myself as I started tossing my things into my suitcase. "One week away from D.C. and you've lost all sense. What you need is a reality check. Just get back home and get to work, get in the thick of things, and . . ."

I went on as I packed, convincing myself little by little, bringing my mind back to a reasonable, logical vantage point.

Sorting through my notes and scraps of paper on the table, I unearthed the Friday edition of the *San Saline Record*—the one with all the gaps, uneven type, the headlines that didn't fit. Running my finger over a blurry picture of Little League practice at Mill Pond Park, I thought about the ice-cream social there, the fireworks . . . the kiss . . .

I thought about True, and my mind went soft again. Wrapping my fingers around the back of my neck, I rubbed the knot of tense muscles, closed my eyes, and tried to decide what I was going to say to True, how I was going to say good-bye, or *if* I was going to say good-bye, and if I was going to suggest a long-distance relationship. . . .

The smartest thing would be to cut the strings, end the fantasy, and go on with real life . . . Clean. Logical. Less painful.

After less than a week of knowing each another, nothing else was very realistic. If I suggested we try to continue on long-distance, True would probably think I was crazy. If I told him I was coming back, he would probably think I was lying, and probably I would be. The minute I stepped off the plane, D.C. was going to pull me in like a whirlwind, and there would be no getting out. Bennett's trial was huge. If it reached as far into the political ranks as Laura said, the story would go on for months, and so would I. My fifteen minutes of fame was at hand.

By the time it was over, I wouldn't be the same, and True would be . . . would be . . . settled into the fairy-tale castle with someone else?

Something stabbed just below my heart, like a broken rib puncturing some essential part of me.

Come on, Collie; don't do this to yourself.

Opening my eyes, I threw the Friday edition on the stack, buried it beneath my laptop, and headed for the door to get it over with, to make a clean break.

When I parked in front of the newspaper office, I could see True standing behind the light table, one hand wound into his hair, the other holding a bit of text, moving it here and there on the page. He looked frustrated, incompetent, charming . . . perfect.

Closing the car door quietly, I stood on the sidewalk and watched him, remembering our first meeting at the newspaper office, when Mrs. Hawthorne tried to push us together, remembering Saturday night, when we stood at the light table putting together the Monday edition, laughing, teasing, flirting, resisting the electricity that drew us together.

A diesel truck rumbled by on the other side of the square, and I turned to look over my shoulder, gazing at the quiet shade on the courthouse lawn, at the empty benches in front of the stores, where the old men would resume their daily vigils tomorrow, at the gigantic cowboy boot swinging lazily back and forth in front of Harvey's Boots-'n'-More, at the cattle pens and the glowing pink adobe of the Sale Barn Café.

Stories whispered in the air like the voices of ghosts—stories about the people, the buildings, the old sidewalk where occasionally bricks could still be found that read *Unlawful to spit on walk*, an effort to control cholera in some long-forgotten time.

How could it be that I felt I had a history here, after so short a time?

Is it possible that some things are meant to be . . . ?

"Any reason why you're standing out here on the curb?" True's voice made me jump, and I spun around unsteadily, slapping a hand over my heart.

He blinked at my reaction and gave me that lopsided grin. "Guilty conscience?"

"No." Not exactly the truth. "You surprised me, that's all."

He stood looking at me for just an instant, as if he were seeing through me, reading my mind. The smile faded, and his brows knotted together beneath a tangle of tawny hair. "Is something wrong, Collie?"

The fact that it showed on my face sent a pang of panic through me. I wondered what else was showing. "I'm . . . umm . . . I . . ." And then the truth spilled out. "I have to go back to D.C. In the morning."

He seemed as if he hadn't heard me or didn't get what I was saying. "Won't that put your magazine articles off schedule?" The wrinkle of concern deepened into a furrow. "Nothing wrong with your family, I hope."

The tone of his voice told me he'd misconstrued my meaning, or maybe he didn't want to understand. He thought I was going back to D.C. for a quick visit, to take care of something and then return to San Saline.

"No, it's not anything like that." I tried to think of how to say it, of what to say. My heart wanted to say nothing at all. "It's . . . a . . . job offer."

The last of his smile disappeared, fell into the grim line of a frown. He stared at the sidewalk, unable to look at me. "This is kind of a sudden turnabout. I thought . . . well, I didn't know you were looking for a job in D.C."

I swallowed the burning feeling in the back of my throat. "Well, I wasn't. I . . . You see, it's . . ." So much to say, and not the words to say it. *I wasn't stringing you along. I really felt something. I was thinking of moving to Texas and becoming a cowgirl until . . .*

Finally I just sat down on the bench beneath the newspaper window and blurted out the whole sordid story—my newspaper career, the political article that had started the trouble, the lawsuit, the termination from my job, the end of my career, the three months of hiding in my apartment, the offer from Laura, the new shake-up in D.C., the offers from talk shows, newspapers, networks. Every piece of the puzzle, scattered like shrapnel on the sidewalk where he stood, looking shell-shocked.

He blinked, clearing the fog from his eyes and seeing me for the first time. A long moment of silence passed between us, as if he were trying to decide what to say, how to react. Finally the warmth went out of his gaze, and there was only empty sky. "Sounds like it's an opportunity too good to pass up." He said it flatly, the way he might have remarked about a good buy on cattle. "I can't blame you for wanting to pursue it."

But I could tell he *did* blame me. I could see it in the way he tipped his chin up slightly, like a preacher sending down a look of disappointment and reproach. I had failed to live up to some unspoken test. I could tell it by the way he leaned against a porch pole instead of sitting down with me. He was keeping his distance—building the distance so he could let me go without emotion.

I felt a crushing sense of disappointment. Some part of me was hoping he would beg me to stay. A foolish, romantic notion.

Looking away from me, he stared across the courthouse lawn. "So when do you leave?"

The lump rose in my throat and my eyes started to burn. Why did I feel rejected, when I was the one saying good-bye? "In the morning. I need to get back as soon as I can. The story's blowing wide-open."

He nodded, watching the pecan trees rustle in the breeze. I wondered what he was thinking, but he wouldn't say. He just stood there staring, indicating that the conversation was over. Nothing left to say.

But there was. "True, I . . ." Saying his name made me ache inside, and I took a deep breath to clear my emotions. "I want you to understand that . . ." *I think I love you. . . .* "I didn't mean for things to turn out like this. I really thought I'd be here for a while, and we'd just . . . well . . . we'd just see what happened." He didn't react, so I went on, as if enough words could solve the problem. "I didn't know things were going to blow wide-open in D.C." *It's your big chance, Coll. You're back on top.* "It's just such an unbelievable opportunity. I could work for years and never be offered jobs like these."

A long sigh passed his lips. "I understand, Collie. I really do." Still leaning against the pole, his arms crossed over his chest, he turned to look at me. "I used to have that kind of ambition. I've sure been married to it. So you don't have to explain to me about wanting to make the big-time. I've been there."

The comparison of me to his ex-wife stung, and I sat there, taken aback. I didn't want to be lumped into the category with the woman who didn't want him if he wasn't going to be a rich lawyer. My situation was completely different. I still wanted him.

He must have realized that the words had wounded me, because he drew a breath and tried to explain. "I understand wanting something more than a sleepy little town like San Saline. Growing up, all I thought about was getting out of here. There was a man who owned a weekend ranch next door to ours—a lawyer from Dallas. Drove big cars and talked about big law cases, and I couldn't wait to go to law school and do what he did. When I got out of college, he helped me get a long way fast. Too fast. I got into a bunch of stuff I didn't have the belly for, and I made up my mind to get out—go to some small town, hang out a shingle and slow things down, raise Melody somewhere safe and decent."

He shook his head, crossing his arms tighter over his chest, trying to keep away the memories. "Things don't always work out the way you plan. My wife ended up married to my law partner, and Melody . . ." His voice trembled with emotion and he shook his head, looking down at the sidewalk.

I sat there numb, thinking of a little girl with True's blue eyes. A little girl who now had a name. *Melody.* I wanted to comfort True, but I didn't know how. "True, that wasn't your fault."

"Yes. It was."

"It was an accident."

"No. It was two adults fighting over furniture while their two-year-old daughter wandered into the swimming pool. Amazing, what things can seem important at the time . . ." He rubbed the pads of his fingers against his forehead, smoothing away the furrows, and the memories. "You know, I shut down after Melody died. I brought her here to bury her, and I never left. I couldn't leave. I didn't want to. I wanted to hide out from the world and pretend all of it never happened."

He turned slowly and met my gaze. I stood up and came close to him, close enough to touch him, but I didn't. I just listened as he went on, "I never thought about what I was doing until you came here. When you came, I woke up and realized I was walking through my life like a ghost. Five years, on hold. Just living in this apartment over the newspaper office, selling tractors, doing business, letting the time go by. But none of it brought Melody back. She isn't coming back. Life goes on whether you want it to or not."

Reaching out, I laid my hand over his arm without meaning to. I could feel his heart beating just below my fingers, slow, like a sleeper's. "Come to D.C. with me." I wondered where the words had come from. I stood breathless, hoping. . . .

His eyes, blue and clear, looked into mine. The corners of his mouth turned up slightly. "And do what? Be a D.C. lawyer?"

I smiled back, wondering at his thoughts, but his face was like a wall, hiding his emotions. "Plenty of work for lawyers in D.C."

Taking my hand in his, he brought my fingers to his lips and brushed them with a kiss. "I can't." The wall cracked, and his face was a tangle of emotion—sadness, love, regret. "Not even for you, Collie." He brought his other hand up and held mine tight against his chest, against his heart. "I don't have it in me to go back to that life. This is me. This place, my family. These are the things that matter. The big-time just isn't me anymore." Leaning down, he kissed me, soft, slow, lingering. Then he pulled away and looked at me again. "Go back to D.C., Collie. Knock 'em dead. I hope you get everything you want."

I want you. But I couldn't say a word. I just stood there, my eyes filling with tears.

He smoothed a stray curl from my forehead and wiped a drifting tear with the pad of his thumb. "Go back to Washington. Hire a good lawyer when you get there. You have strong grounds for a wrongful-termination suit against your newspaper. It's a can't-lose proposition. Good luck, Collie. Good-bye." Then he kissed me on the forehead, let go of my hand, and walked into the newspaper office, leaving me on the sidewalk.

I turned and left without looking back. I knew if I did, I wouldn't leave at all.

The sun was dipping below the hills to the west as I drove around the square. Watching the image of my car reflected in the storefront windows, I remembered the feeling I'd had my first day there—the sense of a place that was constant, frozen in time, too far from the rest of the world to change, or maybe just too stubborn. I remembered that sense of peace, of belonging to the quiet landscape and the drowsy town.

Those feelings were absent now. The peace was lost. I was nothing but another outsider in a rental car in a hurry to get somewhere. Reflected in the storefront windows for a moment, then gone. I felt an overwhelming sense of ending, and it made me want to get on the road, get back to Dallas and on a plane. Forget everything.

I thought about it as I pulled into the driveway at Hawthorne House and stepped quietly from my car, then hurried to the cottage. I didn't want to see Mrs. Hawthorne, or Jasper, or Becky. I wanted to be gone.

Slipping inside, I hurried with the rest of the packing, throwing into a suitcase most of the clothes that would go to the laundry when I got back to D.C. Setting the case on the bench at the foot of the bed, I walked to the table to finish sorting my notes, research materials, and photographs.

Standing at the table, I looked into the darkness

beyond the gently fluttering lace curtains, toward the main house. In one window, I could see Jasper in his favorite chair, watching the Cowboy Channel. In another, I could see Mrs. Hawthorne with her memory book, slowly turning the pages. I wondered what her thoughts were. Was she thinking of me, or of the young woman in the pictures and where she might have ended up if she had chosen to pursue her dream?

I'd probably be an old, fat, lonely lady with some pictures and faded ribbons on my wall. . . . Was that true? Was that really what would have happened? Or was it just easier for her to believe her dream would have turned out that way?

Did she ever regret the path she had chosen to follow? She said not. She said that the other life wouldn't have been so grand, after all. But that is the trouble with the road not taken. Or perhaps it is merciful that you never really know where it would have led.

I looked around the room, wondering why life was filled with such painful choices. This or that, but no in-between. I wondered why it wasn't possible to have both—the quiet and the noise, the racehorse and the ranch land, the big-time and all the little things.

My rush to leave evaporated like a puff of smoke. I wanted to stay one more night, to enjoy the quiet and wake with the peacocks and struggle to wash my hair in the old claw-footed tub.

I wanted to stand just a little longer at the fork in the road, before moving on and leaving one path behind.

I called the airport and booked a flight for the next

day, then settled on the couch and watched a few hours of the Cowboy Channel. It was Tom Mix night, and the old black-and-white movies made me laugh. A commercial with True sitting on a donkey made me cry, and I turned off the television and went to bed.

I dreamed of a slender young woman in bright, billowing silks—amber and gold and violet, like the hill country at sunset. She raced on a sleek black horse, swift and silent as the wind. Her face was my face, her hands my hands. Together we flew toward the hills, racing, racing, trying to reach the horizon.

But the horizon never got any closer. No matter how fast I ran, or how far I traveled, I could never get there. It was an impractical dream, and like all impractical dreams, it remained out of reach. Eventually I had to settle for where I was.

Chapter 14

MORNING slipped beneath the window shades like a thief. When I awoke, muted flecks of sunlight had already ventured to the rug in the center of the floor. The air was silent, and the cool scent of rain was everywhere. I wondered if it had drowned out the peacocks' morning complaints, or if I had slept through the noise.

I glanced at the clock, and my heart lurched to wakefulness. Nearly eight. I needed to be leaving for Dallas no later than nine. Throwing off the covers, I hurried to the bathroom, washed and dressed in a blue silk suit, pinned my hair back, and threw the rest of my things in the suitcases. After loading the bags in my car, I checked the cabin once more, then hurried through the sprinkle of rain to the main house to pay my bill and give the keys to the Hawthornes.

I tried not to look at the empty wicker porch chairs as I waited for someone to answer the door. I didn't want to think about sitting there, talking about forks in the road, and life's hard decisions, and all the chances that come our way only once.

Jasper answered, holding the TV remote in one hand and a flyswatter in the other. He gave me a confused look. "You're not leavin' already, are ya?"

"Yes." The word sounded like an apology. "I have to get to DFW Airport, but I wanted to give you the keys and pay my bill before I left town."

He seemed to think about that for a moment. "Well, you can leave the keys with me, but the missus is already across the road at the café. You'll have to scoot on over there and ask her to figure the bill." The corners of his gray mustache twitched upward, and he raised the flyswatter. "I just fix stuff and swat flies. Paperwork ain't my department."

"All right," I said, considering asking if I could pay the bill by mail. The last thing I felt like doing was going to the café, where True might be.

"The missus will want to say good-bye to ya anyway." Jasper seemed to know what I was thinking. "Reckon that's why she didn't leave the bill here with me."

"I suppose," I said, and turned to leave, then stopped on the top step and glanced back, because I could feel him watching me. "Jasper?"

"Yes, ma'am?"

Do you think I'm doing the right thing? Am I looking too far down the road? Not far enough? "Thanks for everything."

"You're welcome, Collie." His eyes met mine and seemed to read the questions in my mind. "Don't be a stranger. Ye're welcome back here anytime."

"Thank you, Jasper." And I hurried down the steps, through the rain to my car. Thunder rumbled somewhere in the distance as I started the engine and drove to the café.

My heart was in my throat by the time I rolled into the parking lot and looked for the Friendly's truck. I didn't know if I wanted it to be there or not.

I wasn't sure how I felt when it wasn't. Disappointed, a little relieved, hurt, and a mixture of other things I couldn't put into words. There was a sense of ending, a little like going to a funeral. I was glad that the parking lot was full and Mrs. Hawthorne wouldn't have much time to talk. I didn't want to examine what I was thinking or what I was leaving behind. I just wanted to get on the road and not think about anything.

Malachi was waiting under the small front awning when I dashed through the rain. Standing close together in the dry space, we smiled at each other.

"I heard you was leavin' town, Miss Angel," he said, his aged parchment eyes regarding me sadly. "We're sure gonna hate to see you go. You been givin' this ol' place a little sparkle."

I wondered how he knew I was leaving. "I'm going to miss it here." It was the first time I had admitted it.

"This has been quite a trip. It's hard . . . to say goodbye." A lump of emotion choked my throat, and my eyes started to burn.

Malachi seemed to understand. He reached across the space between us and took my hand in both of his with the practice of a man who made a life of comforting others. There was a tremor in his fingers that I had never noticed before. "Well, now, don't you forget we're here. You're welcome at my catfish fry anytime."

Taking a deep breath, I swallowed hard and gathered my thoughts, because I didn't want to make any promises I couldn't keep. I didn't know if I would ever be coming back. Chances were, I wouldn't. "I want you to know that one of the best things about this trip has been meeting you. Malachi, I think you're one of the best men I've ever had the pleasure of knowing."

Malachi hooded his eyes like a bashful child and looked at our intertwined hands. Chuckling, he patted my fingers. "Oh, now, you better stop all that. You'll turn my head." Letting go of my hand, he reached for the door and held it open. "Guess I'd better get on with what I come here fo'. Gotta pick up a sack a' doughnut holes fo' the folks at the rest home." He gave me a sly sideways look as I slipped through the door. "I'm a pretty popular fella over there 'cuz I always show up with a sweet. Them folks don't get much sugar." Following me through the door, he shook his head. "Little sweet never hurt nobody. Makes them poor folks happy."

"I'll bet it does," I agreed, and we parted ways as he

went to the cash register and I moved to the end of the counter to catch Mrs. Hawthorne as she finished pouring coffee for a group of men in cowboy hats at the bar.

The cactus-killing cowboy looked up and tipped his hat at me as I waited. Then he went back to watching the morning news on TV. I recognized Pennsylvania Avenue on the screen, filled with people marching and carrying signs, something about the killing of an innocent African-American man by police, and the lack of opportunity for black men in society.

Home. But it seemed a million miles away.

I glanced at Malachi, wondering if he could hear the speeches as he paid for his doughnuts and turned to leave. I wondered what he would think and what he would have to say about the issue.

"Well, don't that just beat all?" The cactus-killing cowboy waved a forkful of eggs at the TV and turned to the man beside him. "More of them welfare people cryin' about how bad they got it. I don't git no welfare money or no affirmative action, and I ain't cryin'. I have to work my butt off to make a livin'. I'd have a heck of a lot more money if I didn't have to pay taxes to support all them welfare people so they can spend their time marchin' in front of the White House. Trouble with this country is all the damned lazy niggers."

Anger and shame rushed hot into my face, and I stepped back unsteadily, turning to see Malachi shuffling across the floor just a few feet away, too close not to have heard. He paused for a moment in his stride, and I held my breath, waiting for him to turn on the younger man, waiting for him to shake a righteous finger and quote from the word of God.

The room went silent, as if everyone else were waiting, too.

But Malachi just reached out and opened the door, then shuffled through, his lips moving, his words audible only because the room was so silent. ". . . and where there is injury, let me bring pardon . . ." Then the door closed and the prayer was gone along with him.

The cactus-killing cowboy continued watching the TV, oblivious to what was happening around him.

The waitress at the cash register slammed the drawer shut, jolting the room back to life. She gave the cowboy an angry sneer. "Good Lord, Ray! Malachi was standing right behind you when you said that."

Ray turned from the TV with a hollow-eyed look of incomprehension. "Well, shoot, I . . ." He glanced up as Mrs. Hawthorne set a coffee cup loudly on the counter in front of him and began filling it with coffee that sloshed hot onto the red Formica counter. Looking down at his plate, he stammered on. "When I said *nigger* . . . well, I didn't mean him. Malachi ain't a nigger. I've knowed him since I was a kid. He used to give me suckers at the grocery store. Malachi's a good ol' boy."

Mrs. Hawthorne gave him a tight-lipped look, her face angry and red. "Well, Ray, I don't imagine he heard what you *meant*. I imagine he heard what you *said*. That's usually the way things work." Whisking the coffeepot away, she stepped sideways to stand in front of me, leaving Ray muttering.

"Good morning, Collie. Can I help you?" Mrs. Hawthorne's words were curt and quick, and I wondered if she was still mad at Ray, or if she was angry with me.

Suddenly I wanted to be out of there. The magic was gone, and the café seemed like every other place in the world. Same problems. Same prejudices. Same people saying the same cruel things to one another. Just like home. "I gave Jasper the keys to the cottage, but he said I should come over here and see you for the bill. I have to be heading out of town in a few minutes. . . ."

Turning to set the coffeepot on the burner, she glanced around the busy room, then reached to pick up an order pad. "I'll tell you what. Why don't you just write down your address and phone number, and I'll write or call you with the bill. I don't have it figured up yet."

"All right," I said. "You're sure that's OK?"

Nodding, she gave me a quick smile, but then turned away as if she wanted to forget I was asking for the bill on my way out of town. "That'll be fine. I'll figure it up and let you know in a day or two. We sure have enjoyed your visit. You have a good flight home." She tore a page off the pad and laid it in front of me.

"I will," I said, writing my address and phone number on the paper. "Thanks for everything." I glanced at her, but she was occupied with filling a sugar canister.

"You're welcome. Don't be a stranger."

"I won't." I slid the paper across the counter.

"Good-bye, Collie." I had a flash of True saying the same thing.

"Good-bye." And I turned and hurried from the room, hoping I could still catch Malachi in the parking lot and tell him good-bye. I didn't want his last memory of me to be one in which I stood silent while some idiot spouted racial slurs. I should have said something when it happened instead of standing there with my mouth open. . . .

Malachi's old car was just crossing the parking lot as I walked out the door. He stuck his arm out the window and waved at me as he passed, and I waved back. I hoped he understood. . . .

Watching the old cream-colored car disappear down Main Street, I felt my eyes clear as if a fog were being lifted. The sense of magic was gone, and suddenly San Saline looked just like every other decaying rural town on the map. Like Dorothy, I was realizing that Oz was just an illusion.

I fixed my eyes on the centerline of the highway and drove out of town. I could feel the landmarks passing—the café, the newspaper office, Harvey's Boots-'n'-More, Mill Creek Park and the baseball fields where fireworks marked beginnings. I didn't look. I didn't let myself. I stared straight ahead and drove out of town, not looking back, not looking too far down the road. Just driving.

I tried not to think as I drove north and east toward Dallas, toward the real world and everything I had ever wanted. In my mind, I planned what I was going to do when I got home. . . .

Get to my apartment on Mass Avenue. Start making phone calls. Field offers. Maybe get an agent to field offers, if they were as lucrative as Laura indicated. Get to work. See a lawyer. Get revenge. Sail to the top of the heap and have it all.

It's your big chance, Coll. . . .

There is no Oz. Life is the same everywhere.

I repeated it to myself as the miles rolled by, as the countryside gradually turned from jagged, boulder-strewn hills filled with bluebonnets and lacy mesquite trees, to softly rolling grassland, growing more populated, more like home and less like the other side of the world.

The skyscrapers of Dallas rose on the horizon, and traffic closed in around me as I sped closer. I started remembering how fast the rest of the world moved, and a tingle of excitement went through me. I started remembering the person I was three months ago. . . .

A white pickup truck towing a tractor on a flatbed trailer pulled onto the highway from an exit lane ahead of me, and the thoughts rushed away. I stepped on the gas to catch up with the truck, my mind whirling ahead, thinking that maybe . . . by some miracle . . .

. . . *some things are meant to be.*

The man in the driver's seat gave me an irritated sideways glance as I caught up and stared at his truck, reading the sign on the side. *C&M Construction Company.*

Taking my foot off the gas, I let him move ahead again, then leaned my head against the headrest and exhaled the breath I had been holding.

"Come on, Collie," I muttered. "Get a grip. Let's be realistic." But some part of me still wanted to believe in that dream of things meant to be. Some part was still waiting for True to come swooping in like Peter Pan and whisk me off to Never-Never Land, where I wouldn't have to grow up.

I wondered where True was and what he was thinking. I wondered if he was going about his normal routine, working on the Wednesday edition, occupied with his daily business. I wondered if he was thinking about me, or not. . . .

I wondered why he wasn't at the café for breakfast, and if he had wanted to come after me and just wouldn't let himself, or if he just didn't care. I wondered if he really thought I was like his ex-wife, only after money and success.

I wondered if I was. . . .

The airport exit appeared ahead and I thought about passing it by, making the loop around Dallas and heading south again into the hills.

What are you, nuts? . . . Are you high on mesquite beans or something? Laura's voice drummed in my ear.

I turned the wheel to the side and skidded the car across the reflectors and onto the exit ramp. All this self-torture over someplace and someone I'd known only a week was crazy. The truth was that I was trying to make it into something more than it was—the wishful thinking of a lonely heart and a thundering biological clock.

The truth was that if I meant that much to True, he

would have found a way to keep us together. He would have come to D.C. with me—for a while, anyway. He would have planned to call, write, made me promise to come back at some time in the future. He would have been at the café this morning. . . .

The truth was that if it really mattered, he wouldn't have let go of it so easily, and neither would I. The truth was that you couldn't really be in love with someone after only seven days.

By the time I got to the airport, I had myself convinced, hardened, even a little bitter. I crammed my stack of loose notes and photos into an envelope and sent it to Laura from the overnight mail counter, then returned the rental car keys and hurried to the plane, determined to forget all about Texas. I was feeling like Colleen Collins again, and I was ready to get back to D.C. and go for blood.

D.C. was also ready for me, and also out for blood. My first hours back were a nightmare. Word that I was returning had leaked out, and a group of shrewd reporters had gotten the passenger lists for incoming planes—something I would have done in the past. They met me at the gate with cameras rolling, spotlights glaring, and microphones prodding me from all directions. Everyone wanted to know what I had to say about the biggest case to hit Washington in years. Those who had once been acquaintances and friends had now become predators, like a pack of hungry lions turning on one of their own. They shouted questions about my ex-boss, accusations about how much I knew about the blackmail of political officials, and demands that I explain my full involvement in the past libel case brought by Senator Williams.

I pushed my way through the crowd, angry and shaking, and said nothing. It was no fun to be on the other side of my profession. I made up my mind to sign an exclusive contract and get to work somewhere, so everyone else would leave me alone.

A throng was camped outside my apartment building too. Mass Avenue was parked solid with cars and satellite vans, and people were sitting on the curb and the sidewalk as if there were some huge block party going on. I could imagine how the quiet, retired people in my apartment building were taking the excitement.

I paid the cabdriver extra to turn around before they saw me and let me out a block over, so I could sneak in the back way. Luckily, no one suspected that I would carry my suitcase a half mile up an empty drainage ditch to get into the building unseen. Slipping through the back door, I breathed a sigh of relief, then hurried onto the elevator and up to my apartment. Inside, the air was musty and dark. The answering machine was full again and the phone was ringing. With a sense of being out-of-body, I reached over and switched off the ringer, then walked slowly to the window and peeked through the blinds, a prisoner looking out of my cell.

There was a fresh batch of red roses on my breakfast table, with a card pinned to the ribbon. Surprised that the building supervisor would let someone into my apartment to put them there, I reached for the card. I thought of True, and found myself hoping . . .

Welcome home, Collie. Call me. Love, Brett.

Brett didn't need anyone to let him into my apartment. He still had a key. He'd probably been selling tickets and bringing curious reporters in on tours.

Call me. Not likely. Not ever. The only person I was going to call was a locksmith. And my folks. If they'd heard about all this on the news, they were probably frantic by now. I hadn't left a phone number with Dad, so he wouldn't have known how to reach me.

Sinking down on the couch, I picked up the phone and dialed their number. Mom answered. The sound of her voice seemed strange, like something from so far in the past I could barely remember it.

She said hello twice before I could reply. "Hi, Mom." My throat constricted, and I wanted to burst into tears and tell her everything.

"Collie?" She sounded frantic. "Collie, is that you? We've been trying to reach you for days. Are you all right? We've been worried sick!"

"I'm sorry, Mom." The stiff reprimand in her voice did a lot to clear my sentimental fog. "I've been out of touch. I didn't realize what was going on until Laura Draper called me. I've been in Texas doing some freelance articles for her. You remember Laura? My roommate from college?"

"Collie, don't change the subject." Mom was clearly irritated and I was going to hear about it. I suddenly felt ten years old and late for dinner. "Why in the world didn't you tell us about all this business at the newspaper? Brett says you haven't been working there for months."

Heat rushed up the back of my neck at the thought of

Brett discussing my problems with my mother. "I didn't feel like talking about it yet. It's not a big deal."

"Brett says you didn't come out of your apartment for weeks. He says he had to call Laura and get her to send you out on a job."

"Well, Brett doesn't know what he's talking about." I wasn't about to admit the truth. "Brett and I broke up months ago, and now that things have turned my way, he's just trying to get a piece of the action."

"Oh . . . I see." Mom didn't sound at all disappointed about Brett and me, nor was she inclined to defend him. "Well, I can't say I'm surprised. I never liked him." Which had to be the biggest understatement of the year. She despised Brett, and that was part of the reason I didn't see my family much anymore. Things had gotten to the point where it was either him or them, and I, out of stubbornness or stupidity, or God knows what, chose him.

Letting my forehead fall into my hand, I chuckled ruefully. Jobs came and jobs went, lawsuits started and lawsuits ended, but Mom never changed. "I know that, Mom. I guess you were right."

She gave a self-satisfied huff, but stopped short of agreeing with me. "Collie, you don't sound well."

"I'm fine, Mom. I'm tired. I just flew in from Texas."

"I'm coming up."

"Mom, don't, it's—"

"I'll be there tomorrow morning."

"Mom, really, I—"

"Dad's tied up with inventory. I'll get Gran to drive with me."

"Mom, there are people every—"

"Don't worry about a thing. We'll be there tomorrow."

"Mom. Don't!" I shouted. I think it was the first time in my life I had ever shouted at my mother. Both of us were struck silent as the words echoed around my apartment. Sucking in a breath, I tried to take control of the situation. "There's no reason for you to come. I've got a lot of offers, and I'll be pretty tied up the next few weeks. Besides, the street out front is a mess with reporters." I could picture them attacking my mother and my sweet old granny. "As soon as things calm down, I'll come for a visit. I'll tell you the whole story in person. I promise."

"Well . . ." A mixture of resignation and disappointment. "All right. But you call if you need me. Call me by Friday, anyway. I'm tired of getting your answering machine."

"All right, I will. I love you, Mom."

"I love you too, sweetheart. Take care."

We said good-bye, and that was that. The first time I had ever taken control of a conversation with my mother. Apparently I was growing up, after all.

Feeling triumphant, I grabbed a scratch pad and flipped on the answering machine. If I could take on Mom, I could take on anything.

The messages were pretty much the same as the last batch. Reporters wanting information. Offers from three news shows wanting an interview, several irate messages from my mother, one offer from a network TV producer, and four sappy messages from Brett, pretending everything was as it had been before.

I played the last one a second time, tapping my pencil against the paper and wondering how, after six years, he could know so little about me. If he thought I was going to make nice with him after he moved out on me when I needed him, then started dating someone else a week later, he was out of his mind.

Maybe he was afraid I'd tell the FBI that he and Bennett were in on all the political scheming together. Maybe they were. Bennett was the publisher of the newspaper, and Brett was his head of public relations and marketing, right-hand man, favorite dog. They were always whispering together behind closed doors, and Brett had political aspirations. Brett had all kinds of aspirations. . . .

I wondered if it was possible. I wondered if they had picked me to do the story on Senator Williams because Brett thought he could talk me into lying and taking responsibility for the story if a legal matter arose.

Was it possible? Brett had looked as shocked as I that day. Was it possible he was in on Bennett's schemes from the beginning? Or was he merely the spineless weasel I believed him to be?

I picked up the phone and dialed Brett's number. My breath caught in my throat like something solid, choking me as I waited for him to answer. His answering machine came on instead, and I let out a sigh of relief.

"Hi, Brett, this is Collie. I'll be home tonight. Come by if you can. I need to talk to you."

With a sense of satisfaction, I pictured his new girlfriend sitting there listening to the message. Then I wondered if he had found somebody new, or if that was just an excuse to distance himself from me during all the legal mess. If it was the paper or me, he would undoubtedly have picked the paper. *Shmuck.* If I found out he was involved in the political business with Bennett, I was going to bury them both in the same grave. . . .

I thought about the possible scenarios as I rummaged for something to eat. Was it really plausible that Brett could be so devious? Would he knowingly set me up for a fall, after six years together?

I had just finished suffering through an overcooked frozen dinner when a key turned in the door, slicing my thoughts and sending my heart into my throat.

"Collie? It's me." Brett's voice.

When I rounded the corner from the kitchen, he was standing in front of my sofa with another bunch of roses in his hands, looking ridiculous.

I found myself comparing him to True and thinking how pale and small he looked—too perfect in his features, too neatly dressed, not a hair out of place. Like a department store mannequin. It irked me that he would have the nerve to come to my apartment and let himself in with the key. I motioned to it, dangling from his hand. "You don't live here anymore, you know."

He smiled in that smooth, confident way of his, blond lashes descending over hazel eyes, then coming up again. "Sorry about that. I was afraid I'd attract attention, standing there banging on your door."

I walked into the room and sat in a chair, so that he

would have to use the couch, on the other side of the coffee table. "If you wanted to be inconspicuous, you could have skipped the floral treatment." I motioned to the roses with a narrow-eyed look. I wanted him to know I wasn't going to be won by his PR treatment.

He tried it anyway. Setting the roses down, he took off his blazer and loosened his tie, then sat on *my* couch like it belonged to him. "God, it's good to see you, Collie. You look great."

"I wish I could say the same." I crossed my arms over myself, suddenly feeling chilled.

He leaned forward, elbows braced on his knees and palms outstretched. "Come on, Collie, don't be that way. Give a guy a break. I did a stupid thing. I admit it. One stupid thing in six good years. I'd like a chance to make things right." His hazel eyes looked clear and pleading, remorseful and lonely.

To my complete disgust, I felt a pang of something soft for him. I tried to sweep it out of my mind like the dust from some unwanted antique. "Funny you should say that, because there *is* something I'd like you to do for me." I met his gaze, and memories came flooding back to me. Memories of nights at the theater, black-tie parties, expensive dinners, classy jewelry, and pricey gifts.

He leaned forward, interlacing his fingers, looking confident. "Anything. Whatever it takes."

"I want you to tell me the truth about you and Bennett." First blood. "I want to know whether you were involved in any of this political stuff, and if that's why you dumped me."

He sat back in the chair, looking like I'd slugged him. "I didn't dump you, Coll. You left town."

Gripping my fingers over my arms, I tried to control my temper. How dare he deny it now. "I want to know about Bennett."

"I didn't know anything about that, Collie, I swear." He looked truthful enough. He also looked desperate. "I had a few suspicions, but Bennett kept his business to himself. I didn't know he planned to let you go down on the Williams thing, I swear. I wouldn't have done that to you, Collie. I love you."

I sat looking at him, unsure whether he meant that or not and unable to imagine how what he had done to me could fit anyone's definition of love. "You have a funny way of showing it."

He put his palms out again. "I'm sorry, Coll. I really am. I just want to make things right."

I felt a ridiculous twitter of sympathy and an urge to comfort him, as I had four years ago when his father died, and he went off the deep end for weeks. "I'm not interested," I said flatly. "Too much water under the bridge." I glanced away from him and gathered my thoughts, trying to keep things on track. "Do you think the FBI is going to question me?"

I heard an audible intake of air, but by the time I looked at him he had affected a perfect mask of confidence. "It's not likely . . . unless you're planning to go to them and tell them you know something." The mask cracked, and I could see that he was worried.

I wondered again if he was telling the truth about him and Bennett. "I *don't* know anything," I said flatly.

"And I'm not going to invent anything either."

He sank back in his seat like a blowup doll with the air going out. "I didn't think you would." But it showed in his face that he had been afraid I would go to the authorities and make trouble for him. That was why he was trying to get in touch with me through Laura—so he could win me over before I talked to anyone.

"But I will warn you," I said, "that I intend to make use of the opportunities this brings up—probably do a few news interviews, and I may even sign on as a network consultant covering the legal case against Bennett. Seems like it would be poetic justice, doesn't it?" I thought for a minute, then decided to rub it in a little more. "Every paper around wants me now. Even the *Post*."

"I'm happy for you, Coll." But it was clear that he wasn't.

"Thank you," I said, realizing I was ready for him to leave. "I guess there's nothing more for us to say. If you'll give me my key, we can call an end to this"—*Sham? Fiasco? Pathetic excuse for a relationship?*—"to whatever it was we had together."

He twisted the key in his fingers reluctantly, then unhooked it from his key ring and tossed it on the table. "Six years is a lot to give up."

"Yes, it is." I stood up and he stood up with me. "But they say office romances never work out."

He looked over his shoulder and smiled as we walked to the door. "We're not in the same office anymore."

"Very funny," I said, surprised that he could still make me chuckle. I lost the urge to punish him and instead just felt sad. "Take care of yourself, Brett. I hope you meet someone who shares your . . . interests."

He cocked his head and looked at me strangely as I opened the door. "I thought I had." He leaned down and kissed me before I could get away.

I felt . . . nothing. Except the urge to punch him.

"I guess not," he said, then turned and started down the hall toward the elevator. "Be careful, Little Red Riding Hood. The wolves are circling."

Chapter 15

A MONTH in the middle of a big D.C. story is like twenty-four hours anywhere else. It passes so quickly, night runs into day and one day into another, and before you know it, time has gone by. My first three weeks back in D.C. went so fast I barely felt them passing and hardly had time to think, which was probably for the best. I didn't sleep much, and when I did I was so exhausted I fell into a dreamless pit where even memories of Texas couldn't find me. Sometimes, in the few moments before I came to consciousness, I expected to hear the peafowl calling outside, expected to open my eyes and see the adobe ceiling and the rough cedar beams of Mrs. Hawthorne's cottage. But after I awoke, the images faded like bits of a dream, something that never really happened.

After my return to D.C., I had misplaced the notepad

with my handwritten stories. Without that physical proof of my hill-country journey, it was as if I had never been there at all. When Mrs. Hawthorne's bill came in the mail, I kept a copy of it, just left it by the phone where I could glance at it from time to time. At the bottom she had scrawled *Saw you on TV. Don't be a stranger*, and three phone numbers—Hawthorne House, the café, and the *San Saline Record* office. I started to call the newspaper office a dozen times, once even waited several rings until Becky answered, then hung up with my heart pounding and my stomach in my throat.

I spent most of my time working—up before dawn for some morning-show interviews, awake late at night as a special consultant on *Nightbeat*, prowling the town the rest of the time, seeing what I could sniff out about my ex-boss and the impending legal case.

I talked briefly with the FBI, on May Day in the park, of all places. I watched children wind a maypole as the agent conducted what he called an informal interview. It quickly became clear that the FBI already knew more about Bennett's activities than I did, and that was the end of the questioning.

By keeping my nose to the ground, I slowly started to learn more. Bennett had made himself a wealthy man by investing in businesses and then seeing that they got healthy, sometimes fraudulent, government contracts and favorable legislative treatment. He'd used all means of persuasion, legal and illegal, to win the favor of key senators and representatives. His position at the newspaper put him in a perfect spot to learn everyone's secrets. In Washington, the pen is mighty. It controls public opinion. And Bennett had figured out that he could make and break almost anyone. He'd acquired some powerful friends and some equally powerful enemies, but none of them exposed him because he knew the skeletons in their closets.

It wasn't until Bennett tried his bit on an honest man that his house of cards came crashing down. Senator Jeff Williams was fairly new to D.C. and a frightening commodity for most Washington insiders. Williams was leading by a slight margin in the re-election race for the New Jersey Senate seat. Bennett was looking to get approval on a lucrative government-housing contract, and Williams had made a campaign issue of cleaning up fraudulent dealings in government housing. Bennett knew that Williams would be a powerful enemy in the Senate, if re-elected. He went looking for dirt on Williams, and the best he could find was a disgruntled former employee who claimed Williams had taken illegal campaign contributions. Bennett took the story and ran with it, figuring the scandal would knock Williams out of the election. When the allegations were quickly disproven, and Williams took the paper to court for libel, Bennett had more trouble than he could handle.

Somewhere in that process, he came up with the idea of letting me take the fall for writing the article, or perhaps he had planned that all along. It was impossible to know now.

The more I dug into the story, the more it became a crusade for me. I was filled with a heady mixture of vindication and revenge, and caught up in the whirl of my fifteen minutes of fame.

After the story started to die out, it became clear that TV wasn't my thing. I dropped the *Nightbeat* job and made up my mind to sign on with the *Post*, which had been pursuing me since my return. I was suddenly the most recognized print reporter in town, and they knew that would translate into newspaper sales.

So one month after my return, I had an appointment at the offices of the *Post* to sign the deal of a lifetime—a two-year contract with a huge signing bonus and a phenomenal salary, doing news features only—no fluff. It was everything I'd ever dreamed of, yet I found myself stalling at my apartment instead of heading to the meeting. I had changed suits three times, but nothing seemed right. Finally I stood by the phone staring at the numbers on the bottom of Mrs. Hawthorne's bill. I had the overwhelming urge to call the *San Saline Record* office—just once before I signed away the next two years of my life. If True answered, it would be an omen. . . .

The phone rang and I jumped nervously, then stood looking at it, afraid to answer, afraid not to. My heart rocketed to the hollow just below my throat and hammered there like a bird trying to break through a window. I pictured True on the other end of the line.

I picked it up on the fourth ring and choked out, "Hello?"

"Collie? Is that you?" Laura had called me every few days to get updates on my situation, because she hadn't been able to come to D.C. in person. As she put it, she absolutely hated missing all the fun.

"Hi, Laura." I felt a crushing sense of disappointment. Then I shook my head at myself for being so stupid. True wasn't going to call. If he'd intended to call, he would have done it before now. He'd probably forgotten all about me.

"You got a minute?" Laura asked.

"Just one. I'm on my way to the *Post* to sign that contract."

Laura paused as if she were thinking about what to say. That surprised me. I figured she'd be cheering my decision to go with the *Post.* She had been trying to talk me into it for weeks.

"Listen, Collie." The uncertain tone in her voice sent a pang of disquiet through me. "I was just looking through your materials for the article series, and I found this notepad with these stories about the people down there. Did you write these?"

I slapped a hand over my eyes, flushing bloodred, even though there was no one there to see it. "Believe it or not, yes." So that was what had happened to my notepad—stuffed in the envelope to Laura. Good Lord, how embarrassing. "I'm sorry. I didn't mean to send you those. I must have stuck it in there by accident. Those were just . . . well"—*drivel, sentimental meanderings, an out-of-body experience, an altered state, me high on mesquite beans*—". . . sort of . . . like . . . doodles."

Laura laughed. "Oh, don't be so modest, Coll. They're wonderful!"

"They are?"

"Yes, they are." She exploded in a sudden fit of praise, which, for Laura, was unusual. "They made me laugh and cry, and I got that tingly feeling I only get when I read something really good."

"You're kidding." I stood there with my mouth hanging open.

"No. I'm not kidding. I have a friend at a publishing house here in Richmond. I wondered if it would be all right for me to pass these on to him. Do you think you'd be willing to flesh these pieces out into a book?"

"I don't know, I—"

"Well, you could talk about that with him later. I'd just like him to see these."

"All right . . . I guess." Blood rushed into my face again at the idea of everyone reading the meanderings of my hill-country alter-ego. What would the *Post* think of that? "Do you think I'd have to put my real name on them?"

Laura burst into laughter, then ended with a grunt of disgust. "Oh, Collie, don't be so stiff. This is the first piece of your writing that feels like you put your heart into it. I think you really found something while you were down there. You've got a talent for this sort of thing."

Dumbfounded, I muttered, "Who'd have thought?"

Laura chuckled on the other end. "So it's all right, then?"

"I guess so." The digital clock in my bedroom beeped as the hour changed. "I've got to go, Laura. I have to be at the *Post* in thirty."

"All right. Good luck. I'll send these Texas pieces

over to my editor friend." Laura chuckled. "Hey, maybe you should blow off the *Post* and become a wandering story writer."

"Very funny," I said. "Gotta go. I'll call you later and let you know how the meeting went."

We hung up, and I hurried off to make the deal of a lifetime.

But all the way there, all I could think about was Laura and my hill-country stories. I could remember each one now—the prickly pears, Malachi, Dandy Rhodes, the ladies' supper, True and the bush hogs. I recalled the words as clearly as if they were printed on paper in front of me. I felt all the emotions and that strange sense of magic, of understanding and rightness. . . .

I tried to make it all go away as I looked at myself in the glittering mirrored windows of the *Post* offices. Smoothing the wrinkles from my navy suit, I tucked the collar of my shirt crisply under the lapel. I remembered who I was and why I was there. Colleen Collins, at the top of the heap, strolling into the *Post* to sign the dream deal.

The receptionist knew who I was without any introductions. She led me into a conference room as if I were a celebrity. The editor, the publisher, and my new entertainment lawyer were waiting inside. No one complained about my being the last to arrive.

After the introductions were over, we got down to business. Even though we all knew the terms of the contract, we discussed it clause by clause anyway. My mind started drifting again.

"And, of course, Colleen, there will be a signing bonus, biannual bonus, limited editorial control of your work, and a great deal of flexibility in picking your projects." The editor-in-chief, a man who was a legend in the newspaper business, was talking, and I couldn't focus. "We need people of your caliber. Your last piece on the Bennett trial was excellent. Circulation that day was up by . . ."

Maybe you should blow off the Post *and just become a wandering story writer.* My mind drifted back. I started wondering where my notepad was now. Where True was now and what he was doing.

". . . and hits on the Web site up thirty-four percent." I tuned in to the end of the editor's comment.

I snapped my mind back to the present and realized everyone was waiting for me to answer. "That's good to hear. I'm very excited about going to work for the *Post.*" I sounded like a robot. Tomorrow would be the second Saturday of the month. Mrs. Hawthorne would be holding the ladies' supper. I wondered what they would talk about. . . .

I missed another bit of the conversation, then tuned in to the publisher saying, while looking at his watch, "Then I guess there isn't much more to attend to except the signing of the contract. We're anxious to have you aboard, Miss Collins. It's clear that you give your writing a one-hundred-percent effort."

This is the first piece of your writing that feels like you put your heart into it. "Thank you." I watched as he signed the contract and slid it over to me.

My heart started pounding as I picked up the pen and

focused on the words *for a term of no less than two years, renewable thereafter. . . .*

"Two years," I heard myself mutter. My stomach rolled over and acid gurgled into my throat.

The entertainment lawyer straightened in the chair next to mine and gave me a questioning look. "That's what we agreed to, Collie. Remember? We talked about that yesterday."

Suddenly I couldn't remember yesterday. *I think you really found something while you were down there. . . .*

I swallowed hard and tried to shake off the demon possession going on inside me. "There's no limitation on my publishing outside work, is there?" I asked the lawyer. "I think I may have a book offer for something totally unrelated to the Bennett case."

"That's not a problem." The publisher leaned across the table like a used-car salesman impatient with a finicky customer. "As long as it doesn't conflict with your work here, we're happy to have you pursue other interests."

"Good," I said, and picked up the pen again, touching the tip to the line where my name was neatly typed in. "Sign right here?"

"Yes." The publisher.

"Right there." The editor.

"Yes." My lawyer.

Three quick answers. Three anxious men leaning across the table toward me. I felt like a piece of hamburger in a cage with hungry dogs.

Just sign the contract, Collie, and get it over with. This is a godsend. A gift. My fingers flourished a large, round *C,* then *C-o, Co-l,* moving in slow motion. Everything seemed to be moving in slow motion. I focused on the letters and everything else seemed to disappear. *Col-l.*

For a term of no less than two years . . .

Something inside me snapped and I jerked the pen away from the paper. Everyone at the table drew back and regarded me with shock. My lawyer looked like he was going to faint.

I tried to think of some way to salvage the situation. "May I take this home overnight and read over it one more time? I just want to be sure I understand all the terms."

"Collie, we . . ." My lawyer started to speak and I raised a hand to make him stop. He blinked at me in surprise and sat back in his chair again.

"It's not a problem," the publisher offered, but he was glowering at me as he said it. "Take it home over the weekend. Call us on Monday. There's nothing in there that should be a problem."

I put forth my most charming, self-assured smile, but inside I was kicking myself. Not even started on the job yet and I was already causing trouble with the bosses. "Oh, I realize that. After this past year, I'm just a little skittish about legal matters."

Everyone chuckled, and I breathed a sigh of relief, having pulled my head out of the guillotine, at least for the moment.

We stood up and shook hands without too much evidence of animosity between us. The one who seemed most put-out was my own lawyer, who looked like he might pop a double dose of Valium when the meeting was over.

"We'll see you Monday," the publisher said. "And as soon as the contract is signed, you can go to work."

"Sounds good," I said, and we parted ways, them heading toward the offices and me heading toward the door. My lawyer hovered in between for a moment, then followed me.

"Collie, is there something I should know?" he asked, nervously following me out the door.

"No." *Just that I'm out of my mind, having uncontrollable flashbacks, and thinking of becoming a wandering story writer.* "Everything's fine. I just want to look over the contract one more time."

"Do you need my help?" He tried to reach for the folder with the contract in it. "We could go over it at my office."

I held it away from him and proceeded toward my car. "No. It's not a problem. Stop worrying. I'll call you Monday morning and we'll get the papers signed."

He stopped, barring the door to my car and looking at me sternly, tapping a knuckle against his chin, standing closer than was comfortable. "Don't put it off any longer than Monday. This Bennett story is getting to be old news. There's a short window of opportunity here. In a few more weeks you won't be a hot commodity anymore."

"I realize that."

"Now's the time." He laid a hand on my arm. "I don't want to see you miss this chance, Collie."

"I won't." I stepped back and reached into my purse

for my keys, ready to get out of there as quickly as possible. "I'll call you Monday morning."

He stepped aside, and I hurried into my car and out of the parking lot before he could badger me again.

As I drove home, my mind started to spin, going endlessly over the meeting, reviewing everything I had said and done, trying to calculate how much damage I had caused myself. The lawyer was right: There was a short window of opportunity. I couldn't waste it. I had to get a grip on myself. If I didn't get this deal signed, I was history. I'd be lucky if they didn't change their minds by Monday. Signing bonus, flexibility in picking projects . . . But two years . . .

The spinning didn't stop until I was back in my apartment and had locked the lawyer and the publisher and the editor on the other side of the door.

"Stupid, stupid, stupid!" I hollered into the empty room. "My God, Collie, what is wrong with you!"

Sinking down on the couch, I threw the contract on the seat beside me and held my head in my hands, tugging at the roots of my hair as my anger slowly burned away. When it was gone, there seemed to be nothing left in me. I sat there, numb for a long time, then finally curled around a pillow and started to cry. . . .

When the phone rang, my throat was so hoarse I could barely talk.

"Collie, are you sick?" My mother sounded alarmed.

"No." But I knew she had already sniffed out trouble.

"Well, is something wrong?" She was like a hound on a scent.

"No, Mom. It's just been a long day. I had that big

meeting at the *Post*."

Mom seemed to think about that for a moment. "Well, how did that go? Did you sign your contract?"

My lips started to quiver and I gritted my teeth. "No. I brought it home for the weekend to look it over some more."

"Oh." Mom clearly didn't like the sound of things. "Why don't you come up here this weekend? It will give you a chance to relax."

I knew better than to agree to that. Two minutes in the room with my mom, and she'd have the whole story out of me—the hill country, True, the contract negotiations . . . all of it. "I can't, Mom. I've really got to stay here and go over this contract. I'm going to stick close to home this weekend and get some rest. It's been a long few weeks."

"You know you shouldn't sign anything without talking to a lawyer. Dad could get Jim Dugger to give you a call."

I shook my head, rubbing my eyes. "That's all right. I've got a lawyer, remember? I told you about that. He specializes in entertainment contracts. He set up the TV deal for me. He's pretty good."

"Oh, that's right."

I could tell she wanted to linger on the phone, but wisdom told me I should end the conversation before I said the wrong thing. "Well, I'd better go, I guess. I'm going to take a bath and go to bed early tonight. I'm wiped out."

"I'll bet you are. Well, you get some rest. Good night, love."

"Good night, Mom."

And we ended the conversation. But I had a sense of wariness scratching along the back of my spine . . . a feeling that Mom had given up too easily. And when Mom gave up too easily it meant she was undertaking some covert operation.

I awoke early the next morning with a strange sense of nervousness, or maybe a premonition that Mom was up to something. I had an even stranger urge to do some of Mrs. Hawthorne's biscuit therapy, or maybe I just wanted to avoid reading over the *Post* contract again and facing the idea of signing it. Instead of reading the contract, I went to the store and, for the first time that I could remember, bought staples instead of convenience foods. When I got home, I set out the ingredients and Mrs. H.'s biscuit recipe, and started trying to make biscuits. My mind started to clear as the dough came together and I kneaded it into a ball. I envisioned myself back in Mrs. Hawthorne's kitchen, surrounded by the peaceful quiet of a hill-country spring day. . . .

I was almost able to forget that in the next room lay the contract that would determine the next two years of my life.

I was up to my elbows in biscuit dough when the door buzzer rang, and I heard my mother's voice in the hall. For a moment I thought I had imagined it; then I heard my grandmother's voice on the other side of the door as well.

I opened the door, covered with flour and holding a dish towel. Mom's mouth dropped open in shock. Beside her, Gran fluttered her eyelids like she might faint.

"I was making some . . . ummm . . . biscuits," I said, realizing that now they would definitely think I was having a mental breakdown. I stepped aside, and they came into the apartment, peering cautiously ahead as if they were entering the lab of Dr. Frankenstein.

Mom walked to the other side of the room, studying the mess in the kitchen and the biscuits on my newly purchased cookie sheet. "Where did you learn to make biscuits?"

"In Texas," I said, trying to convince her that it was the most natural thing in the world for me to be baking in the morning.

"Oh." Mom clearly had new respect for Texas. "That's wonderful."

Gran stepped forward and touched the top of one of my carefully cut circles of dough. "Texas biscuits." She elevated it to a thing of wonder.

I wiped the rest of the dough off my hands, then hugged them both. "So, not that I'm not glad to see you, but what are you two doing here?" I asked, as if I didn't know already.

"Just having a shopping trip." Mom shrugged, trying to look casual. "I needed some things in the city, and . . . Gran and I thought it was a nice day for a drive."

I knew better. Gran hated D.C.—hated all the crowds, and the noise, and the people wearing foreign clothes and speaking different languages. She came to D.C. only if she was coming to see me, or if Mom forced her.

I knew that Mom was still on the scent of trouble from last night. "We just thought we'd stop in and see you for lunch." She breezed into the living room looking nonchalant.

Gran paused for a moment, craning her neck and giving me a long, critical stare. If there was a nose superior to Mom's, it was Gran's.

"Have you been crying?" she asked finally.

Mom turned to stare at me.

I blushed and pretended to be busy arranging the dish towel on the counter. "No, Gran. I just haven't had much sleep lately. Between those early interviews and *Nightbeat*, I meet myself coming and going. Things will be better now that I'm signing up with the *Post*." At least, I supposed that once I turned the contract in Monday the apprehension would go away, I would begin my new job, things would start whirling again, and I would be off like a feather in a jet stream.

"Uh-huh." Gran clearly didn't believe it. She continued to survey me as we moved to the living area to sit down. She frowned at my outfit—flour-covered sweats and a ripped T-shirt that used to be Brett's. "Not getting dressed today? It's after eleven o'clock."

I chuckled, because the comment was so typical of her. Gran was dressed, curled, and teased by eight each morning, whether she was leaving the house or not. The older she got, the brighter the makeup became, and the more her aim wandered. She looked a little like a circus clown gone awry.

"I just haven't gotten to it yet. Too busy making biscuits."

Gran was not satisfied. "You don't look well."

"I feel fine," I said, combing back my hair and grabbing a barrette from the table. "Really."

"Maybe you should see a doctor," she suggested. "You don't look like you have any spark."

"I'm fine, Gran." I stood up and walked to the kitchen, because I had the uncomfortable feeling they were seeing right through me. "Would you two like some tea? Or lunch? We could have biscuits and . . . ummm, something. . . ." I looked in the refrigerator—glistening and empty except for a can of mesquite beans and a jar of prickly pear jelly Mrs. Hawthorne had given me. "I don't have much here, but I could order out."

"We were going to take you to lunch," Mom called. "Sort of a girls' day out. Why don't you get dressed?"

"All right." And I hurried across the living room, welcoming the chance to be alone for a minute to get my head together.

I heard the phone ringing just as I was finishing my makeup. I hoped it wasn't Brett again, or some reporter asking questions. I could imagine what my mom might reveal.

"She's right here," I heard her say, and she extended the phone to me as I hurried into the room. "It's some man who says he's your lawyer."

Grimacing, I took the phone and said hello.

"Good morning, Collie. I was just calling to touch base with you on the contract." The anxiety was clear in his voice. Why he cared so much, I couldn't imagine. It wasn't like his fifteen percent of the deal was going to make him rich.

"I'm finished with it," I said, hoping to get rid of him quickly. "I looked it over, signed it, put it in the folder. Ready for delivery Monday."

"Outstanding! I'll stop by this afternoon and pick it up."

"No!" The word shot out so quickly and so loudly that Mom and Gran swiveled to look at me. I took a quick breath. "I mean, I'll be gone this afternoon. I have company in town. I'll bring the contract with me Monday."

"You're sure?" He clearly didn't trust me.

"I'm sure. See you Monday."

"Good-bye, then."

"Good-bye."

Hanging up the phone, I grabbed my purse and hustled Mom and Gran toward the door, having the unnerving feeling that the lawyer might show up at my door. I wasn't sure why, but I wanted to keep the contract in my possession until Monday.

The phone rang just as we were leaving. I let it go and stood there listening as the machine picked up.

"Collie?" The voice was familiar, but without its usual ring of laughter. I stepped inside the door, listening. "Collie, are you there? This is Mrs. Hawthorne calling from San Saline . . ."

I threw the keys on the table, rushed across the room, and grabbed the phone, breathless, hoping she would still be on the line. "Hello . . . Mrs. Hawthorne?"

Chapter 16

"COLLIE?" she said, as if she wasn't sure.

"Yes. It's me."

"Oh. I couldn't tell. You sound different on the phone." So did she. I recognized her voice, but the musical cadence, the hint of ever-present good humor, was gone.

A strange uneasiness crawled through the back of my mind. "Mrs. Hawthorne, is something wrong?" I was vaguely aware of Mom and Gran reentering the room and standing near the door, watching me with worried expressions.

"Well . . . yes." Mrs. Hawthorne answered tentatively at first, then started speaking rapid-fire. "I mean, I thought you would want to know. I just thought someone should tell you. I just . . ." She paused to catch her breath, a long, trembling sound, like a sob.

In the instant of silence that followed, my mind rushed with terrible possibilities, then settled on one awful thought. Something had happened to True. "Please, Mrs. Hawthorne," I blurted, suddenly desperate. "What happened? What's wrong? Are you all right? Is True all right?"

I heard her sniff and swallow a low sob on the other end of the phone. "Old Malachi passed away yesterday."

Old Malachi passed away yesterday. I stood there, numb, thinking of the last time I had seen him, waving as he drove out of the café parking lot. Just four weeks—and a lifetime—ago. "Oh, my God. How?" I heard myself mutter as Mrs. Hawthorne drew a long, quavering breath.

Mom and Gran came into the room and sat on the sofa, watching me with expressions of foreboding. I held my hand over the receiver and whispered, "A friend of mine in Texas died." So they would know it wasn't Dad, the twins, or Rob and his wife. Gran laid a hand on the base of her neck and closed her eyes, breathing a long sigh, then muttering a prayer.

I sank into the chair, a black cloud of sadness pouring over me like smoke as Mrs. Hawthorne went on. "He just went in his sleep. His grandkids are going to go ahead and have him buried tomorrow, so everyone can be there. I wanted to have True call you, but he's gone to Oklahoma City. I don't know if anyone's been able to get in touch with him yet." She fell silent, trying to decide what to say next. "I know he'll be upset when he hears. He thought so much of old Malachi. I just thought it might help him to talk to you, but I haven't been able to reach him. We left messages on his voice mail. I imagine he'll get them later on today and head back for the funeral. It would be terrible if he missed the funeral. He thought so much of old Malachi. . . ." She seemed to be waiting for me to offer some solution, but I didn't have one. I didn't know where True was or how to get in touch with him, and I couldn't imagine why she thought I would.

"I'm sure he'll make it back," I replied, still struggling to comprehend the fact that Malachi was gone. "What time is the funeral?" My mind started whirling, making plans, debating flights, rental cars, timing, a contract to be delivered Monday morning. . . .

I glanced at my mother, who was watching me now with confusion—wondering, no doubt, who I could possibly have such a close attachment to in Texas. She would think I was crazy to fly halfway across the country for the funeral of someone I'd known only a few days. . . .

I turned my shoulder to her as Mrs. Hawthorne went on. "It's Sunday afternoon at two o'clock at Malachi's church. I think nearly everyone in town will be there. Everyone thought a lot of Malachi. He's been around here so many years, we just . . . well, sometimes you don't understand how much someone means to you until you realize you'll never see them again. . . ."

I wondered if she was talking about me and True. I wondered if she was hoping the funeral would bring True and me together again.

The idea hatched like a butterfly in my mind. Then I glanced at Mom—frowning, brows drawn together, arms crossed—and I tried to push the image away. I had a contract to sign Monday. An important contract. A life-altering contract. Today was Saturday. The funeral wasn't until Sunday afternoon. I couldn't . . .

I cleared the strangling lump of emotion in my throat. "Is there an address where I could send flowers?" It felt as if somebody else was asking. Something heavy pressed inside me and I stood up, turning my back to Mom and Grandma, closing my eyes as they burned hot. "I'd like to do something." The sadness broke free and my voice started to tremble. "He was such a . . ." *Wonderful person? Good friend? Angel? Godsend?* "I just can't believe he's gone." In my mind, he was still somewhere in the hill country, driving along some winding ribbon of highway in the car with the fluttering wings of tattered vinyl, on his way to someone who needed him. It didn't seem fair that he had been taken away. Heaven didn't need more angels. The world did. I did.

I needed him now, to smile and take my hand, and tell me what to do. Everything was spinning around me. Malachi. The contract with the *Post.* True. The old schoolhouse on the bluff. Life as a cowgirl . . .

I was back at the fork in the road again.

"I guess you could send flowers to the Riverbend Church." Mrs. Hawthorne's voice, heavy with disappointment, pushed away the images. I could tell she'd been hoping I would come.

Laying my hand over my eyes, I tried to think.

Mrs. Hawthorne said again, "Sometimes you just don't understand how much someone means to you until you realize you'll never see them again. . . ."

Or maybe I just heard her say it in my mind. "Thank you for letting me know."

"You're welcome. I just felt that you would want to be told." Silence fell between us, and finally she added, "So is everything else going well there? We saw you on television."

"Things are good." *Then why do I feel like I'm drowning?* "I'm going to work for the *Post* on Monday." *And for the next two years.*

"Well, that's good." And then there was a patch of

static, during which I wondered if we'd lost the connection, until finally I heard, "Collie? My other line is beeping. I'd better let you go." More static. ". . . and take care. Darn this phone. Can you hear me, Collie?"

"Yes. I'll say good-bye, then." But I found myself not wanting to. "Thanks for calling me. 'Bye, Mrs. Hawthorne." I wondered if the other incoming call was from True.

"Good-bye, Collie." But the phone didn't disconnect right away. The line stayed open, and I could hear the distant sound of Mrs. Hawthorne cursing the phone as she tried to answer the other line. I held the receiver to my ear and listened, dreaming that the lines would somehow cross, and I would hear True's voice.

Mrs. Hawthorne faded into static and I stood listening to the buzz, lost in the ether, unwilling to hang up the phone.

The Lawd is leadin' you like a horse to water, but he cain't make you drink, sister. He's wakin' up your heart and all the lastin' things are in there. Malachi's voice came to me so clearly that I opened my eyes and looked around the room. *The mind changes like a river, but the heart is lastin' like the sea. . . .*

And all of a sudden, I knew. Standing there in my living room, I felt the truth rush through me like a breath of spirit—cool, tranquil, constant. And I knew without a doubt where my heart was, where it had been since I first set foot in San Saline, since I first fell in love with True and that place. It may not have made any sense. It may not have been easy for my mind to grasp, but my heart was there. It was constant.

Look with your heart and not your mind. Love with your heart and not your mind. . . .

Now I understood what Malachi was trying to tell me that day beneath the live oaks at the old freedman's school. He could see it in me, even if I could not yet see it in myself. He knew my heart was already there. He was telling me, even now. He was telling me that some things are meant to be.

Wiping my eyes, I took a deep breath, sat in the chair, and told my mother and grandmother everything that had happened in Texas. I told them about the bluebonnets, the rattlesnakes, and the goats. I told them about Mrs. Hawthorne and Becky and Malachi. I told them about True, our first unlikely meeting beneath the Friendly's Tractors sign, the bush hogs, the fireworks, the enchanted schoolhouse, his newspaper, his lost daughter, our final good-bye. I told them about how lost I had been these past weeks back in D.C., like a body with no spirit, about how I couldn't sign the contract with the *Post,* about how I had wished to hear True's voice on the phone line. I told them about Malachi's funeral on Sunday. And finally I told them I was going back to Texas. Probably for good.

When the story was over, I folded my hands in my lap, wondering what they would say, wondering if they would try to talk me out of it.

My grandmother reached out and took my hand, her lips trembling in a smile, tears rimming her eyes. "Oh, Collie, you poor thing. What a choice to have to make. I knew something was wrong with you, but I never would have guessed you had a beau waiting in Texas."

I winced, because the way she said it made it all sound so stupid, and I was afraid she might be giving Mom more ammunition. "I haven't talked to him yet, Gran. He may have changed his mind about . . . things." My throat constricted and I swallowed hard, trying not to consider the idea that things might have changed since I left, or that True might resent me for leaving in the first place. "I just know I can't leave things the way I did. I have to go back." I looked at Mom, worried because she still hadn't spoken. I wondered about what she might say.

Her face was impassive, so I couldn't get an idea of her thoughts. She looked at Gran and then at me, lining up her sights. Now that she had us both in one place, I figured she'd take care of both of us with one quick silver bullet.

"I . . . don't exactly know what to say." She gave me a long, steady, very direct look, carefully considering her response. "I knew something was wrong with you lately, but you've completely stunned me this time."

The words rolled like a bowling ball to the pit of my stomach. Out of habit, I began trying to justify myself, "Mom, I know Texas is a long way away, but—"

"Collie, for heaven's sake, let me finish." She held up a hand, huffing an irritated breath. "What I was going to say was, this all sounds a little crazy. You've never been the type to go off on a romantic notion. Are you sure you're not just reacting to all the stress you've been under these past months? Maybe this . . . True . . . looks so attractive to you right now because you've recently broken up with Brett, you're unhappy with your situation here, and you're looking for an escape."

I gripped the arms of my chair and forced myself not to bow before the queen of amateur psychology. For once, I was going to talk to my mother like a grown-up. "Mom, I hear what you're saying." So far, so good. I sounded like a psychologist myself. "But I don't agree. I have argued those same points with myself a hundred times since I went to Texas, and I keep coming back to the same conclusion. . . ." Now came the part that was hard to explain. The part that defied logic. "Something happened to me there. I found something, I left it, and I want it back. If I don't go there and at least try to see how True feels, I think I'll regret it forever."

Mom sat blinking as if she were seeing me for the first time. She glanced at Gran, who smiled and shrugged her shoulders. Then Mom turned to me again, with a new respect, I thought. "Collie, you're a grown woman. You're the only one who knows what you really want. You don't have to prove anything to me and your father. All we have ever wanted is for you to be happy." Mom sounded a little mechanical, but the words were nice to hear. Of course, she did make sure to finish with, "But I do think you would be wise to keep your options on the *Post* contract open, just in case you get down there and find out you or this man no longer feels the same."

I nodded, relieved. "Thanks for understanding, Mom. I'll keep my options open."

Mom smiled at me and shook her head. "Collie, you've always worried too much about what other people think. You've been that way ever since you were a little girl—too perfect. It's about time you developed a few quirks."

Gran chuckled, and I laughed too, the tension broken.

Mom came to sit on the arm of my chair, combing a hand over my hair as she had when I was a child. "I can't tell you how to be happy, Collie. You're the only one who knows where happiness lies for you." She leaned over and rested her chin on my head, hugging me. "And as for Texas being a long way away, they have airports there. Your dad and I aren't afraid to get on a plane."

"I am," Gran chimed in, then grinned wickedly when we looked at her. "But I guess I could be talked into it."

The three of us sniffed and giggled, dried our tears, then sat there, my grandmother holding my hand, Mom hugging me like a baby, and me making the biggest decision of my life. Three generations, standing at the fork in the road together.

When you have companionship, it isn't such a frightening place to be.

I finally broke it up. "If I'm going to get there today, I'd better get a flight booked and get to the airport," I said, and reached for the phone.

Gran sprang from the couch with remarkable agility. "I'll pack your suitcase. What kind of clothes do you think you'll need?"

"Clean ones." I was only partly joking. My laundry had once again started to form a mountain in the closet. "Some jeans and T-shirts and that navy blue suit to wear to the funeral. Navy pumps, a pair of hose, and some tennis shoes."

"How many days' worth of underthings?"

"Gran!" I rolled my eyes and suddenly the situation didn't seem so grave. The biggest decision of my life had been reduced to *How many pairs of underthings?* Under the circumstances, it was a profound question. "I don't know. Just throw some things in. I'll have to figure it out as I go along." The travel agent came on the line, and I turned to booking a flight while Mom and Gran argued over my laundry and packing a suitcase.

It turned out to be fortunate that they were there to help, because I barely had time to make my flight.

Mom frowned apprehensively, standing in the doorway with me, handing me my purse. "Are you sure you can make that two-twenty flight? You could book a later one. . . ."

"I think I can get there in time." But I knew what she meant. It was all too much, too fast, especially for Mom. "It's the only flight available today, and if I wait until the morning, I'll be rushing to make it to the funeral."

Mom sighed, and we looked at each other for an instant, a silent string of hopes and fears passing between us. "Let us know how things go," she said quietly.

"I will." I leaned down and hugged her, then hugged my grandmother. "Wish me luck."

Gran smiled and nodded. Mom sighed and glanced over her shoulder at the apartment, unable to bear watching me leave. The place looked as if a tornado had blown through. "I think Gran and I will stay the night here and clean up a little. We can get your laundry done. I'm too emotional to drive home today, anyway."

"Mom," I admonished.

But she just waved me off. "We'll be fine." Her voice quavered, and I knew she was about to cry. In spite of the butterflies in my stomach, I felt tears as she braced her hands on her hips, surveying the apartment. "It'll give us something to do. We can drive home early in the morning so Gran won't miss playing the organ at church service."

"All right," I said, lingering in the doorway even though the good-byes were said, and the hugs were hugged, and I needed to make my flight. "There's a bank envelope in the end-table drawer. Let me take you two out to a nice dinner tonight, at least."

Mom nodded, pretending to check the soil in a plant by the doorway. Not too convincing, considering the plant was silk.

Gran made an impatient noise in her throat, reaching out and giving me a push. "Get going. I'll make sure she takes me somewhere nice."

"I'm going," I said, moving toward the elevator. "I love you two." Then the elevator door chimed, and I turned around and ran.

I didn't stop running until I was on the plane and headed for Texas. Then I started thinking about what I was doing and whether it made any sense. About what would happen at the *Post* if I didn't make it back by

Monday. Then I reminded myself that I wasn't planning on coming back at all. I wondered what True would say and how he would feel, and what I would do if he didn't want to make any commitments, or didn't want anything more to do with me at all. I wondered what I would say to him, whether I would admit to the dream I had been painting in my mind, whether I would have the courage to take a leap of faith. . . .

An amazing thing happened in the sky somewhere over Oklahoma. I decided to stop thinking. I was doing what felt right. What my heart knew was right. When I got there, I would know what to say.

The Dallas airport felt like home. The cowboy boots and hats didn't seem odd anymore. I waded into the crowd feeling like I belonged. With each step I took, and then each mile I drove out of Dallas, my heart felt lighter and my mind more at ease. The vibrant blue and the heavy scent of bluebonnets were gone from the roadsides, replaced by the bright red and yellow-orange of Indian blankets, burning like fire on the hillsides. Otherwise everything was as I remembered.

I stopped for gas near Waco at the same service station I had visited on my first trip out. I bought soy nuts and a bottle of water and stood looking at the huge shellacked snakeskin on the wall, thinking about how afraid and out of place I had been my first time there. One girl from D.C., headed for Nowhere, Texas.

The teenage boy behind the counter grinned at my purchases as he punched them into the cash register. "Health nut?"

I laughed. He'd said the same thing last time, right

before he told me there were six-foot rattlesnakes behind every bush, and scared me to death. "Trying to get back in the habit." I wondered if he remembered me, but I supposed not.

He lowered a brow, giving me a baby-faced frown with my change. "Man, you from New York or some-place?"

"D.C.," I said.

"It's a little late in the season for tourists," he offered. "Bluebonnets are mostly gone."

I took my things from the counter and started toward the door before I answered, because it was already evening and I didn't want to get into a twenty-minute snake story. "Just going to visit some friends in San Saline," I said, and started out the door.

"Umm." He nodded as if he approved. "We got a huntin' camp in San Saline. Went snake huntin' there a few weeks ago. They got more rattlers down there than weeds."

I waved good-bye and went out the door, taking comfort in the fact that some things never change.

I smiled to myself as I drove west out of town, heading into the vast azure-and-violet maze of distant hills, toward the crimson ribbon of the sun slowly setting beyond a rim of blazing clouds. Rolling down the window, I listened to the silence passing outside the window. Mile upon mile. No cars. No sirens. No noisy diesel buses. No blaring radios. No voices. Nothing but the occasional complaint of cattle and the low rush of the wind.

Dusk was just settling as I came into the town of

Esther. The street was silent, the stores already closed, the blinking Friendly's Tractors sign the only movement on the street. Stopping beneath it, I looked toward the dark, silent windows of the garage and pictured True there, as if by imagining him, I could bring him to that place. The location of our unlikely first meeting.

Are you lost? he had asked me.

I was. More than either one of us could have imagined. Lost, then found, though I didn't know it at the time . . .

The windows of the garage remained dark and silent, and finally I put the car in drive and started away, wondering where True was, whether he was back from Oklahoma City and whether he knew I was coming.

But then he couldn't. I hadn't told anyone. Even Mrs. Hawthorne would be surprised to see me. I hoped she would have an empty cabin for me to rent. It would probably have been wise to call ahead, but I didn't want her to tell True I was coming. Whatever his reaction when we finally saw each other, I wanted it to be unrehearsed.

I tried not to think about it as I drove the last miles to San Saline. I enjoyed the cool, fresh night air and the millions of bright fingertip-close stars as they twinkled one by one into the hill-country sky.

Coasting into the San Saline valley, I took a deep breath and looked again at all of the things I had tried to push from my dreams—the Friendly's Tractors sign, Mill Creek Park, the courthouse with its giant, heavy-limbed pecan trees, Harvey's Boots-'n'-More, the newspaper office, the café and the sale barn. The memories of those places and the feelings that went with them flooded my mind like water bursting through a levee.

By the time I reached the driveway to Hawthorne House, I felt as if I had never left. I had not an ounce of trepidation as I parked the car and hurried up the steps to the front door.

I could hear Mrs. Hawthorne's heavy steps in the foyer as I rang the bell.

She grinned broadly and opened her arms as she threw back the door. "Oh, Collie, I had a feeling you would come!" she said, hugging me. "I had a feeling, and my feelings are never wrong. I told Jasper that. I told him."

I hugged her in return, a sense of joy filling me. "I couldn't stay away," I confessed, breathless from the bear hug. "I missed the peacocks too much."

We laughed together as she set me on the stoop like a rag doll, eyeing me critically. "You've lost weight."

"Some," I said, smoothing my suit. "It's been a busy month."

"I'll bet it has," she agreed, then reached for a set of keys from the rack beside the door. "Well, you'll need a cabin. The back two are full, but I have the front one empty. It's our best. It has a phone and a . . ." She slapped her hand to her forehead, laughing. "Oh, Collie, what am I telling you that for?" Then over her shoulder she called, "Jasper, Collie's here. I'm going to show her to her cabin." Then to me, "I think he's already nodded off in his chair."

As I had on my first night in Texas, I followed her across the lawn to the cabins, onto the porch, and into my cottage, which was exactly as I remembered it. This time Mrs. Hawthorne came in with me and we stood in the kitchen. "Jasper just redid the floors in here," she said as I stood looking around the place. "And he fixed that darned cabinet door that wouldn't stay shut. But the phone isn't any better. Sorry about that. But you can always use mine in my office, you know, for however long you . . ." She stopped for a breath. I think she had to; her face was turning red. "How long will you be staying?"

I pretended to admire Jasper's work on the cabinet door while I contemplated an answer, then finally settled for, "I don't know. I'm kind of up in the air right now."

"Mm-hmm." She seemed to find that news pleasing. "We haven't heard back from True yet, but I feel sure he's gotten his message and headed back by now for the funeral. It's just like him not to bother to call. I feel sure he'll be there tomorrow."

I could tell she was watching closely for a reaction, so I focused on the new magnetic latch on the cabinet. "I'm sure he'll be there." I couldn't have come all this way for nothing. What if Monday came and I still hadn't seen him? What would I do then?

Shaking off the thought, I changed the subject. "How is Malachi's family doing?"

Her expression turned to one of monumental sorrow, and I regretted having brought it up. "Pretty well, I think," she said. "All of his grandchildren have made it in from college and whatnot, so there's a lot of support there. I took a casserole over there for supper, and they seemed to be getting on all right. I guess this was something they'd expected. Do you know Malachi's doctor told him ten years ago his heart probably wouldn't go another six months? I never knew that. He never told anyone around town."

I looked out the window at the small front porch of the cottage and pictured Malachi unloading my packages after rescuing me from the grocery store parking lot. "That doctor didn't know how good his heart really was," I said quietly. "Or how big."

Mrs. H. sniffled, dabbing at her eyes with the hem of her T-shirt. "Well, that surely is the truth." She glanced toward the main house, starting at a sudden thought. "Oh, my food! I've got things cooking for the wake tomorrow. I'd better get back to the kitchen."

"I'll come help you," I offered.

But Mrs. H. wouldn't let me. "Oh, don't worry about that. I'm almost finished anyhow. You just get unpacked and have a good rest, and I'll see you in the morning." She hustled out the door without giving me another chance to offer help.

After she was gone, I retrieved my suitcase from the car, watched the Cowboy Channel for a few minutes, then gave up and went to bed, feeling exhausted, as if my emotions had run the Boston Marathon in the last twenty-four hours. In the darkness, I lay listening to the silence and thinking about the day—a day that had started with me sitting on my sofa holding a piece of paper that was supposed to give me everything I wanted, and ended with me realizing I wanted something else. Some things defy logic. Some feelings resist explanation. Sometimes you can't put words to what is inside you. The heart doesn't speak. It only feels, and knows, and understands. And that is enough.

Chapter 17

I AWOKE to the sound of rattlesnakes crawling on the roof and someone outside calling for help. Bolting upright in the bed, I looked around the room, realized where I was, and laughed at myself. Propping the pillows, I pulled the quilt up and watched morning wander in around the edges of the window shades. Outside, the clatter reached epic proportions, drowning out the *click-swish, click-swish* of the intruder on the tin roof overhead.

Slowly the clatter faded as the peafowl vacated their perches and fluttered to the lawn to spend the day foraging. The visitor on my roof went with them, and the room fell silent. I lay a while longer, then remembered I needed to call home before Mom and Grandma left my apartment. By now they were probably ready to disown me for not checking in. They weren't likely to understand that it was impossible to use the phone here during peacock-perching hours.

I was surprised when I dialed my D.C. number only to get my own answering machine. I left a message, just in case they were there, or out to breakfast. It was awfully early for them to already be on the road, but with Gran you could never tell. She may have rousted

Mom at four A.M. and insisted they head back so she could warm up the church organ.

I didn't have any real news to tell, anyway.

I took my time bathing and dressing, because I didn't have anywhere to go until afternoon, and I supposed that if Mrs. Hawthorne had tracked down True, she would have called me. With nothing better to do, I left the cottage and walked to the café for breakfast.

Mrs. Hawthorne motioned me to the bar as soon as I entered. With a grim expression she told me that she'd had no word from True, that she had called his folks and they hadn't heard from him either. "I can't imagine why he hasn't called," she said for what felt like the twentieth time. "His mother tried to call him at the hotel in Oklahoma City, and he wasn't registered there anymore, so he must be on his way home."

"I'm sure that's it," I agreed, but I suddenly had no appetite for the café's huevos rancheros. Time was rushing by. If I was going back to D.C., I'd have return to Dallas this evening, then get on a plane. . . .

". . . Collie?" I realized Mrs. H. was talking to me. "I wondered if you wanted to ride with us to the funeral this afternoon, or if you planned to drive yourself."

I thought for a minute. Afternoon seemed eons away. "I'd like a ride." I realized I had imagined myself driving over there with True, as we had on the afternoon of the fish fry. Just for an instant, my mind pictured Malachi there standing behind the cooker; then reality erased the image and put something empty in its place—a hole, like a face cut out of a picture. My eyes started to water. I was thankful that Mrs. Hawthorne had already moved down the bar to pour coffee for some old men.

After a minute, I pushed aside my plate of eggs and told her I was going for a walk around town.

"We'll see you back at the house about one," she said, then went on with her work, but without her usual bounce. The hum of conversation in the café was subdued, no laughter, no loud jokes, everyone dressed in dark, Sunday attire. Even the bell on the door had stopped making noise.

Malachi stayed in my mind as I left the café and walked slowly toward the square, beneath the great swinging cowboy boot of Harvey's Boots-'n'-More, past the dollar store, across the courthouse lawn, where I sat on a bench and stared up at the newspaper office. The windows were dark upstairs and down, the place silent. I thought of the first day I had come there, standing just inside the glass with Becky and Mrs. Hawthorne as Malachi held the door open for True and reminded him it wasn't healthy to carry so many heavy boxes. I remembered myself feeling embarrassed and out of place, and Malachi tipping his fedora hat to me, smiling as if I were someone special. I hadn't realized it at the time, but it made me feel a little better, in a way, welcomed. Funny how you don't always think about things as they happen. Some things don't seem important until later. . . .

I don't know how long I sat there, looking at the newspaper office and thinking. Finally I walked the rest of the way around the square and down to the grocery store. I bought a bottle of orange juice and a pack of doughnuts, then stood at the checkout counter looking at Malachi's bench, which was enshrined with assorted flower bouquets, a wooden cross, and a teddy bear with angel's wings and a halo.

The girl at the checkout stand seemed to realize what I was doing. "The funeral's this afternoon." Her eyes were red-rimmed. "We're going to close the store down at noon, so everyone can go."

"That's good," I said. But Malachi would have told them to keep the store open, so no one would be inconvenienced. "I imagine you'll miss him around here."

"Yes, ma'am," she said quietly. "Malachi's the reason I found God. He used to read that Bible to me when there wasn't no customers in here. I didn't have nothin' in my life. I was just dropped out of school and runnin' around town, and my mama didn't give a rip. But Malachi, he helped me get in school and in church and he told me that God loved me. One time he gave me fifty dollars just because I said I needed it." She picked at the layers of chipping green polish on her nails, a tear glittering against the brown freckles of her cheek. "I never thought about God or anybody else loving me before."

I didn't know what to say, so I just nodded, took my sack, and walked past the empty bench. Tied to the teddy bear with a pink ribbon, there was a rolled-up fifty-dollar bill.

I sat outside the store with my doughnuts and orange juice, contemplating how many times Malachi had traversed the parking lot in his slow, labored gait, how many sacks of groceries he had loaded and unloaded, how many smiles and bits of advice he had doled out, how many lives he had changed. If ever there was a wealthy man, it was Malachi.

When I was finished, I walked back to Hawthorne House, in no particular hurry, watching the highway from the corner of my eye, expecting, hoping, to see the Friendly's truck suddenly appear. But it didn't. And there were no messages for me at the cottage, so I went inside and sat staring at the old TV as the picture waved like a flag on a windy day.

Mrs. Hawthorne came by at twelve-thirty, told me with a worried look that she still hadn't heard from True, and that we would leave for the funeral at one, and that she still felt sure he would be there. And that her feelings were never wrong.

But as I dressed for the funeral, I felt my hope dwindling. I was starting to question the emotional decision that had brought me back to San Saline, and to doubt that all of this was really meant to be.

Even so, it felt right to be there to tell Malachi goodbye. If the trip accomplished no more than that, it was worthwhile. Yet even as I tried to convince myself of that, to prepare for the worst, part of me held stubbornly to the dream. Part of me said that if True didn't show up today, I should wait until tomorrow, or the next day, or the next. However long it took.

But I knew I didn't have that kind of courage. I knew myself too well to believe I could take such a leap of blind faith. I knew that if I didn't see him today, I'd be back in D.C. on Monday handing over that contract.

At one o'clock, Jasper and Mrs. Hawthorne were

waiting on the front porch. None of us spoke as we climbed into the car and headed for the funeral. I knew that Mrs. Hawthorne hadn't heard from True, and I knew that time had just about run out.

Malachi's funeral was a sight to behold. Kings and presidents have been buried with less fanfare, with less adulation. Cars were parked in every inch of the church parking lot and for miles up and down the highway—old cars, new cars, pickup trucks and trailers. Beneath the live oaks at the site of the old log school, there was a carpet of flowers—hothouse lilies and roses, wild Indian blankets, primroses, and the last bluebonnets of the season. The tokens were as mixed as the crowd filing by the porch of the old freedman's school, where a closed casket rested. It was plain and humble, polished wood and simple brass handles. I imagined Malachi wanted it that way.

When the mourners had finished placing flowers, I stood in the thick of the crowd with Mrs. Hawthorne and Jasper, because all of the seats had long since been filled. I felt Mrs. Hawthorne slip her hand over mine as one of Malachi's grandsons took the pulpit and began to eulogize his grandfather.

"My grandfather never had more than a sixth-grade education, yet he understood God's word better than any scholar in any seminary institution. He was born in a time that placed little value on him, a black child, yet he saw the value in each person he met. He lost his father at the age of five, yet he became a father to many who were in need. He grew up with no church in which to worship, yet he built a church with the labor of his hands. He was a man poor in worldly possessions, yet he gave all he had to those who asked of him. He was a man crippled in body, yet strong enough in spirit to carry others' burdens. He was a man weak in his heart, yet he understood the human heart. . . ."

He paused and gripped the sides of the pulpit, his head dropping forward and his shoulders trembling with silent sobs. A hush fell over the grove, and the world was silent. A breeze lifted the petals of flowers, carrying their scents over the crowd, past the old church with the name painted over, through the silent town with the stores boarded up, into the distant hills, toward the horizon, into the vast hill country sky, into heaven. Where Malachi was watching.

I pictured him smiling as his grandson continued the eulogy through a veil of tears, then finally finished, holding Malachi's tattered Bible in his hands. He opened the cover slowly as the crowd around him wept. "No doubt most of you have seen my grandfather with this old Bible. Over the years, he was given many others by many people, but he clung always to this one. It was sent to him by his father, who died on foreign soil, spreading the word of God during the First World War. Inside the cover, my grandfather had pasted this prayer:

"Lord, make me an instrument of your peace!
Where there is hatred, let me sow love
Where there is injury, pardon
Where there is doubt, faith

Where there is despair, hope
Where there is darkness, light
Where there is sadness, joy.
O Divine Master, grant that I may not so much seek to be consoled, as to console.
To be understood, as to understand.
To be loved, as to love.
For it is in giving that we receive.
It is in pardoning that we are pardoned.
It is in dying that we are born to eternal life."

He raised his gaze to the vast blue sky above the live oaks. "This prayer was my grandfather. It was his life. He wasn't a saint; he was just a man. But what he had, he gave. If he were here today, he would tell each of us we have everything we need . . . to do the same." Then he stepped from the pulpit into the arms of his family.

The crowd sat motionless for a long time, then finally started to disperse, people wandering past the coffin, through the grove, toward the cars, into the old white church, like so many lost sheep looking for their shepherd.

Jasper turned and walked toward the church, and Mrs. Hawthorne went with some other ladies to talk to the family about the food for the wake. I stood watching her as the crowd around me cleared; then I turned to walk away.

True was standing in the aisle between the chairs, motionless, waiting for me to turn around.

My heart leaped up and fluttered in my throat like a butterfly ready to burst forth. I took a deep breath and walked forward. My gaze met sapphire blue, and a thousand thoughts rushed through my mind. *I love you. I missed you. I want to be with you forever. . . .*

Instead, I said, "It was a wonderful service." Small talk, of all things. I looked at tiny pink flowers in the grass beneath my feet.

"It was," he agreed. I glanced up and he was smiling, just slightly, confidently, as if he weren't the least bit surprised to see me again, or the least bit curious as to why I had come. I wondered what that meant. "To tell you the truth, I think old Malachi would have been embarrassed by all the fuss. But he would have been proud of Clarence John. That young man has his granddad's gift for putting together a sermon. I don't think he left a dry eye in the crowd. Kind of makes ya ashamed for being petty about things, doesn't it?"

"It does." I wondered if he was talking about me, or about himself, or just making conversation.

If he was wondering about anything, it didn't show. He crossed his arms over his chest and looked completely comfortable. "Saw you on TV a few times."

I grimaced because, after the fact, my TV appearances weren't something I was terribly proud of. "I discovered I wasn't really much of a TV correspondent. I'm pretty glad to have that over with." I held my breath and waited for him to ask what I was going to do now. I wondered if he cared. After I had flown all the way to Texas to see him, it was pretty stupid to be coy, I guess, but I couldn't help it. Part of me was just plain . . . chicken.

Two of Malachi's grandsons walked by carrying

some of the flowers, and True paused to talk to them, then ended up helping them carry things to their cars. I helped too, carrying armload after armload of flowers to the cars waiting to go to the cemetery down the road. Among the bouquets were small tokens of love—bits of scripture, photographs, donation envelopes with money inside. I untied them from the flowers and handed them to Malachi's daughter, a nurse from Dallas.

Beneath the flowers on the old freedman's school porch, one of Malachi's grandsons discovered an envelope marked *For Malachi's baptistery*. A five-thousand-dollar bank draft was inside with the sender's name anonymous. No one had seen who delivered it. No one ever admitted to being the sender. But everyone knew that Malachi's church would now have a baptistery with hot and cold running water. *Praise the Lawd.*

I stood on the church steps with True as the cars departed for the graveside service, which was to be only for family. Mrs. Hawthorne and Jasper were inside with some other community members, getting things ready to take to the wake at one of the grandsons' houses.

True didn't say anything for a while, just leaned against the rail and looked at the sun, sinking toward late afternoon in the vast expanse of sky.

I didn't know exactly what to say either, so I stood there looking also. Feeling afraid. Wanting to back out. But I knew I'd never forgive myself.

I felt him look at me from the corner of his eye. "So

I need to drive down the road and feed my cows. You want to come along?"

My heart twittered into my throat again. I swallowed hard. "I don't know. Is your cow going to kiss me again? Because I have on good clothes."

He chuckled. "Could happen. She missed you while you were gone." He held his hand out and I slipped mine into it and started down the steps, feeling as if I were walking in a dream.

Mrs. Hawthorne's voice drifted from inside the building, and I was reminded for an instant that we weren't the only two people in the universe. "I'd better tell her I don't need a ride home," I said, stopping at the bottom of the steps.

True gave my hand a tug. "She knows. I told her already."

He grinned that lopsided grin, and I fell in love with him all over again. "You're awfully sure of yourself," I said.

He shook his head, ducked his chin, and kept walking. When we reached the truck, he opened my door, then went around and climbed in his side.

The rumble of the diesel engine felt good beneath my feet, familiar, like home.

"So how was D.C.?" True asked as we started down the highway.

I thought about it for a minute, but it all seemed to have faded from my mind, like something unimportant. "Fast," I answered finally. "D.C. is always fast."

He nodded, and we went on talking about things that weren't important. I sat there waiting for the conversation to get around to the things that mattered, but every time I tried to steer the subject in that direction, he found a way to bring it back. I started to wonder what was in his mind and how I was going to get from where we were to what I needed to know. Time was running out.

I looked up and realized we were turning in to a familiar gateway. The mass of cedar had been cleared, but I recognized the place anyway. It was ingrained in my mind from my unfortunate encounter with the bull snake. It came to me all of a sudden that we were headed to the old schoolhouse.

True motioned to the gate and nodded at me.

"No way," I said.

"Old cowboy rule," he reminded me. "Passenger gets the gate."

I leaned close to him, close enough to kiss him. "But I'm not an old cowboy. So you're out of luck."

He laughed, hopped out and opened the gate, then climbed back in and drove through. The cattle were near the gate and swarmed the truck. True moved through them, honking the horn, and then stepped on the gas. Biscuit stuck her head out and wailed, giving chase, but finally surrendered the effort as we moved into the open pasture.

Laughing, I watched her give up her pursuit of the back bumper; then I turned and looked at the pasture ahead. The hillside had been cleared and new grass seeded, the road straightened and covered with fresh gravel. "Somebody's been working in here," I said, looking up the hill toward the grove of trees where the schoolhouse stood hidden.

"Just about ready to start on the house," he said, watching the road ahead, but with an intensity that told me he was measuring my reactions. "Took me three weeks to get the cedar cleared."

"You really bought it!" I said, with more excitement than I meant to show.

True seemed pleased. He nodded as we jostled up the hill into the live-oak grove. A new driveway wound through the ancient trees to the edge of the old schoolhouse fence. The grass had been mowed and some of the loose tin and lumber cleared away, but otherwise the place was just as I remembered. Just as I had dreamed.

We stepped out of the truck together and walked to the bluff above the river, then stood there in silence, looking over miles and miles of watercolor country.

I heard True take a deep breath and felt him slip his hand over mine. "I guess the matchmakers were right, after all," he said chuckling.

I leaned my cheek against his shoulder, drinking in the cool breeze that smelled of water and limestone, grass and sky. "I don't know." I couldn't help smiling, because I understood what he meant. "You had Mrs. Hawthorne pretty worried. She thought you weren't going to show."

"Well, it wasn't because I didn't try." I stepped back to look at him, and he smiled sheepishly. "Let me tell you, it's a heck of a long way home from Oklahoma City through Washington, D.C." He must have noticed my chin dropping off the cliff, because he broke into a full, wicked grin. "Funny thing, the girl I went there to see wasn't home. Met your mom and grandmom, though."

In shock, I stumbled backward. "You saw my *mother* and *grandmother?*" I choked. "Oh, my gaaa . . . what happened?" I had a horrifying vision of my mother and grandmother making mincemeat of poor True.

He seemed a little offended that I didn't think he could handle them. He laid a splay-fingered hand on his chest, pulling me away from the bluff and closer to him. "I was charming, of course." He raised a brow indignantly. "We had a nice supper. They said you were paying the bill, so all three of us ate lobster and drank expensive wine."

I blinked at him in shock.

He went on, enjoying himself immensely. "Then I told them good-bye, hopped in a cab, and hurried like heck to the airport, which, now that you mention it, is about the worst place to spend the night I've ever seen. Some strange things go on in D.C. in the middle of the night. I wasn't sure I'd come out alive. But here I am, four connections and several thousand frequent-flyer miles later, back with you, in Texas."

I stumbled away from him, fell to a seat in the grass, and started to laugh. "I can't believe you went to D.C. Why in the world did you decide to do that now?"

True sat beside me, taking on a serious expression and shaking his head. "I'll tell you, Collie, that was the strangest thing about it." He looked hard at me. "You're going to think I'm nuts, and if you tell anyone about this, I'll drop you in the middle of the pasture and sic Biscuit on you. I was in Oklahoma City on business, sleeping in my hotel room night before last, and I had this dream about Malachi and about you. I woke up at six-thirty in the morning and I swear, I could smell that darned aftershave of his right there in the hotel room. I kept seeing him shaking his finger and giving me that sermon about love. I got up, got dressed, and got on a plane to D.C. I was on the way to your apartment when I checked my voice mail and found out he had passed away that same night."

The look in his eyes was filled with meaning, and I shook my head and rubbed my hand over the lump in my chest. "I guess it is possible that some things are meant to be," I whispered.

"I guess it is," he agreed, then looped his elbows over his knees and looked out over the bluff. "But listen, Collie, I don't want to be the reason you give up everything you've worked for. Life doesn't have to be here. We can work out something else."

I watched the profile of his face, trying to get some hint of his emotions, trying to decide whether he really meant it. For the first time, I knew that he really, truly loved me as love was supposed to be, and that I loved him that way also.

"I don't want that anymore." The words came from my heart and not my mind. "It's like you said that day before I left. That life just isn't me anymore." And I knew without a doubt that it wasn't. I didn't want to go back; I wanted to go forward, into something new.

He rested his chin on his clasped hands and looked sideways at me as if he doubted what I'd said.

I went on before he could question me. "It's too busy. Too fast." I smiled, hoping the pounding of my heart didn't show. "I think I know where I can get a nice, quiet newspaper editor's job."

True reached across the space between us and ran his hand over my hair, then pulled me close. "You're hired," he said, then his lips met mine and it didn't matter where we were. There was nothing in the world but him and me.

We spent that night at the site of our future home. With a little creative thinking, hay tarps make a pretty decent tent and horse blankets fairly decent bedding, when they've just been washed. True's mom had sent food for the wake, but we never made it there. We toasted Malachi on the porch of our home-to-be with leftover Dairy Queen silverware salvaged from the truck and food meant for the wake. We didn't figure Malachi would mind. He got what he really wanted.

That night I went to sleep for the first time in the arms of someone I loved with all my heart, in a place where I knew I was meant to be.

I dreamed of the old stone schoolhouse high atop the river bluff. I dreamed of the broken windows replaced and the roof repaired to keep out the rain. I dreamed of a blond-haired girl playing with a calf who looked just like Biscuit, who kissed her on the mouth, then bolted. I dreamed of the girl laughing, rolling in the grass, then sitting up, turning to look at me, with True's blue eyes.

As I was waking in the morning, as I sat up and looked at True asleep beside me and at tomorrow slowly coming over the far hills, I heard a whispering inside me. It was the voice that Malachi had told me about. The voice that is inside all of us, that knows our hearts and leads us to where we are supposed to be. It is the voice of the spirit, of the heart, of God. It knows the things that are lasting. It is as Malachi said.

If you listen hard enough, it will lead you home.

Center Point Publishing
600 Brooks Road • PO Box 1
Thorndike ME 04986-0001 USA

(207) 568-3717

US & Canada:
1 800 929-9108